# Praise for *Get the Meeting!*

"*Get the Meeting!* is one of those rare books where ideas literally leap off the page, sparking your creativity to ignite campaigns as you star in the role of a very successful contact marketer."

— *Willis Turner, president/CEO of sales and marketing at Executives International, Inc. (SMEI)*

"I've always admired the way Stu Heinecke thinks. He has a no-limit mind-set. He makes the impossible happen. There is no person on this Earth he can't reach with his engaging approach. He crafts an emotionally significant experience and if you read this book and follow his advice you'll be empowered to get out of this world response rates."

— *Gerhard Gschwandtner, founder and CEO of* Selling Power *magazine and* Sales3.0 *Conferences*

"*Get The Meeting!* is hands-down the most innovative and practical book on achieving meetings with hard-to-reach prospects I've ever read. Every strategic sales professional and marketer should read this book."

— *James Muir, CEO of Best Practice International and author of* The Perfect Close

"I love this book. Stu Heinecke has written one of the most innovative and cutting-edge guides on marketing I have ever read. *Get The Meeting: An Illustrative Contact Marketing Playbook* gives you very powerful strategies that completely reinvent your marketing plan. Finally a guidebook that gives you exactly what you need to get above the white noise, stand out, get noticed, and create raving fans in a marketplace that is so overcrowded. I think *Get the Meeting!* is brilliant and a must-read for anyone building a business today!"

— *Meredith Elliott Powell, business growth strategist and sales expert*

"You're so lucky you only have to seek meetings here on Earth—and you have a book like *Get the Meeting!* to help you do it."

— *Seth Shostak, senior astronomer at The SETI Institute*

"If you are a marketer or seller who needs to get someone's attention (and who doesn't?), the one book you need is Stu Heinecke's *Get the Meeting!* It's a jam-packed lovefest of audacious ideas that real people dreamed up and harnessed to produce brilliant results, complete with step-by-step how-to's that you can follow. You'll enjoy super stories from big spenders as well as mind-boggling results from penny-pinchers with big imaginations. And you'll meet genius technologies priced for even the smallest companies and solopreneurs. An astounding collection of inspirations that will keep you busy opening big doors for years!"

— *Dr. Barbara Weaver Smith, coauthor of* Whale Hunting

"Choose any account, take aim, and get the meeting! Stu's book makes it that simple."

— *Sangram Vajre, author, podcast host, and founder of FlipMyFunnel*

"Gene Simmons once said, 'Rock stars have a license to be outrageous.' *Get the Meeting!* gives sellers that same license. Be outrageous; get meetings! Peace, cheers, I'm out."

— *Kraig Kleeman, "the world's greatest cold-caller"*

"In sales, you can't win if you can't connect with buyers their way, and that's getting tougher every day. Breaking through the noise of messages that buyers simply ignore will be made so much easier if you read Stu's new book, *Get the Meeting!*, a companion to *How to Get a Meeting with Anyone*. You can thank me later!"

— *Barb Giamanco, vice president of sales/marketing at ECHO Listening Intelligence*

"Stu's nonconventional but results-driven advice truly stands out. If you want to get a meeting with anyone to launch a business, close a deal, start your nonprofit, or anything else, then this is the book for you."

— *Nicholas Loise, president, Glazer-Kennedy Insider's Circle*

"When you're faced with filling a gaping pipeline with leads and sales, it can be intimidating. The remedy is smart and fanatical prospecting, and that starts with getting the right meetings with the right people at the right time. *Get the Meeting!* can help you do just that."

— *Jeb Blount, author of* **Fanatical Prospecting**

"Bombarded by noise, the speed of changes they need to make, and the pressure of making the right choices, it is getting increasingly harder to cut through all the clutter for your salespeople to get a meeting with the right people. That's why I loved Stu Heinecke's book *Get the Meeting!* He blends his experience as a *Wall Street Journal* cartoonist and skilled marketer to offer really fantastic strategies to get a meeting with anyone. His perspective is both pragmatic and modern—the right mix of practical and strategic for our new digital age of selling. Get this book, read it—and put his ideas to practice. You will be happy you did."

— *Scott Santucci, founder of Sales Enablement Society*

"Empathy is key in securing meetings with potential buyers. If you can't demonstrate that you understand a day in your buyer's life, you will be quickly disqualified. In *Get the Meeting!*, Stu Heinecke gives the reader a trove of delightfully unique ways ways to demonstrate to prospects that they do indeed 'get them.'"

— *Colleen Stanley, author of* **Emotional Intelligence for Sales Success**

# Praise for *How to Get a Meeting with Anyone*

"In a super-connected world, we're actually anything but. Stu reminds us that in business, you actually have to connect on a human level to really succeed, and he is the Master guide on how to do that."

— *Bob Guccione, Jr., media entrepreneur and founder of* **SPIN** *Magazine*

"With this book, Stu gives you everything you could possibly need to get all of the meetings you could possibly want."

— *Bob Mankoff, cartoon editor at* **The New Yorker**

"Stu says, When you hear 'Executive Assistant,' think instead, 'Vice President of Access.' This is so true—our role is to ensure that you speak to the right person at the right time during the decision-making process. I highly recommend that all salespeople read Chapter 15 at least three times!"

— *Bonnie Wooding, president of Hywood Services and executive assistant to top business leaders for over 30 years*

"Stu is a master innovator and creative virtuoso. What he has put together in this book is a true gift to the reader. If opening important doors is important to your success, you can't afford NOT to read this book!"

— *Dan Monaghan, cofounder of WSI Digital*

"Building trust and adding value are critical to cultivating profitable business relationships. Stu Heinecke and his Content Marketing Strategies have greatly contributed to our success."

— *David Rosuck, vice president of marketing and innovations at Pacific Life*

"Go ahead and list a dozen or two impossible-to-reach, off-limits people that could change your life or career. Read and follow Stu's guidance. Then change your life forever."

— *Dean Batson, assistant director of the Arizona State University Alumni Association*

"Stu is one creative dude. Who else can run a campaign that catches the attention of a US President? Almost as crazy as using an AI to schedule a meeting :)."

— *Dennis Mortensen, CEO and founder of x.ai, producers of the world's first artificial intelligence assistant who schedules meetings for you*

"Stu's ideas helped me get a meeting with Amblin Entertainment and Stephen Spielberg, and continue to produce results for my company. Thanks to *How to Get a Meeting with Anyone*, now the entire world can get in on Stu's precious secrets!"

— *Jay Silverman, creator and executive producer of* **The Cleaner** *on* **A+E Networks**, *director of* **Girl on the Edge**, *and president of Jay Silverman Productions*

## OTHER BOOKS BY STU HEINECKE

How to Get a Meeting with Anyone

# GET THE MEETING!

# GET THE MEETING!

## AN ILLUSTRATIVE CONTACT MARKETING PLAYBOOK

**Stu Heinecke**

BenBella Books, Inc.
Dallas, TX

BenBella

**BenBella Books, Inc.**
10440 N. Central Expressway, Suite 800
Dallas, TX 75231
www.benbellabooks.com
Send feedback to feedback@benbellabooks.com

Printed in the United States of America
10 9 8 7 6 5 4 3 2 1

Library of Congress Cataloging-in-Publication Control Number: 2019007197
ISBN 9781948836449 (trade paper)
ISBN 9781948836692 (electronic)


Editing by Debbie Harmsen
Copyediting by Miki Alexandra Caputo
Text design and composition by Kit Sweeney
Proofreading by Sarah Vostok and Karen O'Brien
Indexing by WordCo Indexing Services, Inc.
Cover design by Emily Weigel
Cover photo © Shutterstock/koosen and
    studioworkstock; photo editing by Emily Weigel
Printed by Versa Press


Distributed to the trade by Two Rivers Distribution, an Ingram brand
www.tworiversdistribution.com

**Special discounts for bulk sales are available.**
**Please contact bulkorders@benbellabooks.com.**

"DIVIDE $200,000 BY THE
COST OF A CUPCAKE THEN
MULTIPLY BY A HUNDRED. I GET
5 MILLION PERCENT ROI."

———————

Dedicated to all who
understand that one meeting truly
can change everything—and to those
bold enough to make it happen.

# CONTENTS

# FOREWORD

The first thing I did after reading *Get the Meeting!* was walk it down to my sales team. It's that good. It's that important.

This is an easy read that will spur you to consider the value of Contact Marketing, replete with examples including a new replacement for business cards—Pocket Campaigns—plus forward-looking practices and real-world uses of video, social media, visual metaphors, gifts, digital marketing, artificial intelligence, augmented reality, virtual reality, and more—all in the service of getting important meetings.

If Phil Kotler is the father of marketing, Stu is the father of Contact Marketing. He coined the very phrase in his first book, *How to Get a Meeting with Anyone*, while applying a lifetime of success stories that gird his mastery. In this book, Stu makes a freshly compelling case for approaching Contact Marketing as a strategic asset for anyone looking to rapidly expand the scale of their network and thus their careers, businesses, and lives.

As Stu is fond of saying, "One meeting can change everything." But you cannot innovate without creativity. You cannot be creative without imagination.

You cannot imagine without inspiration. And that is precisely how Stu's new playbook on Contact Marketing fills the gap. It will be an inspiration to anyone who feels stymied by the increasing difficulty of reaching decision makers in every sector of commerce, and really, in life as a whole.

Because we all need to get meetings.

Whether you're a sales development rep, a CEO, or somewhere in between, nothing happens without contact with the right people. Few topics receive more attention in the field of marketing than the notion of friction-free experience design. Stu rightly points out that in the B-to-B world, gaining access is the number one source of friction today.

And who better to write a book like *Get the Meeting!* than Stu himself. He's not only an author and marketer, he is a *Wall Street Journal* cartoonist. That killer combination led him on a journey, first to discover the magical effect of cartoons as contact devices. And then to discover this mysterious, shadowy form of marketing, something that has been quietly used for years to make critically important connections happen, often with explosive results.

But I must warn you, as a level-headed businessperson, you may find what Stu shares in this book rather shocking. Perhaps even upsetting. You will read about metrics that should be impossible. When he asserts that the new baseline for response to a Contact Marketing should now be 100 percent, you're probably going to find it hard to believe. And when you read that the new ROI record for a Contact Marketing campaign has reached into the *millions* of percent, your head will spin.

And it ought to. This isn't another unoriginal book the world didn't need about sales or marketing or business. It's a shocking call to up your game by orders of magnitude. But it is also a practical guide to show you how to do it all, step by step.

One could argue the most meaningful point in a customer journey is the first contact. After reading this book, and fully implementing the Contact Marketing model within, I think you'll agree with Stu: One meeting really can change everything.

**— Russ Klein**

*CEO, The American Marketing Association*

"Hey listen, we got your proposal
and we like everything except
having to pay you."

# INTRODUCTION

If you've ever seen the movie *Hitch*, you've seen Contact Marketing in action.

Thirty-three minutes and thirteen seconds into the 2005 feature film, a secretive matchmaking consultant named Hitch (played by Will Smith) sends a contact device to reporter Sara Melas, played by Eva Mendes. A courier walks into her office and hands her a box. As Sara signs for it, her curiosity steadily rises. "What is this and who sent it," she wonders as she hands the pen and manifest back to the courier.

Sara excitedly opens the box and finds something surprising inside. A walkie-talkie. It's already turned on. She picks it up.

"Hello?"

Hitch is on the other end, waiting to engage. His mission? To persuade Sara to go on a date with him.

While the ultimate aim of Hitch's Contact Marketing piece wasn't to sell something, it did have a meeting as its intent, and it's easy to see how a tactic like the walkie-talkie in a box could work for just about anyone trying to gain the attention of an important account or prospect.

If you read my debut book, *How to Get a Meeting with Anyone*, ploys like Hitch sending a walkie-talkie in a box sound familiar. You may recall Dan Waldschmidt's sending of swords to break through to CEOs of distressed companies, Rick Bennett's contact letter run as a full-page ad in *The Wall Street Journal*, and Nowait's brilliant personalized videos delivered on iPads—not to mention the pigeon used to arrange lunch and a $250,000 deal with one of the most famous CEOs in the world.

You may also remember the story I tell in the book of my own experience with using cartoons in a "contact campaign" to connect with just two dozen vice presidents and directors of circulation at the biggest publishing houses in New York. It was a campaign that produced a 100 percent contact rate and a 100 percent conversion-to-sale rate and launched my business. It was worth millions of dollars to me, and it all came from a campaign that cost less than a hundred dollars.

So you might wonder, "How is this book different from the original? What does it add to the Contact Marketing story?"

The first book has resonated with people all over the world who really needed to get meetings. Naturally, those who sell for a living see the value in breaking through to virtually anyone immediately. But there are also entrepreneurs who recognize that the ability to make critical connections quickly is essential to their success and nonprofits that perceive the significance of making contact with more megadonors. Job seekers, too, understand the unfair advantage it gives them to stand out to prospective employers.

I know because a lot of those people shared their stories with me. But they also unanimously expressed one unfulfilled wish after reading *How to Get a Meeting with Anyone*: They wanted to *see* what the campaigns looked like. What did it look like when Dan Waldschmidt sent those swords? What does it look like when I send cartoons to help enterprise sales teams break through to their top accounts and prospects?

Those are important questions, and I sought to address them in this book. The intent was to produce a collection of case studies with photography, to give readers a better look at successful contact campaigns. But the book quickly took on a bigger scope. The change happened as I was googling "the coolest business cards in the world." I discovered there was a collection of the same cards showing up over and over.

There was Kevin Mitnick's lock-pick card made of etched stainless steel, and Remo Caminada's card-sleeve combination for a dentist that was so involving it was easy to see why the card regularly generates new business for the doctor. Then there was Poul Nielsen's sheet-rubber card that changed everything. It suggested an entirely new paradigm for the results we should expect from our Contact Marketing campaigns, which already reach as high as 100 percent. I'll just say it can go even higher.

These and other cards in the compilations all had one thing in common: They didn't follow the strategy that defines every business card on the planet. And they suggested an even more radical strategy that has business cards directly generating sales, revenue, metrics, and ROI. I have dubbed these "Pocket Campaigns" in this book.

Then I started looking at the roles technologies such as artificial intelligence, augmented reality (AR), and virtual reality (VR) might play in future campaigns. And again, an astonishing new paradigm emerged. The more I looked, the more the book transformed from a collection of case studies to an entirely new *playbook* for Contact Marketing. Even a new *manifesto* for what Contact Marketing should become.

Some of the insights into how much Contact Marketing has evolved and how profoundly it can contribute to rapid, sustainable growth didn't even occur to me until I reviewed all the chapters together. What emerged was a shocking set of conclusions, which combine at the end of the book, where I describe "The Perfect Contact Campaign," a step-by-step guide for your own campaign.

This isn't all theory and no practice. There are still plenty of case studies of even more audacious things people have done to break through to their most important prospects and accounts. They're amazing and now fully illustrated with photography and art. There is a lot to see and reference for your own campaigns.

*How to Get a Meeting with Anyone* includes twenty categories of Contact Marketing campaigns. They are all still valid and all still generating strong results. This book shows a few of the campaigns described in the first, but most of it is new. You'll find new sections on AI, AR and VR, LinkedIn, personalization, digital marketing, jewel boxing, unsolicited proposals, perseverance, video, and the aforementioned Pocket Campaigns. They are all additive to my seminal book.

There is also a fascinating look into how Hollywood has either portrayed Contact Marketing in film or used Contact Marketing directly to arrange Tinseltown tête-à-têtes. One story in particular, about a young singer-songwriter gaining the attention of Johnny Cash, will utterly inspire you. That story alone confirms the expression "Fortune favors the bold" so completely that you will never again doubt the value of audacity in your own client outreach.

When Amazon first announced it would be seeking a location for a second headquarters, cities, states, and municipalities were invited to submit proposals. The company received more than 250 submissions, but some contenders went much further, turning Amazon's HQ2 search into one of the biggest Contact Marketing stories in recent history. Tucson sent Amazon a twenty-one-foot-tall saguaro cactus. The city of Stonecrest, Georgia, offered to change its name to

NBBJ/Sean Airhart

**AMAZON'S SEARCH FOR A SECOND HEADQUARTERS**

*"Amazon Spheres," part of the company's headquarters campus in downtown Seattle, Washington. Amazon's search for its "HQ2" location set off a frenzy of Contact Marketing activity among cities, states, and municipalities across North America, hoping to gain the company's attention.*

Sun Corridor Inc.

**TUCSON'S HQ2 BID OPENS WITH TWENTY-ONE-FOOT-TALL CACTUS**

*The community-development authority for the city of Tucson wasted no time getting Amazon's attention to propose locating the company's second headquarters in the Arizona desert. Their contact device was a twenty-one-foot tall saguaro cactus on a flatbed truck, quickly dispatched to Amazon's Seattle headquarters.*

Amazon. Another set up giant Amazon packages all over the city, with wireless devices to issue tweets to the company about the benefits of locating its new headquarters there.

We all know how the Amazon story turned out, but the big message is that Contact Marketing has grown, and that is the focus of this second book in the series. Even though it produces response rates and ROI figures well beyond those of other forms of marketing, we are still only beginning to see how far it can go. Contact Marketing is expanding and evolving rapidly. It is also quickly becoming mainstream, as it proves its worth as a sales growth strategy.

I was expecting to write a book about case studies, but it turned into something much more. It turned into an entirely new model for Contact Marketing, one in which we expect to regularly generate 100 percent response rates, support the impetus for any given sale all the way through completion, and provoke more sales from existing clients.

We live in an amazing age, one in which we can connect on LinkedIn with the authors of our favorite books, ask questions, and share stories. I've heard some amazing ones from the readers of *How to Get a Meeting with Anyone*, particularly about the difference that book has made in their careers and lives. In the later paperback edition, I included the story of how Dom Steinmann used Contact Marketing to leapfrog from a freshly hired sales development representative (SDR) just out of college to sales manager of a multibillion-dollar company in the span of just one year.

Since then, other stories about startups using the book to quickly spool up have poured in. Some readers keep piles of the book on hand to give out as gifts. Others use it as a training manual for their sales teams.

What is clear is that Contact Marketing is an important tool for sales, business development, job searching—really any activity that requires contact with the key people with the power to change everything, if only they could be reached. Contact Marketing gives us that ability. And as you're about to read in the coming chapters, it has evolved into a miraculous tool for exploding the scale of our careers, businesses, and lives.

Let's jump in, shall we?

# PART 1

## CONTACT MARKETING BASICS

# CHAPTER 1

## MAKING CONTACT

What is the greatest friction point in every career and in every business? It's not the absence of customers or investors. It's not resistance from a hypercompetitive market. It's not a shortage of capital. It is the lack of access to important people. It's getting meetings—the right meetings. With the people who can become dream clients, sponsors, strategic partners, employers, or investors. With the people who have the power to change everything.

Amazing things could happen, *if only you could get through*.

If you had the ability to get meetings with anyone, at will, all the friction-causing issues above would disappear. You'd have access to customers, investors, and an abundance of revenue. You'd slice through competitors. And you'd have all the capital you want. Or you'd get that job interview with that dream employer. Doesn't that sound like a skill worth having?

The ability to make contact is a universal human need. And challenge. Everything we do in life requires making connections. As a marketer, I need to make connections. And I have had tremendous success in doing so. You see, I have a secret weapon that gets people's attention—among other things, I'm a cartoonist for *The Wall Street Journal*. Being able to craft cartoons as a device to make connections is a great advantage. I've used them to reach presidents, prime ministers, celebrities, countless CEOs, and other top decision makers. It has always been easy for me to break through.

I used to think my cartoon-drawing talents gave me an unfair advantage, but I was wrong. Well, partially wrong. It *is* an advantage to use a creative approach in making contact with someone, but you don't have to be a professional cartoonist to be a successful Contact Marketer. For my first book, *How to Get a Meeting with Anyone*, I interviewed the top hundred sales thought leaders in the world and asked them how they were breaking through to their top-level connections. If you've read that book, you'll know that they had some of their own brilliant, creative ways to do so. I later discovered that every time I spoke to a group and asked if someone had a can't-miss method for breaking through, there were always hands raised.

As I interviewed sources for that first book, I also learned that no one had a name for what we were doing—using inventive, audacious means to connect. It's surprising that something so commonly used wouldn't have a name, so I gave it one: Contact Marketing. And ever since, the term has been catching on all over the world. I'll provide a more elaborate definition later in this chapter, but briefly, Contact Marketing is a disciplined ability to make contact with our most important prospects, investors, partners, mentors, and others.

# 100 PERCENT RESPONSE RATE AS YOUR BASELINE

My first experience with Contact Marketing came at the start of my career. I wanted to create direct mail campaigns for the big magazine publishers, and I quickly picked up assignments from *Rolling Stone* and *Bon Appétit*. The mailings both featured cartoons with personalized captions, so even my first contact campaign used personalized cartoons.

Those first test campaigns for the two magazines set new response records, and I wanted to share the story with the rest of the big publishers. That meant connecting with about two dozen highly placed contacts at Time Inc., Condé Nast, *Forbes*, *The Wall Street Journal*, Times Mirror Magazines, and more.

The campaign included an 8" × 10" framable personalized cartoon print and a letter explaining the approach and new results. I suggested that we use the same device in tests for their titles. The campaign generated a 100 percent response.

I connected with all the target executives, and they all became clients. That's a 100 percent contact rate and a 100 percent conversion. It is the campaign that launched my business. It was worth millions of dollars, and it stemmed from a campaign spend of less than a hundred dollars.

What I just described to you is supposed to be impossible. No one gets 100 percent response rates to any form of marketing. Many are content with just a few percentage points, and while some campaigns score higher, many digital forms eke out tiny fractions of a percentage point for response.

Similarly, marketing campaigns are meant to produce at least as much as was spent. If they get multiples of 100 percent, management is pretty happy. But Contact Marketing campaigns regularly produce returns on investment (ROI) of over 10,000 percent, or even well over 100,000. In my research, I've found that the record percentage return for a Contact Marketing campaign is in the *tens of millions*.

In ads for *How to Get a Meeting with Anyone*, the headline reads, "One meeting can change everything." It most certainly can. When I think back on all the best things that have happened in my life, they involve first making extraordinary connections with people in extraordinary positions.

I met my wife after spotting her in a magazine. Obviously, we wouldn't have gotten married if I were not able to meet her. Every one of the major accounts in my Contact Marketing agency came as a result of making extraordinary connections. This book exists because of remarkable connections. My cartoons appear in *The Wall Street Journal* because of life-changing editorial connections. All the interviews that informed my books came from making important connections.

I am sure if you think about each milestone in your life, you'll have a similar story. They all come from making remarkable connections. Thus, this could be one of the most important books you could ever read to advance your career, your business, and your life.

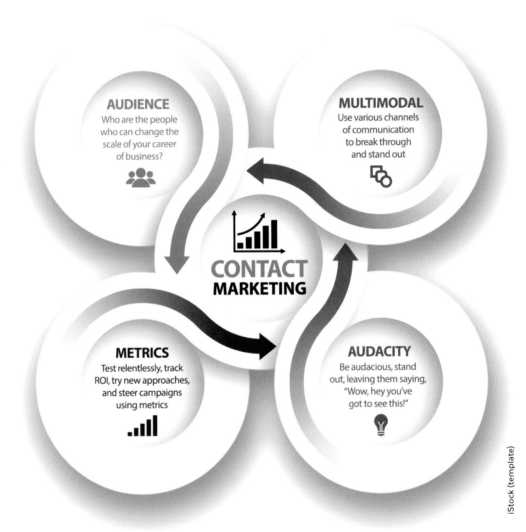

iStock (template)

### THE CONTACT MARKETING MISSION

*The Contact Marketing mission is to create explosive growth through contact with the people who can change the scale of your career, business, or life. Marked by careful selection of target contacts, multimodal communication, audacity, and gravity-defying metrics, Contact Marketing is a high-growth, low-risk strategy.*

# PUTTING IT ALL TOGETHER: CONTACT MARKETING 101

This book is part of a series that began with *How to Get a Meeting with Anyone*. The two books are different in scope, and if you haven't read the first in the series, you'll probably want to pick it up to read about the many strategies, stories, and tools I include there, and learn about the twenty categories of Contact Marketing campaigns that are not part of this book. The intent of both books is to empower you to make any connections you want, with anyone you choose. To do so, you need to know some basics about Contact Marketing and connecting with important people at will.

> If someone asks you, "How could we do a million-dollars' worth of business right now?" you ought to be ready to answer.

These basics include the definition of Contact Marketing, the notion of executive assistants as your ally, the ability to develop a VIP statement, the idea of going after the CEO—the Center of Enterprise Opportunity—and the fundamentals of a million-dollar phone call. I cover these in depth in *How to Get a Meeting with Anyone*, but here is a look at those concepts briefly.

---

**Contact Marketing:**
A fusion of marketing and selling in which often-audacious forms of marketing are used in support of specific, high-level sales approaches to VIP prospects and accounts, resulting in extraordinarily high levels of response, ROI, and explosive growth of the enterprise.

---

## Executive assistants are your ally

Most sales reps refer to executive assistants as gatekeepers and wonder how they can circumvent them to get to the executive. Ironically, that attitude is what prevents them from breaking through. Assistants meter access, but their job is also to bring relevant sources and people to their bosses' attention.

They are always watching for interesting opportunities their executives might otherwise miss.

Think of executive assistants as vice presidents of access, or talent scouts. They wield tremendous power and are some of the sharpest people in their organizations. Your job is to package yourself as someone who belongs and is welcomed. Assistants should be part of your campaign. Include a few contact elements just for them.

Remember also that executives rely on their assistants' judgment of callers. They'll ask how the caller treated the assistant. They'll ask the assistant's opinion of the caller. Assistants often have the power to say, "You need to talk to this person." Engineer your contact campaign to ensure executive assistants always become your allies.

## Develop a VIP statement

When you first break through to a target executive or their assistant, you have only a few seconds to entice them. That's when you should be ready to deliver your VIP statement. Try to confine it to a dozen words or fewer. Ultimately, as *SHIFT!* coauthor Craig Elias says, it should contain a bold promise that has them asking, "How would you do that?"

My VIP statement is a bit different. I often send a cartoon to connect. Before sending, I contact the executive assistant and say this: "Hello, my name is Stu Heinecke. I'm one of *The Wall Street Journal*'s cartoonists, and I'm sending a print of one of my cartoons about your boss." It's almost an ambush. Who wouldn't want to continue the conversation? You must come up with your own quick statement of introduction that does not allow the prospect or assistant to dismiss your call.

## The goals have changed

Every campaign must define the "desired response" it will produce. In Contact Marketing, we want recipients to respond, "I love the way you think!" But as you will read, the mission has changed a bit. Now we're looking to incite evangelism with our campaigns. Now, the desired response is, "Wow, hey everyone, come here! You've got to see this!" They're still impressed with your thinking, but now we want to motivate recipients to share your campaign with colleagues.

### CEO—"Center of Enterprise Opportunity"

It's nice to connect with actual CEOs—that is, chief executive officers—but there are many times when it's unnecessary. As *Eat Their Lunch* author Anthony Iannarino explains, you want to reach *the CEO of the problem you want to solve*. Imagine "CEO" to mean "Center of Enterprise Opportunity" and target the person who really has the authority and acute need to do business with you. It will make your campaign far more effective.

### Your million-dollar phone call

When you get the right person on the phone or in a meeting, you should always be aware not only of what you want but how to get it. That means always being ready to make a million-dollar phone call. If someone asks you, "How could we do a million dollars' worth of business right now?" you ought to be ready to answer.

If you wanted to do a million-dollar program with my agency, I already know what the structure, pace, scale, and expected results would be. You should be similarly prepared for your prospecting calls.

## Critical Next Steps

For each chapter of this book, you will find an objective related to the chapter along with a set of critical steps to follow and important questions to ask yourself, based on the types of Contact Campaign ideas presented in the chapter. Use these steps and questions to form your new, transformative strategy. Take time to record your answers. Your notes will guide your Contact Marketing strategy. By the end of the book, you will have everything you need to press ahead, connect with anyone, and grow your business.

**OBJECTIVE:** Adapt your approach to make the connections you desire.

### Step 1. Ask yourself, "What do I want to change?"

Chances are you bought this book because there is something about how you do business (or even how you do life) you want to change. That is, you want the outcome to change. If making contact is the biggest friction point in business, what is your commitment to changing that source of friction in yours? Keep in mind, Contact Marketing is more than a collection of clever tactics for connecting. It is a change-management program meant to create rapid growth, greater market share, and unfair strategic advantages. So what do you want to change?

### Step 2. Take stock—What have you tried so far?

We all have experience with reaching out to people who are important to our lives. What have you been doing so far, and how has it been working? Are there elements that are unique to you that should be integrated into your future approaches? What hasn't worked and why?

### Step 3. Confront what you like least about prospecting.

When you think of cold-calling, what thoughts immediately come to mind? Is prospecting your least favorite business activity, thus something you avoid? If it is, give thought to what may be holding you back. The Contact Marketing strategies in this book will help you break through, but first you've got to get past your own mental blockades.

# POINTS TO REMEMBER

✔ Making contact is the biggest friction point in business.

✔ The ability to break through to those most important to our success is a universal human need.

✔ The purpose of Contact Marketing is to give you an unfair advantage in your marketplace.

✔ Contact Marketing is actually a change-management initiative that drives the enterprise toward rapid growth and market dominance.

✔ Contact Marketing produces unusually high levels of response and ROI, well beyond any other form of marketing.

✔ Contact Marketing is a fusion of marketing and selling. Combining the two disciplines results in an unusual level of cooperation and shared objectives for the greater good of the enterprise.

✔ "Contact Marketing" is the name I gave to the practice of using audacious, clever means to connect with important contacts.

✔ This book does not replace *How to Get a Meeting with Anyone*; the first book explains Contact Marketing in depth and contains strategies and twenty categories of Contact Marketing campaigns that are not in this book. Each complements the other.

✔ Be sure to record your answers and observations for each step listed in the Critical Next Steps section at the end of each chapter. By the end of the book, your notes will define your Contact Marketing strategy.

✔ Remember, one meeting really can change everything.

# CHAPTER 2

# THE POWER OF PERSEVERANCE

Two words float in our vocabularies, often interchangeably, that are often uttered with a tone of admiration—unless they're used to describe the actions of salespeople: perseverance and persistence.

If entrepreneurs persevere over several years to launch a business and then sell it for hundreds of millions of dollars, they're heroes. If a saleswoman persists through ninety-seven calls and finally makes an appointment on the ninety-eighth, she's a pest. Yet both have produced, through their perseverance, enormous value from their efforts.

In this section, we'll explore the nature and meaning of these two words in the context of making good things happen in business. We'll examine amazing stories of success produced through sheer determination, and we'll look at how persistence and perseverance can be systematized in your own business activities.

But first, let's look at the difference between the two words. The dictionary defines perseverance as "steady persistence in a course of action, purpose or state, especially in spite of difficulties, obstacles or discouragement." It's interesting that perseverance is actually defined by the display of persistence. Meanwhile, persistence is defined simply as "the act of persisting, the quality of being persistent."[1]

> " *Persistence is the simple act of continuing relentlessly. Perseverance requires awareness, intent, and character.* "

Both words are defined with the word "persistence," but the word "perseverance" shows up in neither definition. So what's going on here? We know that a cough can persist, but it doesn't persevere. A noxious odor can persist, an annoying noise can persist, but they're never described as persevering. Persistence is the simple act of continuing relentlessly. Perseverance requires awareness, intent, and character.

Persistence is the act of repeated action. Perseverance is a character trait. Perseverance is the strategic driver of why we persist. When we persevere, we use persistence to make it happen.

Perseverance is often said to make the difference between success and failure. There are many stories of deals achieved in which persistence alone was the driving force. It tells the buyer you're for real. It shows them how interested you are, how consistent the quality of your work is, and how you handle adverse conditions. It provides a preview of the relationship ahead. It gives assurance that you'll always be there when needed. And that can greatly improve your odds for a successful outcome in your Contact Marketing campaigns.

## PERSEVERANCE BRINGS BREAKTHROUGHS

To research this chapter, I returned to the top sales thought leaders in the world who were the original sources for *How to Get a Meeting with Anyone*. For that

---

[1] Dictionary.com, definitions of *perseverance* and *persistence*, based on *Random House Unabridged Dictionary*, 2019.

book I asked, "When you absolutely must connect with someone important, someone nearly impossible to reach, how do *you* do it?" This time I asked, "What is the nature and value of perseverance in sales and in business?" And once again, they shared superb insights and techniques.

The group's unanimous conclusion is that perseverance is a required trait for success in business, and certainly in sales. They all have stories of people who have persevered through daunting circumstances, emerging with great rewards on the other side. *New Sales Simplified* author Mike Weinberg can trace the acquisition of his present home to one account in particular that he won as a result of relentless perseverance.

The famed Hollywood movie producer Brian Grazer, whom we'll revisit in chapter three, is an expert at getting meetings with literally anyone. He is an obsessively curious man, which fuels the consistently excellent quality of films he and partner Ron Howard produce for our enjoyment. How does he satisfy that relentless curiosity? He seeks out fascinating people for meetings, or what he calls "Curiosity Conversations." Over the course of his career, Grazer has met with Jonas Salk (the man who saved millions of lives by discovering a cure for polio), Jim Lovell (Apollo 13 astronaut), Edward Teller (inventor of the hydrogen bomb), and Fidel Castro as well as countless artists, musicians, scientists, entrepreneurs, politicians, journalists, and philanthropists.

It must be nice to be an Oscar-winning Hollywood producer, but the secret to Grazer's success at getting meetings doesn't stem from his fame. He attributes his success to one thing: perseverance. In his book *A Curious Mind* (coauthored with Charles Fishman) he tells fantastic stories of perseverance. In one case, Grazer left messages for a year before breaking through for a meeting. Even in his vaunted position, perseverance is a must. It turns out Grazer is just like the rest of us.

If perseverance is necessary for our selling success, can it be taught? Can it be reduced to a process? Our experts were split on this question. *High Profit Prospecting* author Mark Hunter believes it is imperative to hire someone for whom perseverance is already a native trait. In fact, he advises clients to put new sales rep candidates to the test. At the conclusion of the first interview, the hiring manager promises to call back in two days, but never does. It's only after the prospective rep calls back a second time that they reconnect for a second interview. If the candidate doesn't pass that simple test, they never get hired.

Does this mean all is lost if you weren't born with a knack for perseverance? Perseverance is a character trait, not a personality trait, which means it can be developed—and like any character trait, it takes desire and discipline and lots of practice. As Hunter's example shows, those who have developed perseverance already have a big advantage—but it can be cultivated in anyone. As you'll read in some of this chapter's case studies, some sales reps discovered simple techniques that can smooth the way and help anyone become more persistent. It begins with following a plan.

# MAKE AN APPOINTMENT WITH YOURSELF FIRST

Many of us miss the simplest point about being persistent. We move through our days, perhaps making lists of what we want to accomplish. We think we're being efficient, but mostly, we're just busy missing the mark.

In a rush to check off as many items as possible, we attack the easy things first. Order a copy of that report. Check. Make sure the invitations to that event were sent. Check. Call IT to change a password. Check. Order those shoes from Amazon. Check. But at the end of the day, that critical deal outline is still left unfinished. In fact, not even started. There's always time tomorrow.

> *Persistence needs to be a priority. It needs to show up in your calendar.*

Meanwhile, unexpected client needs intervene all day long. It's pretty easy to be busy all day and never notice you got very little done. That is especially true of the things you perhaps didn't want to do in the first place—like following up on sales outreach. As *Your Sales Management Guru's Guide* series author and *Forbes* contributor Ken Thoreson points out, "People don't like to do things they don't want to do." His advice is to do the hard things on the list first but also to set appointments with yourself throughout the week for prospecting and follow-up. Persistence needs to be a priority.

So how do we persevere in giving persistence the place it deserves? It needs to show up in our calendars.

**TACTICAL EXAMPLE**
# Putting Persistence in Your Calendar

**TACTIC:** Be strategic with your time and leads by creating a persistence campaign.

**BACKGROUND:** There are many stories of deals achieved in which persistence alone is the driving force. *New Sales. Simplified* author Mike Weinberg points out that most salespeople try once or twice on a sale and then give up.

**CHALLENGES:** It makes sense that if you don't book time in your calendar for follow-up, it won't get done. It certainly won't get the attention it deserves, and continually failing to follow up is what causes requests for contact—and sales—to fail.

**CAMPAIGN SPECIFICS:** A persistence campaign has two requirements: a defined process for follow-up that maps out the touches, tools, and scripts to be used over the course of a scheduled set of steps, and a disciplined use of time to ensure the process is followed.

What does this look like? First, you build follow-up time into your schedule. Simply carving out daily two-hour blocks in your calendar, six weeks in advance, helps you corral the inevitable day-to-day interruptions that monopolize the most productive uses of your time.

**WHY IT'S NEEDED:** We keep hearing it takes seven to twelve touches before a buyer responds. The logical conclusion is that setting up time for regular follow-ups immediately raises the likelihood that your Contact Marketing outreach will be successful. But if you don't book time in your calendar for follow-up, it won't get done.

**WHAT TO KEEP IN MIND:** Admittedly, just inserting regular appointments in your calendar to be persistent sounds like a simplistic solution. But remember that perseverance is a pattern, a product of timing and discipline. And a lot of people simply never get around to it. If you constantly find yourself working down a daily to-do list, being very busy, but seldom accomplishing your goals, setting firm appointments on your calendar is an easy solution.

# TIMING, DISCIPLINE, AND MINDSET

Perseverance is important for anyone in business. For the entrepreneur, perseverance drives the vision forward, attracts investors, and fills the client roster.

For the manager, it powers their rise through the ranks as successes mount. For the business owner, it is the difference between a flourishing enterprise with exit-strategy potential and a bankrupt flop.

But for the sales rep, perseverance is even more serious. In the daily sink-or-swim reality of their careers, they must be naturally persistent or drown in a series of missed quotas until they're finally fired. This is not just a heartless push by management to produce sales. It's the central mission of the company: profit or perish.

Perseverance is more than a personality trait—it is also a mindset, a mental toughness merged with an unyielding confidence that the solution you're offering will substantially improve the client's business. *Hacking Sales* author Max Altschuler says it's best to adopt an immigrant's point of view. Many grew up in tough circumstances and learned to fight and persevere to get what they wanted. And they employ that mindset throughout their lives, often giving them an unbeatable advantage over native citizens who've had it too easy and lack resilience in the face of disappointment.

> *How do you make the process of beating your head against the wall every day fun?*

But you don't have to come from a third-world country to create an unbeatable advantage in the perseverance race. *High Profit Selling* author Mark Hunter reminds us that there is always a reset button. If today was tough, hit the reset button and come in refreshed the next day, ready to make amazing things happen. He says one key is to make the process fun.

But wait, how do you make the process of beating your head against the wall every day fun? As a first step, stop seeing it as beating your head against the wall. Then you can build a process to follow that actually is fun because it works.

## CASE STUDY
# Ram Tool's Persistence Process

**BACKGROUND:** Sales expert Mike Weinberg tells an inspiring story about Ram Tool, a company that sells construction supplies. Ram Tool faces stiff opposition in its markets from entrenched competitors with long-standing relationships with the major contractors in their areas.

**CHALLENGES:** Relationships are built over time. Ram's sales reps wouldn't stand a chance of breaking through by calling on their construction accounts' offices. They needed to be out on the job sites, meeting with the foremen who make purchasing decisions as needs arise.

**CAMPAIGN SPECIFICS:** Every working day, Ram Tool reps head out to construction sites in their territories, clad in visibility vests, work boots, and construction helmets. They're there to run their process, a prescribed ten-step persistence campaign that

Mike Weinberg

### RAM TOOL'S TEN-STEP PERSISTENCE CAMPAIGN

*How do you break through to new accounts? Ram Tool has devised a simple process that can be taught to all its reps, resulting in predictable outcomes. At the end of ten weekly visits, buyers conclude, "It seems like you're really serious. Let's take a look at a few things we need."*

consistently wins new business. The campaign is a series of weekly visits to the job superintendent, each time delivering a little more value, asking a few planned questions. The reps are courteous, always respect the foreman's time, and always end each encounter with a promise to show up again in a week.

**RESULTS:** For Ram Tool, perseverance isn't some loose concept of never giving up in the face of adversity, of never saying "No." It is a well-defined, ten-wave campaign that produces consistent, predictable outcomes. Note that this is not a sales-automation operation. It is a process of personally showing up, of demonstrating commitment to the buyer's success.

Ram Tool reports its ten-wave campaign produces a roughly 80 percent conversion. The campaign generates business based on programmed perseverance. Each rep uses the same process and gets roughly the same outcome.

By the tenth week, Ram Tool's prospects often remark, "It seems like you're really serious. Let's take a look at a few things we need." That is a direct result of perseverance and the commitment it demonstrates to the buyer. Perseverance wins business.

**KEY TAKEAWAY:** Perseverance can show up as a natural course of events driven by the rep's push to develop business. Perhaps there is a natural cadence to their outreach and follow-up actions. It could be a demonstration of the rep's mindset, sense of timing, and discipline. But as Ram Tool's campaign shows, persistence can easily be translated into a program that produces uniform follow-up and results.

Your Contact Campaign should be built around that same personal persistence. Since our Contact Marketing mission is to break through, and do it in a way that has the target executive saying, "I love the way you think," a demonstration of tenacity and commitment can be a powerful contributing factor to your success.

# VALUE OVER TIME

To persist is to contact, over and over and over. That can either lead to a lot of frustration—on both sides—or a successful outcome. Some sales reps wonder why they're not breaking through. They send a lot of emails and follow up regularly but still receive no response from the contact. Others build contact over time, which leads to relationships and trust, and ultimately to sales.

The same apparent level of work is producing very different levels of business. What's causing the difference?

In most cases, it is a matter of delivering cumulative value. But let's pause for a moment. Isn't the goal of Contact Marketing to help you break through to your toughest prospects on the first try? Well, yes, it is. It's far less work and a greatly shortened sales cycle if you can get in and start selling right away. But whether you make immediate contact or it takes several efforts to make the connection, perseverance sets the stage and plays a central role in moving the contact forward.

> *Whether you make immediate contact or it takes several efforts to make the connection, perseverance sets the stage.*

One of the best ways of making that happen is to continually deliver value. It shows that you care about the contact target's business, and it models the kind of relationship you'll have before they commit to any business with you.

Most executives treasure insights and information they can't get anywhere else. If you become the source of that value, you earn the status of trusted business adviser, a necessary step toward capturing scale-bursting levels of business.

## HOW TO DELIVER VALUE

How can you deliver value? Three sales veterans and authors weigh in with three steps you can take to provide value to prospective clients. These actions give you valuable content to use in a persistence campaign.

**Be a fountain of information:** Tibor Shanto, author of the *Objection Handling Handbook,* says delivering value can be as simple as sending articles from publications the executive might not otherwise see, that touch in some way upon issues in their markets and industries. Articles should always be sent with a quick narrative, explaining the relevance of the piece to their business.

**Be on even footing in terms of knowledge:** *Your Sales Management Guru's Guide* series author Ken Thoreson recommends reading voraciously to create equal business status with targeted executives.

**Start an advisory board:** Thoreson also advocates convening a "customer advisory group," a set of executives from eight of your clients, to discuss challenges, trends, and problems they're seeing in their marketplaces.

---

**Channel your inner news reporter**: Tom Searcy, *Whale Hunting* coauthor, takes the delivery of value a great leap further, with a formula to quickly penetrate markets. His approach is to conduct TV news-style interviews of a dozen thought leaders in a given market. The interviews are transcribed into a book and the videos shared with each executive's company. This makes it easy to penetrate any company, simply by calling its PR department and offering to do it all at no cost. The approach allows Searcy to deliver an overwhelming amount of value to the targeted executives, leading to lasting contact and valuable relationships in a newly conquered market.

**Your Next Step**: Consider if any of these will work with any of your prospective clients. If so, schedule some time on your calendar for reading articles, thinking through the best candidates for your advisory group, or planning an interview.

---

Consistently delivering value is the best way to employ the power of perseverance in your Contact Marketing efforts. It's the difference between being a pest and generating startling new levels of business. If you're continuing to ping your prospects with the message "Hey, I was just checking in to see if anything changed," you're wasting their time and yours. But if your messages change to "I thought you might find the transcripts from last week's Gartner Conference useful," you may quickly earn a chance to do business. How the contact sees you has changed, and the new perception works in your favor.

Contact Marketing is intended to shorten the cycle of making critical connections happen. Whether you break through right away or it takes several tries, you're just beginning a journey toward a relationship meant to last and help your clients improve their businesses. It's a long-term process, and it should always be fueled by the exchange of value and insights.

# SERVING FINAL NOTICE

We've all experienced stalled proposals. You've had several conversations with the client, they love what you've been telling them, and you eagerly await sign-off on your proposal, which you're assured is in the works. Then nothing. Crickets.

You know you need to break the silence and get the ball rolling again if you ever hope to get the business, but what if you've exhausted your personal limit of follow-up calls or your persistence process has run its course? At this point, many would be ready to give up and move on. They'd sigh and think, "Well, it wasn't meant to be." I know how you feel. It can be a time of peak frustration. But for me, it's actually one of the most enjoyable stages of a campaign.

How can that be? Because now we get to unleash the mischief, to serve notice that it's all about to end, that they're about to miss out.

*Ultimate Sales Machine* author Chet Holmes once shared a wonderfully devilish method for getting people to finally respond. His tool of choice was a miniature trash can, stuffed with a wadded-up copy of his final contact letter. The letter started by saying, "I've sent you several letters in the past, to which you never have replied. Since I assume you must have thrown those all in the trash, I thought I'd save you some time with this one . . ."

My old friend Chet was using a classic Contact Marketing visual metaphor to get his point across, that the recipient's lack of response had been quite rude. He took a risk with this approach, sure, but these packages were going to potential clients who weren't responding. He knew he had to do something or they'd drift away forever.

Another favorite method of "serving final notice" is one of my own. I explain it in the next case study.

## CASE STUDY
# A Beautiful Giclée Art Print for Their Office

**BACKGROUND:** Proposals stall all the time. They probably stall far more often than they succeed, leaving us all at some point to wonder what to do next. What we need is a foolproof method to restore momentum.

**CHALLENGES:** If you've had proposals stall, your prospects have probably had other priorities pop up, displacing your proposal from their immediate focus. Or they've lost interest. Or they haven't noticed they're delaying anything. Whatever the reason, saving the proposed sale requires immediate action.

**CAMPAIGN SPECIFICS:** My solution is to have a fine art giclée print made up, featuring the cartoon at the beginning of this book. It shows an executive with his sleeves rolled up and the phone cradled on his shoulder as he leafs through some papers on his desk. The caption: *"Hey listen, we got your proposal and like everything except having to pay you."*

The print is packaged in my own custom fold-over folio piece, made of corrugated cardboard covered with enlarged mezzotint cartoon art. Inside is a handwritten note saying, "Sorry it didn't work out this time. Maybe next time." The reactions are often priceless.

**RESULTS:** The giclée print piece, combined with the handwritten note, immediately prompts recipients to pick up the phone or reach out by email, restoring forward motion to roughly 50 percent of the stalled proposals. They often call to apologize for the delay and immediately approve the proposed project.

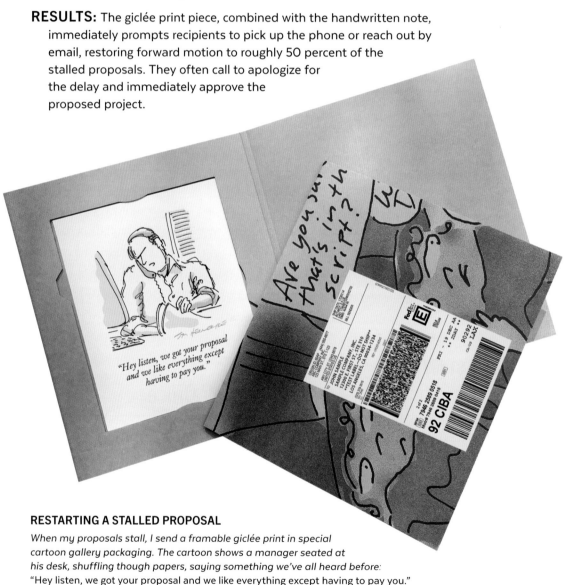

### RESTARTING A STALLED PROPOSAL

*When my proposals stall, I send a framable giclée print in special cartoon gallery packaging. The cartoon shows a manager seated at his desk, shuffling though papers, saying something we've all heard before:* "Hey listen, we got your proposal and we like everything except having to pay you." *At least half of the proposals spring back to life and the projects move forward.*

**KEY TAKEAWAY:** The people I'm reaching out to have not been responding to my proposal or follow-ups. I need an effective means to reach them, and creativity helps. Sometimes prospects aren't actively avoiding your call but have fallen into a rut. They're embarrassed that they haven't called you, and the longer it goes, the deeper their embarrassment. The "serving final notice" humorous contact piece interrupts all of that.

# VARIATION

I have other cartoons at my disposal that I send as greeting cards to prospective clients to prompt replies. One that I've used frequently shows a guy standing at a pay phone at an old, broken-down gas station in the middle of the desert, probably somewhere along Route 66. He's speaking into the phone, saying, "Hi Bob, it's me again. Listen, I don't know if you've been checking your voice mail all last week, but I'm still here at the same number, waiting for your call." Of course, with the name "Bob" in the caption, I'm sending it to someone named Bob. Chances are, if Bob has not been answering my calls, he will now.

"Hi Bob, it's me again. Listen, I don't know if you've been checking your voice mail all last week, but I'm still here at the same number, waiting for your call."

**HEY, ARE YOU STILL THERE?**

*This gas station card goes out when a contact has gone cold. The caption is personalized and the effect is often magical. If the prospect is embarrassed about not calling back, the cartoon melts the ice and contact is reestablished.*

I find these kinds of campaigns to be quite valuable. While they may seem a bit silly, they are also utterly disarming. Who wouldn't crack when presented with a tiny trash can with a final contact letter wadded up inside? It takes a lot of nerve to send a letter that way, but what do you have to lose? Remember, these campaigns are going to people who have not been responding. They will probably be gone forever without some forceful intervention.

# SET AN EXPIRATION DATE

When a persistence campaign nears the end of its tether, you have a few choices. Letting it lapse seems like a waste of a lot of invested effort. Serving a final notice can be effective. There's also a third option: Invoke an expiration date.

Sales thought leader and author Tibor Shanto says it's a basic law of human behavior: People want what they cannot have. Putting an expiration date on a proposal makes use of that law. If prospective clients have a serious interest in your service or product, a deadline can cause them to act as they become aware of the closing window of opportunity. Advertisers bank on this principle all the time, and effective sales representatives build it into their strategies for closing deals as well.

> *It's a basic law of human behavior: People want what they cannot have.*

## CASE STUDY
## This Is About to Expire

**BACKGROUND:** Despite our best attempts to woo them, clients sometimes don't take action on our proposals. Gaining leverage in those situations can be difficult, so you need to let the dynamics of human behavior work in your favor—entice people to go after what they cannot have.

**CHALLENGES:** There is a risk that an expiration date might backfire, but Shanto feels the rewards far exceed the risks. If the prospect doesn't like the idea of a deadline imposed by a vendor, Shanto reasons, then they're not a serious prospect. It's best to know that early.

**CAMPAIGN SPECIFICS:** Sales tactician Tibor Shanto gets people's attention with deadlines. If a prospect knows that she must make a decision within a given time frame, she's more apt to respond. Shanto employs this tactic in various ways, but the most common is putting it in writing at the pitch stage. When Shanto formulates a proposal to a prospective client, he simply adds an expiration date and time—for example, "This proposal expires on June 12 at 5 PM." Shanto pushes it even further by contacting a prospect the day before a proposal expiration date with a reminder that his proposal is about to expire. He also offers to extend it by a week if the prospect needs more time.

In other instances, a deal has been approved, but it is stalled. In these cases Shanto again implements his "expiration date" campaign. If a deadline has already passed and a client asks, "What can we do to get this back on track?" Tibor responds, "Let me know what you want to do. I've moved on." The message is clear: "My deadlines mean something. Next time, pay attention." If there wasn't a hard deadline in place because everything had seemed a "go," but then faltered, Shanto still likes to indicate to the client that the window of opportunity has closed. For example, Shanto had an assignment to train executives in June one year. The engagement had been approved in January, but by the end of April, it remained stalled. So Shanto sent a note to the client that said, "Unfortunately the dates you were looking at are being bid away. When you're ready, let's talk again."

He took this approach knowing there was still a week's leeway in the actual deadline. He could have said, "If you don't act in a week, we'll have to cancel the dates." But going ahead and canceling now, the moment he sent the note, meant Shanto had time to reinstate the program if the client suddenly said, "Hey, wait! We want to do it!" It gives clients the chance to play the "Now that I can't have it, I want it" game and allows Shanto to set the rules of engagement going forward.

**RESULTS:** The results of this approach have varied for Shanto, but he says that even how prospects respond to the deadlines yields fruit. If prospects take the extension he offers, Shanto says it indicates a commitment to a serious review and, perhaps, a pending deal. When they're not concerned with the deadline, he knows there is no possibility of a deal, at least not within that period.

**KEY TAKEAWAY:** Withdrawing an opportunity by limiting its availability can push your negotiations into hyperdrive. People often respond positively to a pitch when they know they might not be able to get what they want if they wait.

## VARIATION

Rather than deciding on the expiration date yourself, you can use the decision on the date as an early engagement opportunity with your prospective client. With this approach, you make it known there will be an expiration date for your proposal, but ask the prospect what they see as a reasonable date. This promotes early dialogue between the two of you. Another method would be to use a document management platform and set an expiration date on the document link. You still let the prospect know when it expires, and you include it at the top of the proposal.

While some sales experts, like Shanto, use actual deadlines to prompt prospects, others employ the expiration-date principle in other ways. For example, when a prospect resists contact, Art Sobczak sends an email that addresses a previously discussed goal, such as increasing a prospect's revenue. The email might say, "I've reached out to you multiple times, and I'm going to assume increasing your revenue is not a priority at the moment. If I'm wrong, just reply 'Yes' or 'No.'" The email clearly puts the ball in the prospect's court, with the implication that Sobczak is moving on if he doesn't hear from the prospect.

Being persistent is always part of the process of engaging buyers. But there comes a point when your efforts may be more productively focused elsewhere. When that happens, it's worth reaching out with a final notice or an expiration-date tactic to see if you can move toward a closed deal.

Note that I used the word "persistent" above. I am not suggesting that, if a given deal doesn't happen, you should abandon a buyer who is worth pursuing. If you have identified someone of value, you can continue to persevere with the pursuit, even when you drop a particular persistence effort to reach them.

*Full Funnel Marketing* author Matt Heinz recommends keeping those people in a perpetual system of follow-up based on value. If you're constantly producing new content, they should be included. Heinz recalls one prospect who couldn't get his manager to sign off on a purchase. They stayed in regular contact while the fellow left the original company, took a job with another, then returned to the old company as the manager. It took a few years to pursue, but Matt's persistence paid off. He persevered and won.

Perseverance always matters. Even when you reach the expiration date, you can still persevere over a much longer period and win the business.

# WHEN DOES "NO" REALLY MEAN NO?

Art Sobczak says there's a difference between being uninterested and simply being hard to reach. If you were pursuing a connection with someone who hadn't been responding, how would you know which factor was in play?

Perseverance is really the only way to know. Some people want to respond positively to you, but they're nearly impossible to get on the phone. I once had a client at the *Harvard Business Review* who had an active campaign with us, and yet I couldn't get her on the phone. I left messages, but she wasn't calling back. I didn't think she was avoiding me, but I could have taken her lack of action as a "no" response to continuing the campaign. Instead I persevered, and we ended up creating a bit of history for the magazine with a record-setting campaign.

Sobczak recommends using a bit of social media research to make your outreach efforts more relevant and welcome, even if they don't produce a response for a very long time. Some people engage in the pursuit for a year or more. Tibor Shanto shared a story of a woman who pursued an executive at a Fortune 50 company. It took her a year, sending sixty messages, each with an evolving theme, to finally break through. Was prospect's lack of response to the first fifty-nine messages truly a "no"? Um, well, no. Meanwhile, Matt Heinz says it's not unusual for some prospects to remain in his pipeline for four or five years before they start doing business.

*The Emigrant Edge* author Brian Buffini has perhaps the best story of persisting in the face of repeated "no" responses.

## CASE STUDY
# One Giant Step for Neil Armstrong

**BACKGROUND:** Brian Buffini is a famous speaker, trainer, and real estate coach who evangelizes the powerful effects of referrals in sales and business. To attract paid attendees to his events, he often books impressive guest speakers to increase the draw. At one point, Buffini set his sights on Neil Armstrong as his blockbuster guest speaker for an upcoming event.

**CHALLENGES:** The first man ever to set foot on the moon was notoriously reclusive, shunning media interviews and speaking engagements, even when hosted by NASA. He truly was *impossible* to get.

**CAMPAIGN SPECIFICS:** Buffini's method of connecting with high-profile personalities was to send handwritten cards, followed by phone calls. The cards always explained why he was reaching out and why he wanted the recipient to join him onstage. His tools were handwritten cards and a great deal of perseverance.

**RESULTS:** Buffini sent card after card, but Armstrong's response was always "No." Buffini continued the cards, and at some point Armstrong had had enough. "When will you stop sending me these cards?" he asked, to which Buffini replied, "As soon as you agree to speak at my conference." That sealed the deal. Armstrong had refused to speak anywhere for years. But it was Buffini's perseverance that made the difference.

**KEY TAKEAWAY:** Perseverance can turn a temporary "no" into a "yes." Not giving up truly makes a difference.

NASA (Armstrong photo); iStock (card image)

**NEIL ARMSTRONG FINALLY STEPS ONSTAGE**

*Neil Armstrong wasn't shy about stepping onto the moon, but he certainly was about stepping onto a stage. Brian Buffini broke through all of that with a simple and unrelenting persistence campaign, landing the legendary astronaut as a coveted guest speaker for his event.*

# PERSISTENCE TAKEN TO THE EXTREME

There are all sorts of stories of triumph achieved through unreasonable persistence: the grandma in Korea (Cha Sa-soon) who finally passed her driver's license test on her 960th attempt; the French postman (Ferdinand Cheval) who built a palace using just pebbles over the span of thirty-three years; the inventor (Thomas Edison) who failed nearly ten thousand times before perfecting one of his greatest inventions, the light bulb; and the entertainment mogul (Walt Disney) who went bankrupt and failed several businesses before starting his famous empire.

And then there's the story of how one sales rep finally got one particularly elusive prospect to connect.

## CASE STUDY
## Outrageous Persistence

**BACKGROUND:** A sales rep needed to reach a prospect, a vice president of marketing for a national retail chain.

**CHALLENGES:** VPs—or any VIPs, for that matter—can be difficult to reach, even when you're persistent. Sometimes perseverance (and creativity) need to be taken to the extreme.

**CAMPAIGN SPECIFICS:** The rep did his research and began the campaign by reaching out to the prospect with sixty email messages and phone calls that elicited no response. Then he sent books with personal notes and Polaroids. Still nothing. Most reps would have given up, but he just got more fired up. Like any good Contact Marketer, he redoubled his efforts, hunting for a way in.

His persistence campaign continued when he managed to get on the guest list of an event to be held by the prospect's company. The prospect was expected to be there, so it would have been a perfect opportunity for the rep to introduce himself. When the rep arrived, he discovered the prospect would not be attending the event after all. Undeterred, he used the opportunity to get to know others in the organization. He handed out a few business cards and regrouped.

Then he placed more phone calls. He sent more emails. And still there were crickets.

Next, the rep devised a plan to appeal to the prospect's sense of humor. He had a coworker shoot a video of him locked in a closet, hands and feet bound, pleading for the fellow to connect. "They're not going to let me out of here until we connect. Please, I'm begging you."

Finally, there was movement. The prospect responded with the promise of a meeting, along with the company's CFO. But in the ensuing weeks, the crickets were back. He tried to make contact but could not connect. Still, every time he was spurned, our story's hero only became more determined to make the connection happen.

Finally, he reviewed his research and found the fellow's home address. A few keystrokes later, he found a listing of the prospect's house on Zillow, including a gallery of photos. The rep and his colleagues went to work again, this time shooting snapshots of themselves jumping in the air, sitting at a cafe table, sipping cocktails, and more. Next, they isolated their images and placed them into the Zillow shots. Suddenly, they were jumping on the prospect's bed, sipping martinis by his pool, and hanging out in the kitchen. Five composited shots became centerpieces for a succession of Facebook posts, tagged with the prospect's name.

**RESULTS:** After eighteen months, countless phone calls, emails, a hostage video, more calls and emails, and, finally, a series of staged celebratory shots in the prospect's home, the persistent rep was in. That night, the VP replied, telling the rep to stop by his office the following day at 1 PM. And the connection was finally made.

### WHO COULD SAY NO TO THIS?

*The rep in this story went to great lengths over an eighteen-month period to connect with a prized prospect. He sent countless emails, notes, social media messages, and even filmed himself in a hostage video. It wasn't until the rep composited photos of himself and a colleague in Zillow photos from the prospect's house—then posted them on Facebook—that he finally scored a meeting.*

**KEY TAKEAWAY:** This certainly is an entertaining story of persistence. It makes me smile as I write it, and I expect it has the same effect as you read it. But it also has tremendous instructional value. Not only did our protagonist not give up, he found renewed inspiration every time he was disappointed by the prospect's lack of response. It would be easy to conclude the prospect simply did not want to connect and move on. But this story shows it's never time to give up if the opportunity is valid and valuable. It also shows that rejection can be used to refuel efforts rather than deplete them.

Prospects learn something about us each time we reach out. Are we the kind of people who give up in the face of adversity? Or do we keep moving forward, always with the end goal in sight? Which kind of person do you think most buyers want as their vendors? Which one eventually wins their business? In that framework, the answer is obvious. Those who persevere win. Those who don't, do not.

# PERSISTENCE ON AUTOPILOT?

What if the persistence element of our campaigns could be automated? That seems to fly in the face of what we typically think of as persistence—unending personal effort. But it turns out that some of our persistence can be automated. That was one of the very exciting discoveries made during the research and writing of this book.

I will tell you more about my discoveries related to this in chapter nine, which looks at assorted uses of digital marketing, including retargeting and geofencing. These automated technologies can play a pivotal role in how we apply persistence in our campaigns and even to a new Contact Marketing model. I believe persistence elements using automated technology will play a major role in pushing response to our contact efforts to unprecedented levels. That same element of our campaigns can then be applied to the sales cycle itself, helping to advance the impetus for a sale through to completion.

# PUTTING IT ALL TOGETHER

Albert Einstein reportedly said, "The definition of insanity is doing the same thing over and over and expecting different results." Does that define perseverance and persistence? Hardly.

As our experts have repeatedly said, persistence isn't about calling over and over, just to check in and see if anything changed. That would fit Einstein's theory. But if your persistence is marked by ever-changing modes of communication with ever-evolving messages and real value, you're not doing what Einstein described—you're adapting and trying something a little different each time, just like Edison and his light bulb. When you take this approach, you're not suffering insanity. You're running a persistence campaign that will generate connections.

The stories in this chapter illustrate the value of perseverance and persistence. Our experts have shown that personal expressions of perseverance do win business.

We see that regularly reserving time for follow-up, creating a persistence process, injecting value into our follow-up, serving final notice, and setting expiration dates all make a big difference in sales outcomes. These examples demonstrate that when we are unrelenting, we will prevail. We're following Edison's example, not Einstein's theory.

If Contact Marketing is a secret weapon for salespeople, perseverance and constant persistence are the secret weapons within that secret weapon. They are essential tools in a Contact Marketer's tool kit. Over and over, persistence proves to be the deciding factor in winning business. It is unimaginable to expect to generate new business relationships without it. By employing persistence and persevering, you can easily win business away from any other sales rep who is unwilling to stick with it.

Perseverance is important in sales and has become critical in Contact Marketing. It is the primary factor for adding 100 percent as the new baseline for response to the new Contact Marketing model described in this book.

## Critical Next Steps

**OBJECTIVE:** Make persistence a central feature of every campaign.

### Step 1. Decide what type of impression you want to make.

Before you begin (or continue) your campaign, you want to position yourself for success. You need to understand that as you interact with a prospect, you are making an impression. Persevering is the act of beginning a relationship. Our contact campaigns are auditions for those relationships. As we persevere, we demonstrate character and value. We show how we handle difficult situations, because the very act of reaching out and persevering is arduous. So ask yourself, "What impression do I want to make?"

> *Persevering is the act of beginning a relationship.*

### Step 2. Use a mix of manual, social, and digital modes of persistence.

The stories in this chapter all describe manual processes involved with persistence efforts. But you should use a blend of social and digital persistence, too, which you can learn more about in chapters nine and ten. Plan to use a blend of all three forms in the persistence elements of your campaign process.

### Step 3. Make persistence a permanent fixture in your process.

In the beginning of this chapter we looked at the importance of making an appointment with yourself to schedule persistence. You need to act on that now. Process is how we hardwire persistence into our campaign. Every action to be taken throughout the campaign should be mapped, defined, and plotted into our calendars. Gantt charts are helpful for diagramming steps across a time line, much like the Ram Tool case study in this chapter showed, with its ten-step construction site process. The more defined your process is, the better your team will perform its persistence mission within your Contact Marketing program. How can you make persistence a permanent fixture in your process?

# POINTS TO REMEMBER

- ✔ Persistence is the act of repeating an action over and over. Perseverance is a prized personality trait.

- ✔ Perseverance is the root of success throughout every field of human endeavor.

- ✔ To persevere, start by making an appointment with yourself by reserving time in your calendar just for follow-up.

- ✔ Perseverance is also a positive mindset; it assumes a positive outcome every time.

- ✔ Persistence can be taught, even converted into a program with great effect, as shown by the Ram Tool example.

- ✔ For persistence to work, each touch point with a prospect must contain unique new value.

- ✔ Value can come in the form of shared articles, insights, research, predictions, best practices, trade show synopses, and other modes that are relevant to the recipients' interests.

- ✔ Sometimes, serving final notice before moving on can open contact or win a sale.

- ✔ Expiration dates on proposals can also have a positive effect. People often want what they cannot have.

- ✔ When a prospect says "No," it's helpful to interpret that to mean, "No, not right now."

- ✔ Perseverance shows prospects how we deal with adversity and demonstrates our value.

- ✔ For Contact Marketing purposes, creativity in our persistence efforts is key, but we ideally want to use a balanced mix in our persistence campaign elements among manual, social, and digital approaches.

# CHAPTER 3

# LEARNING FROM CELEBRITIES

*"Let's take a meeting."*
*"Have your people contact my people."*

Hollywood has always been in on the act of getting and taking meetings. Like any other, the movie industry is heavily dependent on meetings to collaborate and create. The whole notion of "getting discovered" is about getting a meeting with someone powerful enough to propel one to stardom. The story that generated the expression supposedly happened when a director discovered sixteen-year-old Lana Turner innocently sipping her drink at the soda counter. The rest, they say, is history.

Chance meetings like this have played a leading role in Hollywood stories for decades, and they affect projects, too. *The Blair Witch Project*, for example, would never have happened without the chance intersection of the lives of the film's sixteen-year-old producer Robin Cowie, his father, their neighbor with his new camera, and the neighbor's bikini-clad daughter. And the neighbor's mailbox.

Meetings are critical on-screen, too. The challenge of meeting someone important has proven to be a great source of inspiration for movie storytelling.

As you might have guessed from my earlier mention of it, one of my favorite films is Kevin Bisch's *Hitch*, starring Will Smith and Eva Mendes. The entire premise is about getting meetings, although these encounters are romantic in nature, rather than for business. But the two missions are nearly identical. Both are about creating connections that can be life changing. Both are about gaining someone's attention and parlaying that into a meaningful relationship.

Another of my all-time favorites, *Contact* focuses on the ultimate life-altering meeting, our first contact with an intelligent alien species. In the film, scientists discover a series of transmissions, which become a grand blueprint for a space-time travel apparatus, which gets built and sends Dr. Ellie Arroway (played by Jodie Foster) to a distant world—and back—in an instant. Many of the characters in the film doubted the trip ever took place, but Dr. Arroway went through an experience that profoundly changed her life. She learned, from the aliens, that we are mostly alone in the universe, all of us doing our best to cope, understand, and love. The aliens did a wonderful job of humanizing themselves, just as we must as Contact Marketers. Their transmissions, the ones that led to the building of the travel device on Earth, served as the ultimate contact device. And it got the entire world's attention.

Hollywood understands the importance, demands, and nature of meetings. So it's essential to examine its teachings. The following stories are not shared as replicable methods for us to incorporate into our campaigns. Rather, they are presented as a source of inspiration, as so many Hollywood movies are. What we can learn is how to be more audacious and more confident in the significance of our actions and the events they trigger in the minds of those we truly want to meet. Ready to be inspired?

## STAR EXAMPLE
## How Kris Kristofferson Met Johnny Cash

Kris Kristofferson and Johnny Cash made up half of the legendary, badass country quartet the Highwaymen (Merle Haggard and Willie Nelson completed the group). Onstage, they seem like lifelong friends, but how did they first connect?

In Kristofferson's case, he was the younger man of the four and started with his nose pressed against the glass, wanting to get in. Kristofferson is a Hall of Fame singer-songwriter now, but back then he was just another unknown who came to Nashville to become a star.

Kristofferson had just returned from military service abroad and had managed a few chance encounters with one of his true heroes of the music world, Johnny Cash, but he still hadn't broken through. He worked as a janitor in the studio where Cash recorded, sneaking demo tapes to Johnny's guitarist for two years, only to have his efforts lead nowhere. He even managed to get a tape into the hands of Johnny's wife, June Carter Cash, but when she gave it to him, Johnny discarded it into a heap of other hopefuls' tapes.

But Kristofferson was not someone to be ignored. You know the expression "Go big or go home"? Kristofferson might as well have coined it himself. He knew it was time to take bold action and stand out.

In the military, he had been a helicopter pilot. In his new civilian life, he continued as a weekend reservist in the national guard. His position gave him just what he needed. The meeting took place when Kristofferson

iStock (helicopter); Shutterstock (pilot)

**KRIS KRISTOFFERSON DOES A DROP-BY**

*Unable to draw Johnny Cash's attention to his music demo tapes any other way, aspiring singer-songwriter Kris Kristofferson finally resorted to landing a helicopter on Johnny's front lawn to make a personal delivery.*

commandeered a national guard helicopter and landed it on Cash's front lawn. Kristofferson stepped out of the helicopter, blades still whirling overhead, and handed Johnny Cash yet another demo tape.

This time the door opened and Kristofferson was on the path to stardom. He appeared with Cash in the Newport Folk Festival in the late '60s and became one of his closest friends and collaborators. Cash remembered the stunt as Kristofferson "stepping off the helicopter with a tape in one hand and a beer in the other," but Kristofferson credits Cash's version as a tribute to a deeply creative mind. "Y'know, John had a very creative imagination," he once explained. "I've never flown with a beer in my life. Believe me, you need two hands to fly those things."

I don't know if Kristofferson was thinking about Contact Marketing when he borrowed the helicopter, but he surely knew he had to do something drastic to get Cash's attention. He wasn't getting through with his timid demo tape hand-offs to the people around Johnny; in fact, he later discovered every one of the tapes had been tossed in the pond on Johnny's property.

## Lessons to Learn

**WHAT'S THE SCENARIO?**  Like so many of us find in our careers, Kris Kristofferson was stuck in a role he didn't want. A musician without a professional outlet, he had a desire to work with his hero, Johnny Cash. He aspired to be his bandmate and his equal.

**WHAT'S THE CHALLENGE?**  Kristofferson's many attempts to gain Cash's attention failed, requiring even more drastic measures. To break through, he needed to take stock in who he was and what he possessed. What is it that made him unique, other than his talent and desire to be a recording artist? What skills or traits did he have? How could he stand out?

**WHAT'S THE TACTIC AND HOW DID THE CELEBRITY USE IT?**
Kristofferson has musical talent and he tried breaking through with many attempts at getting his demo tapes to Cash, but he wasn't being taken seriously. He wasn't being seen. He needed a different approach in order to break through. In the end, he was able to stand out by tapping into his access and ability to fly a helicopter, a skill he'd acquired from another daring mission in his career as a military man. Kristofferson flew a borrowed helicopter, landed on Johnny's lawn, and put a demo tape in his hand. This time, he wasn't a dime-a-dozen musician trying to make it big. Kristofferson's helicopter stunt became part of Nashville mythology.

**WHAT INSIGHTS CAN WE GATHER FROM THIS EXAMPLE?**  Think about Kristofferson's dilemma. He'd been introduced to Johnny Cash several times, knew his wife and bandmates, and had regular contact with him while he worked as the janitor in Cash's recording studio. He had access, but he hadn't made himself stand out. He hadn't done anything yet to establish himself as a peer who could become part of Johnny's inner circle. Flying that one mission elevated Kris in more ways than one. He humanized himself spectacularly in Cash's eyes.

Cash was deeply impressed with Kristofferson's ploy to meet him and get him to listen to his demo tape. And as we know, he and Kristofferson went on to become bandmates, collaborators, even best friends. Without that one bold move, Kristofferson would have lived a very different life.

While we can't all commandeer helicopters to land on our prospects' front lawns, we can take great inspiration from Kristofferson's audacity. It serves as a successful example of how determination, perseverance, positive outlook, and boldness can combine to produce tremendous results. Kristofferson's approach should be a springboard that prompts us to assess our own levels of audacity in our campaigns. I guarantee we can all benefit from being bolder than we already are.

> *I guarantee we can all benefit from being bolder than we already are.*

## Acting with Audacity in Contact Marketing

Kristofferson's larger-than-life rise to fame is a story that could easily have been penned by a scriptwriter. Its protagonist is thwarted at every turn, and at his lowest point the plot has an outrageous twist that catapults him from frustrated custodian to famous country musician. It's one for the books, one for the big screen. It's not a story defined by response rates and return on investment—or is it? It is a story of friendship and lifelong collaboration. The two made music history together, and isn't that a lot like what we're all seeking with our top accounts and prospects? In our contact efforts, aren't we seeking long-term relationships that produce extraordinary results?

The mission of Contact Marketing campaigns is to humanize yourself to your most important accounts and prospects, and do it in a way that leaves them saying, "I love the way you think." That doesn't come without sacrifice and risk. We are often required to take bold steps.

Kristofferson could have been fired from his job at the studio or arrested for misappropriation of government property. He even says, "I still think I'm lucky [Johnny] didn't shoot me that day." But he weighed the risks and rewards, and opted for acting with audacity. The decision changed his life.

## STAR EXAMPLE
# *Hitch*: The Greatest Contact Marketing Movie Ever Made

*Hitch: Do you know the definition of perseverance, Miss Melas?*

*Sara: An excuse to be obnoxious?*

*Hitch: Continuing a course of action without regard to discouragement, opposition, or previous failure.*

In Contact Marketing, bold outcomes require bold decisions and actions. Still, when Kevin Bisch set out to make his first movie, *Hitch*, I doubt he had Contact Marketing in mind. He was simply writing a script about a character who was an expert at hooking people up and who fell into a love connection of his own. But somehow, Bisch nailed the mission of Contact Marketing, of making connections that are important, that last, that leave all participants in a better place. Hitch, the film's protagonist played by Will Smith, was an expert in the concepts that drive Contact Marketing.

Throughout the film, we see examples of methods for getting the interested party noticed by the focus of their fancy. Accidental meetings, perfect gifts, perfect opening lines, all offered up by the perfect coach. In the movie, Hitch is the consummate Contact Marketing consultant for singles looking to become couples.

But it's not until Hitch himself gets involved with his own pursuit that we see the real Contact Marketing begin. That's when he spots his love interest, Sara Melas (played by Eva Mendes), for the first time in an upscale Manhattan lounge, suffering through yet another unwelcome, inept approach from an unwanted suitor. Sensing her frustration, Hitch steps in, posing as her late-arriving boyfriend to shoo off the interloper.

What happens next is a move straight out of *How to Get a Meeting with Anyone*. Hitch does his research and has a live walkie-talkie delivered by courier to Sara in a nice, neat gift box. She opens it and picks up the walkie-talkie, and Hitch asks her out on a date. She accepts. Then the courier steps in with a second box containing a wet suit and instructions to meet Hitch at the Battery Park dock.

When she arrives, Hitch is waiting with a pair of personal watercraft, ready to whisk them away to Ellis Island, where he reveals her grandfather's signature in the immigration rolls. The movie goes on from there, and being a movie, there are complications at every turn. For one, Sara is unwittingly out to extinguish Hitch's secretive matchmaking practice with an exposé in her employer's newspaper. Hitch is already an urban legend, but Sara has no idea who it is she's actually dating. So Hitch must choose to persevere in his pursuit or let her go to save his business.

At its heart, the movie is about the same thing we seek with our Contact Marketing campaigns: an important, life-changing connection; a meeting that has the possibility to expand the scale of our lives.

## Lessons to Learn

**WHAT'S THE SCENARIO?**  In *Hitch* the title character is a love-connection consultant who quickly finds himself in unfamiliar territory. Always the behind-the-scenes sage, guiding his clients on how to connect with their soul mates, he is suddenly in need of his own advice. At a New York lounge he catches sight of Sara drinking her Grey Goose martini with a don't-bother-me vibe about her. She will clearly be hard to get.

**WHAT'S THE CHALLENGE?**  Sara is being standoffish when Hitch first meets her, even after he rescues her from a would-be suitor who can't take a hint. He needs to follow up with a creative Contact Marketing approach that will get her attention and bring breakthrough.

**WHAT'S THE TACTIC AND HOW DID THE MOVIE CHARACTER USE IT?**
Hitch is full of tricks, and he conducts a profile scrape on his target, discovering where she works and her grandfather's connection to Ellis Island. With the research complete, he sets about making contact in a creative way.

**WHAT INSIGHTS CAN WE GATHER FROM THIS EXAMPLE?**  Movies are said to be fantasy, barely reflective of real life. Some feature impossibly lucky chase scenes or shoot-outs where every bullet misses. And there is always one plot element that seems utterly unrealistic. That is, the protagonist is always bolder than any real human being. Here, Hitch is spectacularly confident in his reasons for connecting and his belief that he belongs in Sara's company. His boldness is contagious, playing a major role in his eventual success. Hitch's boldness is an example set for all of us to be bold in *our* approaches and to expect nothing less than 100 percent results in our campaigns.

But there's more going on here. In the most basic terms, people—the ones who will become Hitch's clients—are having a tough time making important connections. They try but awkwardly fail. They keep trying the same things over and over again, only to see the same failures over and over again. Even though we're examining a film, the actions and outcomes are indeed like real life. The mistakes the would-be suitors are making are just like the way people approach one another in business. Sales reps send endless streams of emails, wondering why they aren't standing out. They leave voice mails saying they're "just checking in" and are surprised when no one calls back. They're not being bold or creative enough to break through.

Hitch gives us a startlingly simple message: humanize yourself. Make yourself stand out. Intrigue the person you want to connect with. Do your homework. Understand who they are. Take bold action, but do it thoughtfully, creatively, and courageously.

There are other guidelines inspired from the movie we can take to heart: Avoid using crowded channels; they won't help you stand out. Use multiple modes of communication; people respond to varied stimuli. Take time to understand the reasons why someone might tilt toward the kinds of decisions you seek.

iStock

### *HITCH* IS CLASSIC CONTACT MARKETING IN ACTION

*Thirty-three minutes and 13 seconds into the movie Hitch, viewers are treated to a classic demonstration of Contact Marketing. That's when the film's main character, Hitch, has a gift box delivered to his love interest, Sara, with a live walkie-talkie inside. When she picks it up, Hitch is on the other end, waiting to connect.*

## Hitching Your Wagon to a Star

*Hitch* plays like an instructional film about being strategic in your approaches and audacious in your actions. It's a source of inspiration about watching people making life-changing connections. The movie implores us to have the patience and perseverance necessary to make the most meaningful connections in our careers come to life and flourish. It is one of two movies I recommend you keep on hand if you want a boost for your Contact Marketing efforts.

## STAR EXAMPLE
# Brian Grazer: Curious Minds Want to Know

Legendary producer Brian Grazer is the cofounder of Imagine Entertainment with an equally legendary partner, director and former child actor Ron Howard. The duo is responsible for several of the most successful films to emerge from Hollywood in recent memory, including *A Beautiful Mind, Apollo 13, Splash, The Da Vinci Code, Angels & Demons, Fun with Dick and Jane*, and *Backdraft*.

Grazer's also known as the guy with the hair—the crazy hair of an electrocuted clown. And he's a guy with an insatiable curiosity to meet and connect with people who have experienced the unbelievable and improbable, and the people who shape our view of the world. To satisfy that curiosity, Grazer has been arranging meetings with some of the most intriguing people in the world, to sit down together and have what he calls "Curiosity Conversations." He's had hundreds of them; his list of notables include Jim Lovell, Jeff Bezos, Muhammad Ali, Jonas Salk (discoverer of the vaccine for polio), Edward Teller (father of the hydrogen bomb), and Fidel Castro.

In his book *A Curious Mind*, Grazer shares stories from these meetings that have informed much of his work in film. For example, his conversations with Jim Lovell, one of the three astronauts aboard the ill-fated Apollo 13 space mission, and Veronica de Negri, a woman who found the courage to survive being held captive and tortured for months during Augusto Pinochet's reign of terror in Chile, helped form the foundation for the movie *Apollo 13*.[1]

It must be nice to be able to call someone and say, "Hi, I'm an Oscar-winning Hollywood producer and I'd like to learn about you." Who wouldn't take that call? It turns out there are a lot of people who wouldn't. Oddly enough, this famous Hollywood producer is just like the rest of us. He has the same challenges we all do when reaching out to important people. Even Grazer has trouble getting appointments.

---

[1] *A Curious Mind: The Secret to a Bigger Life* by Brian Grazer and Charles Fishman, Simon & Schuster, 2015, pp. 69–75.

His bids for contact start with phone calls from his assistant, asking to set a meeting. As Contact Marketers, we recognize this as a powerful way to establish equal (or superior) business status, by having an assistant arrange our meetings. It communicates our importance, our worthiness for a meeting. However, the biggest weapon in Grazer's arsenal is simple persistence. He never gives up. His persistence campaigns for meetings can sometimes span years. His perseverance is rooted in the belief that the resulting conversation will be fascinating, that the insights gained will be valuable for his work. But he also knows it will instill deep personal value to those pursued, to know that the conversation might show up in some way in a future blockbuster movie.

Grazer is firm in his belief that the curiosity conversations will be worthwhile, so he doesn't quit until he gets the interview he wants. One way or another, these conversations will take place. It's just a matter of helping the person on the other end understand the inevitability and value of the connection. And to that end, he has amassed a separate and equally impressive body of work in the meetings he has had with extraordinary people.

## Lessons to Learn

**WHAT'S THE SCENARIO?**  As a storyteller, Grazer understands he must immerse his mind in characters and stories. To do that, he has been conducting meetings—what he calls "curiosity conversations"—throughout his career with people who have fascinating real-life stories.

**WHAT'S THE CHALLENGE?**  Just because Grazer is an Oscar-winning, world-famous movie producer doesn't mean he automatically gets meetings with his curiosity conversation subjects. In fact, just like any Contact Marketer, he often has a difficult time getting meetings. He experiences that universal struggle just like the rest of us. His challenge, like ours, is to persist until he breaks through.

**WHAT'S THE TACTIC AND HOW DOES THE CELEBRITY USE IT?**  Grazer starts with the "big shot" approach, having his assistant call the assistant of his prospect (the rough equivalent of the old Hollywood expression "Have your people call my people"). If that doesn't work, he puts his targeted interviewees on a follow-up cadence, sometimes from his assistant, sometimes from Grazer himself.

**WHAT INSIGHTS CAN WE GATHER FROM THIS EXAMPLE?**  Grazer has a few advantages most of us don't. He's famous; we're not. He can put his target contacts in a movie or even make a movie about their lives; we cannot. Still, he has the same trouble getting meetings we do. But like many of the characters in his movies, Grazer presses on with unreasonable assuredness, fully confident in the outcome he desires, and bold in his continued outreach until the meeting takes place. Even when we remove the mask of "Hollywood producer," Grazer shows us the value of positive mindset and expectations, and steady perseverance. What is your mindset when you go after a hard-to-get prospect? What are your expectations? Do you have the stamina to maintain steady perseverance until you break through?

In addition to his mental outlook and gritty persistence, Grazer uses techniques to increase the probability of getting meetings. Peer-to-peer communication works between principals, but it is equally powerful between executive assistants. A monthly call between the two demonstrates his commitment and the significance of having a meeting. Eventually it wears away the prospect's resistance, and the meeting is on.

## The Curious—and Persistent—Bird Gets the Worm

The results of Grazer's curiosity-driven meetings are clear. He breaks through to essentially anyone he chooses. His methods are simple and they work. And the value of the meetings is also made clear when you read his book. Grazer's products—his movies—are made richer through the enormous bank of experiences and wisdom gathered through the meetings.

> *I guarantee all the success you see others around you achieve is a result of creating connections with the people who could help them make it happen.*

Grazer shows us that, no matter who you are, no matter how famous or impressive you may be, getting meetings with important people is never guaranteed. No matter who we are, we must approach the Contact Marketing mission with perseverance and vision. Nothing worth doing is easy or simple, which is why the difficult task of breaking through to important people is left to the enterprising few who are ready to meet the challenge.

If you need inspiration, look around. It can be found everywhere, especially among people like Brian Grazer who've applied their vision and done the work to make it happen. I guarantee all the success you see others around you achieve is a result of creating connections with the people who could help them make it happen.

If you need further inspiration, read Grazer's book. It contains stories of breaking through to incredibly impressive people and learning something extraordinary from each of them. It's what helped Grazer bring deep insight into every movie he and partner Ron Howard have put on-screen. It truly is an Oscar-winning performance in itself.

## STAR EXAMPLE
## *Contact*—The Ultimate Contact Device

If *Hitch* is the best Contact Marketing movie ever made, *Contact* is the best movie ever made, period—in my humble opinion, of course.

Conceived and written by the great astronomer and cosmic thinker Carl Sagan, the movie contemplates what our first contact with an alien intelligence might look like, and, more important, what it will mean for humankind. The film is breathtaking. It starts with the best opening scene I have ever seen, with the camera leaving Earth to sail past the moon, through the asteroid belt, then past Mars, Jupiter, Saturn, the rest of the solar system, and beyond.

It continues past star systems, accelerating farther to exit our home galaxy, the Milky Way. As it exits our corner of the universe, the radio and television emissions from our planet grow more and more ancient, and the camera accelerates beyond the speed of light to show how far those electromagnetic waves have gone— traveling at the speed of light—since the dawn of radio and television.

What a magnificent way of communicating how immense the universe truly is. And how alone we are. Into this thought-provoking scenario, Jodie Foster and Matthew McConaughey are cast as astronomer Dr. Ellie Arroway and the Reverend Palmer Joss, whose divergent life views must come to grips with what surely would be the most significant event in human history—the moment we make contact with an intelligence beyond our own.

Dr. Arroway starts the action when her installation receives the radio transmission the SETI (Search for Extraterrestrial Intelligence) Institute has been waiting for the past thirty-five years. What starts as a series of repetitive numbers and characters resolves into the blueprint for an enormous apparatus and an invitation to meet. For the sake of humanity, countries pitch in to build a series of giant towers and interlocking rings, with a tiny one-person capsule to take a trip of a lifetime roughly twenty-five light-years from home.

Foster's character is chosen as humanity's emissary for the trip, placed in the capsule, and then . . . nothing. The capsule simply drops through the giant counterrotating rings and falls into the water below. Only something did happen. Dr. Arroway went on an astonishing journey to the Vega solar system. Greeted there on a sandy beach by her deceased father, the form the alien beings thought would be most comforting for Foster's character to take in their message, they explained that we're mostly alone in the universe and we need to value one another.

This is Contact Marketing writ large and in the extreme. The importance for contact between species was obvious. This was a meeting worth having.

The value to the recipient of the campaign was also obvious. It answered perhaps the biggest question of human existence: Are we alone? And the method of contact was certainly audacious. "Here is a device you must build. It will cost quadrillions of dollars to complete and will require all of humanity to pool its resources to build it." That is one impressive involvement device. It connected and involved everyone on the planet!

## Lessons to Learn

**WHAT'S THE SCENARIO?**  If the most important contact story in human history were to happen, it would have to be connecting with an alien civilization. But how would it happen? And how would we react as the contacted party? In the movie, Dr. Ellie Arroway, played by Jodie Foster, is going to find out. However, let's also look at this from the perspective of the writers and studios that brought this fictional story to us.

**WHAT'S THE CHALLENGE?**  Earthlings meeting intelligent life elsewhere in the universe is a story that has been told thousands of times since the Roswell UFO incident, and it always seems to happen the same way: bright lights whizzing through the sky at impossible speeds, occasionally stopping to shock the hell out of whoever happens to be nearby. So the writers and producers took on the colossal challenge of telling this story in a unique way. And isn't that the main challenge we face as Contact Marketers? How do we stand out? How do we set ourselves apart? Interestingly, the space creatures in this movie faced the same dilemma: How can we get the attention of those earthlings? How can we stand out against all of their distractions? How can we get a meeting?

**WHAT'S THE TACTIC AND HOW DOES THE MOVIE CHARACTER USE IT?**
The client's contact device is delivered in a most intriguing way, starting as obscure signal patterns received by SETI's desert array of radio-telescope dishes. The patterns turned into digits, vectors, and soon, a grand master set of plans for a travel device humanity must find the resources to build. They didn't just land somewhere in a saucer. That would have been too pedestrian. They made it a riddle. Humanity had to work for it. They directed their message where it was most relevant to our species, sending it in a form to be received by those who were looking for a signal. They made it relevant, mysterious, and irresistible. The humans, surely, loved the way these aliens were thinking.

**WHAT INSIGHTS CAN WE GATHER FROM THIS EXAMPLE?**  If we think of this as a contact campaign, the alien's approach is the very definition of audacity. The contact device was so massive, extreme, and expensive that it required all of humanity to pool its resources and bring together its best minds.

This is, of course, a movie. But even as a work of fantasy, it gives us an opportunity to explore the outer fringes of outreach and audacity in our own campaigns. After watching this movie, you are apt to conclude that no idea is too extreme, outrageous, or expensive as long as it produces the desired results and ROI.

Another message for Contact Marketers: If something is worth doing, it's worth doing in a big way. The lessons of *Contact* are inspiring examples to follow of audacity and going to the extreme and then reaping the results.

Seth Shostak

**SETI CONTINUES TO LISTEN**

*The SETI Institute is the scientific nonprofit research institute that operates the famed Allen Telescope Array, pictured here, that constantly searches for signs of extraterrestrial life. It was SETI's scientists who discovered the alien radio transmissions that led to contact with an alien civilization in the movie* Contact.

## Connecting on the Big Screen—and Beyond

Maybe it is a bit obtuse to link contact with another species to our mission to connect with the people most important to our own success here on Earth. But the best stories, whether told in film, written in a book, or simply spoken, offer lessons we can adapt to our own use. At their best, Hollywood films teach us deep lessons that can have a life-altering impact.

I think it's more than a coincidence that two of my favorite movies—*Hitch* and *Contact*—are about making life-changing connections. It reflects the deep significance that activity has in our lives. Nothing happens until we make connections with others. And the greater the importance of those connections, the bigger the results from the ensuing collaboration. Getting important meetings is a central theme to human life. That is the message we can take from these extraordinary films.

It's worth having both on your business bookshelf, ready to reach for when you need a boost.

## STAR EXAMPLE
# Blair Witchcraft Beginnings

This is not a story of witchcraft or sorcery for getting meetings, but it is a story of how divine intervention can sometimes play a role in making important meetings happen. It's the story of how the movie *The Blair Witch Project* came to be, which reads like a Hollywood script itself . . .

The opening scene is set in South Africa, where the Cowie family is preparing to emigrate to America. The family's patriarch, Les, is having a conversation with friend and former Formula One world champion driver Jody Scheckter, also a native of South Africa. "You'll be sued within the first six months you're there," Scheckter tells him. Cowie takes it in but is determined. "We're going anyway," he says.

Still, Scheckter's words remain lodged in Cowie's brain. "Better be careful. Better not get sued."

The next scene jumps to a beautiful Sunday afternoon in the family's adopted hometown in Georgia, where Cowie is teaching his young son, Robin, to drive. Robin is at the wheel when something grabs his attention. One of their neighbors is having an impromptu photo shoot on the front lawn with a very attractive young lady in a bikini.

Naturally, and right on cue, Robin crashes the family car into the neighbor's brick mailbox structure, knocking it to pieces.

"Oh no," the elder Cowie thinks to himself. "This is it. We're going to be sued."

As the four participants in the scene converge, Cowie apologizes to the neighbor, promising that his son will clean up the damage and replace the mailbox installation. But the neighbor has a surprising reaction. He's not angry, he is apologetic for the obvious distraction he has caused. He explains he'd just gotten a new camera and was trying it out with his sixteen-year-old daughter, who was the same age as Robin.

As they engage in conversation, it emerges that Robin is a budding filmmaker. And their neighbor is an investor in films made by young filmmakers. They talk some more, and suddenly, Robin's first feature film, *The Blair Witch Project*, is funded. The movie goes on to earn rave reviews at the Sundance Film Festival, gets picked up for distribution by Artisan Entertainment, and grosses nearly $250 million. Quite an achievement for a first-time filmmaker not yet out of high school. It's a true-life, fairy-tale story that ought to be made into a movie itself.

Would the film have achieved all this if that fateful meeting hadn't happened? Perhaps. But the fact that the felled mailbox precipitated the connection that led to funding the film seems more than just a coincidence.

## Lessons to Learn

This is a story without much point, other than this: Believe in the magic of chance. Some things just happen, with no plan required. The key is to be open to chance encounters and the serendipity they may bring.

Cowie might have had other plans for seeking funding for his film project, but even in disaster, new opportunities arose. The conversation simply needed to shift toward exploring whom fate just presented to one another and how they might help each other.

There is nothing repeatable here; nothing to include in your contact campaign process that can be relied upon for predictable results—or is there? Chance

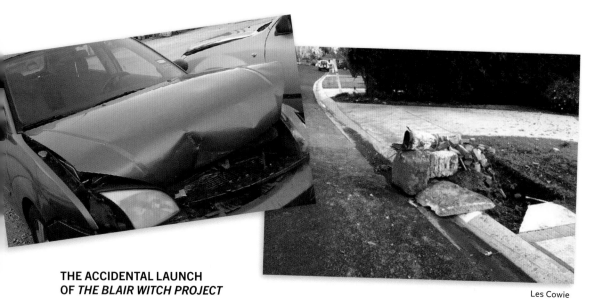

**THE ACCIDENTAL LAUNCH
OF *THE BLAIR WITCH PROJECT***

Les Cowie

The Blair Witch Project *is the highest-grossing student film of all time, but it might never have happened if fate hadn't intervened. The film's creator was taking a driving lesson from his father when he crashed into the mailbox of the man who would become the project's first investor.*

encounters can happen anywhere at any time, with people we never expected to meet. But suddenly, there they are. So there is a lesson to be learned: Be prepared.

If you wonder how anyone can be prepared for valuable chance encounters, you will find chapter seven quite interesting. It examines a new kind of Contact Marketing form called a "Pocket Campaign," which launches just like a business card but includes elements of engagement and persistence to make sales happen out of thin air. Sort of like what happened to the Cowies. Their experience, and many more like it, encourages us to be open to and prepared for unexpected providence.

## Moviemaker Mindset

Having the right mindset has obvious implications, but it also has hidden ones. When the Cowies crashed the front-lawn photo shoot, what do you suppose led them to talk about the film project or the neighbor to mention his investing in independent, youth-generated films? I would argue they were all caught up in a vortex of their visions, and regardless of their reason for connecting that day, it was bound to emerge in their conversation.

Some of the spiritually inclined among us might offer, "If you want something to happen, put it out to the universe." Others might politely dismiss that advice. "Things happen for a reason, and I intend to be that reason," they might counter.

Either way, stating our intention to make something happen and living those intentions can often mysteriously produce the results we desire. Whether or not it looks like coincidence, it's always worth keeping those intentions clearly in your thoughts. As Contact Marketers, we aim to accomplish what many think is impossible. But we must first believe our greatest dreams can indeed come true.

# PUTTING IT ALL TOGETHER

Just like any other sector in business, Hollywood players must make critical connections happen quickly or watch their dreams perish. People in Hollywood are always talking about how connected they are to the rich and famous of film, television, and music. It is one of the most connection-dependent environments in all of business.

The people who drive the Hollywood machine—the actors, agents, artists, producers, writers, and directors—happen to be some of the most creative and expressive among us. They're also among the most meeting-hungry.

Naturally, their stories often reveal insights into this most universal of human needs, to connect. And in that way, Hollywood can be a powerful source of insight and inspiration for all Contact Marketers.

# Critical Next Steps

*OBJECTIVE:* Use inspiration from Hollywood to up your game.

### Step 1. Take a page from Hollywood: Get bold to get results.

We often wonder why a character would dare walk into that dark room in a horror movie, or what made the main character in pretty much any movie act so boldly. Hollywood knows boldness is necessary to move its stories along and make us care. You must adopt that same ethos to move your story along. Be bold, be audacious, and get results.

### Step 2. Take inspiration from Hollywood as well.

Hollywood is a concept, a maelstrom of popular entertainment, but it is also simply a business. People in the industry talk about taking meetings and brag about powerful people who will take their calls. Perhaps because filmmaking is such a collaborative process, they understand more than most the value of getting meetings and making connections. Your own quest for meetings with important prospects is just as valid and just as necessary as any in Hollywood.

### Step 3. Take solace: Even celebrities have a tough time getting meetings.

Everyone in the film business struggles at times, just like we do, to get important meetings. Remember this fact when you encounter difficulties. Everybody goes through it. Don't take it personally; just resolve to break through it. Be just like one of those unreasonably bold characters in a Hollywood movie.

# POINTS TO REMEMBER

✔ Hollywood has always understood the value of meeting with important contacts.

✔ Just like in our lives, nothing worthwhile in Hollywood happens without meetings.

✔ In movies, protagonists are often recklessly brash in their push for desired results, but their actions are almost always rewarded with success. That same thirst for bold action can be highly effective in Contact Marketing campaigns.

✔ Hollywood stories can be inspirational and instructive about the value of taking big risks to make great things happen.

✔ Kris Kristofferson's helicopter stunt was a bold move that changed the scale of his life and career.

✔ *Hitch* is perhaps the best movie for watching Contact Marketing in action.

✔ Producer Brian Grazer's pursuit of "curiosity conversations" with important character sources demonstrates the value of perseverance and the shared experience of struggling to get meetings at any level.

✔ The movie *Contact* portrays the need to make important connections as truly *universal*.

✔ *The Blair Witch Project* filmmaker Robin Cowie's story reminds us to be open to and prepared for chance encounters with important contacts.

✔ Mindset is important. Believing something will happen is often a good portion of why it happens.

# PART 2

## TANGIBLE TACTICS

# CHAPTER 4

# PERSONALIZATION: GOING DEEP AND WIDE

The definition of personalization is shifting, even splitting into two distinct forms. The first is based on referencing facts, interests, and occurrences uncovered through intensive research of each prospect. The other is based on assumptions applied across a list of contacts, in which each prospect gets the same standardized (albeit personalized) outreach campaign.

At the start of my career, I created direct marketing campaigns for the major magazine publishers. That is, I produced subscription-acquisition campaigns that were mailed to millions of recipients at a time, featuring single-panel cartoons with captions written to include the recipient's name. The experience helped me to understand what moved people to take notice and take action.

The effect was so compelling that it produced many new response records, while creating a different sort of reaction to direct mail. People often treated the cartoons as keepsakes, keeping them on their refrigerator doors for years, even framing them.

Today, I'm using those same techniques in Contact Marketing campaigns to produce huge wins for my enterprise sales clients. When prospects receive our cartoon pieces, they show them off to colleagues, take selfies with the contact pieces, and send thank-you letters to the reps who are seeking meetings. And recipients are agreeing to connect and meet at record levels.

This is all based on careful assumptions about everyone on the list. We assume, for example, they all like to think of themselves as successful and smarter than their competitors. So when we send a cartoon commemorating their success, our top-level executive targets respond quite positively.

That's one version of personalization. The other produces some pretty astonishing results as well. By listening, watching, and acting when triggering events or market opportunities occur, some Contact Marketers are responding with relevant offline contact pieces and communiqués. And they, too, are creating breakthrough results.

The process of researching relevant interests and events is getting easier with the help of new AI platforms. They keep a constant watch through their robot eyes on deep data and constant crawling to bring relevant facts to the Contact Marketer's attention so they can take action.

# BEYOND BASIC CUSTOMIZATION

*Merriam-Webster's Collegiate Dictionary* defines the verb *personalize* as "to make personal or individual." That's no longer enough. We need to update the definition to differentiate the two forms of personalization: "Wide" and "Deep."

"Wide personalization" refers to any form of data-driven application of a recipient's most basic data in order to produce an individualized and highly positive effect on response. It can be applied to physical or digital contact devices that derive their magic from including a recipient's name somewhere in the piece.

> **Wide personalization**—The application of readily available data in a uniform way across an audience.

"Deep personalization" refers to the activity of first gaining deep personal insight into each potential contact in order to formulate a custom outreach effort, in physical or digital form, to elicit a highly positive response.

> **Deep personalization**—The application of individualized research findings to produce unique outreach elements, one by one.

# DIGGING DEEP OR GOING WIDE?

Which type of personalization is right for your campaign?

Both types of personalization, Deep and Wide, can produce strong results—up to 100 percent response and a highly effective impression.

One of the biggest challenges for Deep personalization is its granular nature, which means it cannot be mass produced. If the requirement for success is time-consuming research of each targeted executive, scalability becomes a big issue. If each prospect has a distinct campaign piece, there is a lack of uniform branding.

Wide personalization, however, doesn't have those challenges. Branding is tightly controlled. Scalability is not an issue. The only elements of personalization are first and last names, sometimes the recipient's address, city or state, or company name. Thus, Wide personalization can only be enabled by basic data from a list.

Of course, marketers still must do something interesting with the data to produce results. This is true for whichever form you choose for your campaign.

I share five stories in this chapter to show you the different forms of personalization in action. And really, many of the stories throughout the book are illustrative of how personalization can be used to supercharge response to your contact campaigns.

## CASE STUDY
# Lee Hamilton's Big Bet

**BACKGROUND:** Lee Hamilton is an energetic, seasoned bus-dev rep who reached out to me shortly after the release of *How to Get a Meeting with Anyone* to share his debut with a bold personalized Contact Marketing campaign after reading my book. It's a unique story of determination and persistence.

**CHALLENGES:** Hamilton had just started with Proxios, an IT operations outsourcing service, and wanted to make a mark. He knew there were a dozen or so accounts that no one in the company had been able to penetrate, so he selected those as the targets of his first Contact Marketing campaign.

**CAMPAIGN SPECIFICS:** To connect with each account, Hamilton researched the personal social media accounts of each company's CEO. He was looking for items of personal interest that could be incorporated into cartoonish illustrations he commissioned a local artist to create. Hamilton then had each illustration produced as a 24" × 36" stretched canvas print and sent them to each prospect with a note asking for a meeting. When Proxios's CEO, Frank Clark, saw what Hamilton was doing, he remarked, "That will never work." Hamilton insisted it would, quoting my book as his expert source. The disagreement then turned into a lighthearted competition. "I'll make a bet with you that it won't work," Clark said, and the wager was on. Hamilton sent each canvas print in plain corrugated packaging via courier to each of the dozen prospects and then followed up by phone to set appointments.
   So who won the bet?

**RESULTS:** Much to the CEO's surprise, the campaign produced a 100 percent response. All twelve of the previously unreachable accounts had been penetrated. This was an especially welcome outcome for Hamilton, as he became an instant hero to the company's leadership.

**KEY TAKEAWAY:** Hamilton's stretched-canvas print campaign succeeded on many levels. Obviously, it allowed the opening of important new accounts the company would have otherwise missed. It also helped Hamilton win his bet with the CEO and create an important connection within his own company. And the CEO also came away with a big prize—important new accounts no one else had been able to secure. It was a productive bet to lose.

Print courtesy of Lee Hamilton

### LEE HAMILTON'S BET WITH HIS CEO

*When Lee Hamilton's CEO saw what he had in mind to connect with his top accounts, he told Hamilton it would never work. So they made a bet. The CEO lost, as Hamilton's campaign generated a perfect 100 percent response. So really, they both won.*

But the bigger win is for Contact Marketers. This is a classic demonstration of the power of Deep personalization. To do it successfully requires deep personal attention for each targeted executive and the contact device must be one of a kind, something that could only be sent to each target contact. It requires a blend of research and creativity to pull it off.

Hamilton found a way to incorporate important personal details in a contact piece that will surely be kept on display in recipients' offices for years to come. If you are the recipient of a Deep personalization effort, it must be hard not to respond to the person behind such a grand gesture. Clearly that was the case, since Hamilton's gambit yielded a 100 percent response rate from a tough-to-reach group.

## CASE STUDY
# Deep Personalization Captures Flock of New Accounts

Dom Steinmann is a reader who contacted me with a story so amazing that I featured it as a preface to the paperback edition of *How to Get a Meeting with Anyone*. The story is about a young sales development rep who discovered that, using Deep personalization, he could connect with valuable accounts that had been previously unreachable by company reps. Noticing his new success, the rep's fellow SDRs asked for his help.

**BACKGROUND:** Steinmann explained to me that he'd been recruited twelve months earlier, straight from college, to serve as a sales development rep for a late-stage tech startup. He soon discovered he'd stepped into a meat grinder. Each rep was required to make a hundred cold calls per day, which rarely produced even a single worthwhile conversation. It was a grind he lamented to a friend one night at dinner, who recommended that Steinmann read *How to Get a Meeting with Anyone*.

He did, and became deeply inspired. He decided to start his Contact Marketing efforts by targeting accounts no one in the company had been able to penetrate, while still maintaining his hundred-calls-per-day duties.

Steinmann's first target was an executive who, he discovered through diligent profile scraping, was interested in family, cooking, and technology. Calling on his recollection of personalization in the book, he commissioned a barbecue apron embroidered with a quote from noted futurist Arthur C. Clarke: "Any sufficiently advanced technology is indistinguishable from magic."

The apron went out and Dom followed up with a call. This time, the executive engaged, resulting in a six-figure deal. It was a major victory for the young, straight-out-of-college SDR. Pretty soon, his colleagues noticed his success and asked if he'd help them do the same. The first collaboration targeted yet another account no one had been able to reach, and the campaign for this prospect is the one we'll look at here.

**CHALLENGES:** The account selected is one that had been entirely unresponsive to previous contact efforts.

**CAMPAIGN SPECIFICS:** Steinmann explained that his method started with research to identify personal markers

Mike Syring/Mike's Falconry Supplies

### DOM STEINMANN'S BRILLIANT USE OF DEEP PERSONALIZATION

*Dom Steinmann knows how to combine deep research with Deep personalization to produce results. Discovering one of the company's most important accounts was headed by someone deeply interested in falconry, Dom and a colleague sent this spectacular glove as a gift. That hundred-dollar investment resulted in several six-figure deals.*

that might motivate the prospect to take action. Steinmann and his colleague discovered the prospect was deeply interested in falconry. They visited an online falconry shop, spoke with the owner, and asked for his recommendation for a gift. Falconry is the sport of working with birds of prey in a unique partnership to hunt. Through the sharp, crushing grasp of their talons and powerful beaks, falcons are lethal hunters. Falconers need protection from friendly fire from these weapons, so they wear thick gloves, which are often ornate and can be true works of art. The shop owner recommended a glove and they placed the order.

Their next step was to send a photo of the glove in an email to the prospect, explaining that the glove is on its way, sent as a gesture of interest in making a connection to talk business.

**RESULTS:** When the prospect received the photo, he responded immediately. While he was appreciative of the gesture, he explained he was not a good prospect for the company's service. But when the glove arrived, everything changed. The prospect excitedly called back to thank the rep for the glove. He then remarked, "Remember I told you I'm not a prospect? Well, I'm not, but I know three chief information officers who are looking for what you offer right now, and I'm going to make introductions." And new deals ensued.

But the story doesn't end there. The more Steinmann helped his fellow reps, the more deals they started to win. That's when upper management started to notice the change in results. They inquired, and all fingers pointed to Steinmann as the catalyst. That led to an immediate promotion, putting him in the new position of sales manager. But events were still progressing, as the company was soon acquired by a Silicon Valley tech giant for $4.5 billion.

Contact Marketing propelled Steinmann from new college recruit to sales manager in the span of a year—for a $4.5 billion multinational company. It changed the way the company did business. And it all stemmed from some clever uses of one-to-one Deep personalization.

**KEY TAKEAWAY:** Deep personalization gives enterprise sales teams plenty of firepower to boost their results, especially when it is a collaborative and supportive effort. Because of Steinmann's efforts to enable his team to create breakthroughs, the entire company benefited. Steinmann's story also shows the power of Contact Marketing to change individual careers and lives. He went from recent college graduate to a position of great responsibility thanks to the results he and his colleagues were able to achieve by using Contact Marketing and Deep personalization.

# CASTING A WIDER NET

While the Hamilton and Steinmann campaigns produced strong results, we should also recognize the limitations of Deep personalization. Steinmann and Hamilton executed their strategies with great discretion. Their instincts were right on target concerning the gifts and messaging used in their campaigns. But entrusting such brand-defining choices to legions of individual reps leaves a lot of room for error—and virtually no room for cohesive branding.

This is where the power of Wide personalization comes into play, because a Wide personalization campaign can make branding uniform and produce the contact device at any scale for distribution to a larger field. While Deep personalization is a one-to-one approach, Wide is one-to-one on a broad basis.

One of the most illustrative uses of Wide personalization would be my own use of cartoons in Contact Marketing campaigns. I was originally drawn to the use of cartoons in marketing because of editorial readership survey results. Publishers discovered those simple drawings with captions were disproportionately attracting all of the attention in their publications: According to readership surveys, cartoons are almost always the best read and remembered part of magazines and newspapers.

> *Humor has the power to heal and redirect our emotions.*

Also important, cartoons are a form of humor, which is a potent force in our lives. It has the power to heal and redirect our emotions. Doctors tell us laughter is good for our health, and I know this to be true firsthand. One of my cartoons once got someone laughing so hard, it helped him pass a kidney stone. That's a pretty direct health benefit.

At its core, humor is about truth revealed in a twist of irony. It's why we find ourselves saying, after a fit of laughter, "That's so true!" An example: a woman standing at her desk, talking on the phone, saying, "Listen, you're the expert, so let me tell you how this is going to work . . ." It's funny because it's something we hear throughout our time in business. Clients hire us for our expertise, then often overcontrol the situation and interfere with the application of that expertise. Because we've all been through it, the cartoon has the ability to resonate with anyone in business.

That's really important. The cartoon has the ability to grab anyone's attention, pull them in, and get them to laugh. Even better, it immediately plants a point of agreement: Not all clients listen well, which hinders our ability to deliver results. Wouldn't it be nice if we could eliminate that problem? Can't you already feel your head nodding in agreement? That's the power of cartoons as a marketing device.

It is also how personalization—and powerful results—can be achieved at scale. When I produce a cartoon for a campaign, and when I direct that campaign at, say, marketing directors at Inc. 5000 companies, I'm quite safe assuming I can speak to them about universal experiences in business. Like, let's say, if I focus on how successful they are. If I have produced the cartoon properly, it will elicit a strong, excited response from just about every recipient.

Note that I don't need to know the name of their dogs, the size of their pools, or what they like to cook. It's not relevant to our mission, which is to make a connection themed around doing business, not striking up a conversation about their cats or favorite foods. Those things may come up as we genuinely get to know one another, but they're a distraction when we really should be focused on solutions, results, and doing business.

The style of personalization I use in my cartoon campaigns stems from the many direct marketing campaigns I created at the beginning of my career. These were mailings that sometimes went to millions of people who we knew were likely to be stock investors, fishing aficionados, or pet owners. The effect of the cartoons with personalized captions was magical.

At a time when true junk was jamming millions of mailboxes with fake checks, misleading "teaser copy," and cheap pencils forming lumps in envelopes, the cartoons kept on doing what they do in publications: They made the campaign piece stand out over anything else in the stack of mail that day. They got recipients to notice, open, and engage with it. People often clipped the cartoons and saved them on their office walls or at home on refrigerator doors. They stuck around for years. When we offered the personalized cartoons as suitable-for-framing prints with their paid subscription orders, recipients responded at record rates. In fact, those cartoon mailings earned me nomination for membership in both the Direct Marketing Association's and American Marketing Association's halls of fame.

There has always been something very special about cartoons, a fact that still drives Contact Marketing campaigns to extreme levels of response today. Part of that effectiveness comes from the nature of cartoons and our built-in reaction to them. But another part comes from their great applicability as a vessel for Wide personalization.

## CASE STUDY
# Insurance Company Producer Campaign

**BACKGROUND:** Many insurance companies go to market through a vast network of independent agents, known as "producers." Since the agents represent products from a long list of insurance companies, they tend to be aloof toward the insurance companies. The producers are in demand; they know it, and they act like it.

**CHALLENGES:** Some insurer-producer relationships are downright frosty. Still, every producer counts. The reps at the insurance company in this case study wanted to reactivate dormant relationships with important producers. The challenge was that the producers simply did not want to be bothered by the company's reps. The question running through the reps' minds was the same one we all find ourselves asking when we're trying to get a meeting with someone difficult to reach: "How do we get them to notice us and engage?"

**CAMPAIGN SPECIFICS:** The campaign was based on using my cartoon BigBoard contact system. BigBoards are 18″ × 24″ foam core boards, with a personalized cartoon on one side and a personal message from sender to recipient on the other. The piece is sent in custom corrugated cardboard packaging that makes it appear to be an art print coming from a cartoon gallery. As the piece was sent, reps called producers' assistants to let them know a print of a cartoon about their bosses by one of *The Wall Street Journal's* cartoonists was on its way. Follow-up emails were sent to assistants with all the details, including FedEx tracking info. This process resulted in many of the assistants acting as inside coordinators, ensuring delivery of the BigBoard and further conversation with their bosses.

**RESULTS:** The sixty producers chosen for the test were both inactive (they'd had no correspondence within the six months before the campaign) and of great value to the company, based on their proven ability to generate revenue. After the shipment of the boards, only one producer did not respond, setting the contact rate at 98 percent. The other fifty-nine recipients were thrilled. Some sent personal thank-you notes, some even sent selfie pictures, posing with their BigBoards. Meanwhile, the producers did what they do—they produced. Within the first three months after the test, the company received orders worth $2 million, an initial 13,000 percent ROI that continued to mount monthly as the producers continued to sell.

**KEY TAKEAWAY:** If cartoons are the best read and remembered part of publications (they are), it's obvious why they are also incredibly powerful contact devices. But the key takeaway here may surprise you—you don't have to be a

Box by WoodGiftBox.com

### BIGBOARD PROTOTYPE GOES WIDE AND DEEP

*This BigBoard format mixes Wide and Deep personalization, with hand-drawn personalized captions in a multipanel cartoon format focused on what the recipient does. A custom wooden box with laser-etched branding detail finishes the piece.*

cartoonist to be an effective Contact Marketer. This book and *How to Get a Meeting with Anyone* are filled with contact campaign approaches you can put to use in your efforts.

---

## VARIATION

Cartoons are wonderfully malleable tools, so big foam core boards are not the only form these can take. They can be produced as giant stretched-canvas art pieces or even sets of personalized coasters. They can be offered in a series, so once a prospect receives the first, they're incentivized to participate with reps to complete the collection. The cartoons don't have to be personalized to be effective, either. Just think in terms of a point of agreement you want to deliver and the right cartoon will do the rest.

---

# DEEP AND WIDE TOGETHER

Dom Steinmann's and Lee Hamilton's approaches are brilliant, and they produced results any company would be thrilled to have. Similarly, my own use of Wide personalization with cartoons has been producing highly desirable results. This really isn't an "either-or" proposition. Both approaches work, and the two dimensions—Wide and Deep—reinforce the rationale for injecting personalization into any campaign.

Most of the stories in this book employ some form of personalization, even though they appear in other sections. Dan Waldschmidt's sword campaign in chapter six follows the same one-to-many personalization used in my cartoon campaigns. Every recipient gets the same type of sword, the same messaging, and the same packaging. But each piece is initiated by a trigger event—a missed earnings report—so there is some element of deeper personalization than simply sending a series of packages out to a list.

So it appears the two forms of personalization can, in some cases, be combined. Engagio marketing director Charlie Liang did this brilliantly with a campaign that combined elements of social media profile scrapes with a Wide personalization, one-to-many format.

## CASE STUDY
# Engagio's Bobblehead Campaign

**BACKGROUND:** Engagio provides a platform that helps marketers organize, coordinate, and monitor their account-based marketing (ABM) activities. As a startup at the time of the campaign, the company's goal was to create deep awareness among prime sales enablement and operations prospects. Engagio's marketing efforts to reach the audience drew them to their exhibit at a trade show.

**CHALLENGES:** At the trade show, Engagio would be competing with many other companies to win business from attendees. Engagio needed a way to stand out and get selected attendees to engage in conversations leading to new business.

**CAMPAIGN SPECIFICS:** The campaign required individual profile scrapes, as all Deep personalization schemes do, but Liang's primary focus was harvesting profile pictures. Engagio staff scoured profiles of 150 prominent sales enablement and operations professionals who were likely to attend the trade show. The profile pictures were harvested and used to have a customized bobblehead doll made for each prospect. A social media, direct mail, and email campaign followed, inviting recipients to stop by the Engagio hospitality suite to pick up their personalized bobbleheads.

**RESULTS:** Twenty-five percent of the targeted executives visited the Engagio suite to pick up their dolls, giving reps and prospects a chance to connect in person. The remainder of the bobbleheads were delivered after the show. Many of the recipients responded through their social media feeds with selfies and congratulatory notes to Engagio, further enhancing the campaign's reach to other sales-enablement professionals.

While in-person responses produced immediate conversations, the misses also provided opportunities for additional touch points, as arrangements were made to ship the bobbleheads and talk later. Liang reports that "a fair amount of the responses have already turned into immediate opportunities," and that the campaign produced an immediate win worth $70,000, which more than covered their costs.

The cost of each unit was approximately $100, a total spend of $15,000. That first sale put the ROI at 466 percent, a great start as the campaign continued to generate wins, deals, and revenue.

**KEY TAKEAWAY:** Engagio's bobblehead campaign had elements of both Wide and Deep personalization. It required more than a simple name-and-address

Charlie Liang/Engagio

**ENGAGIO'S PERSONALIZED BOBBLEHEAD CAMPAIGN**

*When Engagio marketing director Charlie Liang faced the challenge of connecting with Engagio's top accounts, he devised a clever use of personalization. Using LinkedIn profile photos, custom bobblehead dolls were made for each contact on the list. Recipients were then instructed to stop by the Engagio booth at an upcoming industry event to pick up their dolls.*

list, and the intel required couldn't be purchased in bulk; the booth guest list had to be determined based on research, and the pictures then had to be painstakingly located, verified, and extracted.

The production vendor then had to carve new heads and bodies for each one to match each recipient's photo. This wasn't data fed into a terminal for a rapid digital output, like a mail campaign. There was a lot of custom work, but there was a lot of uniformity as well.

These are important findings because they show the effectiveness of Deep and Wide personalization used together to produce winning results. Even when the lines between the two forms are blurred, personalization can produce a very positive result. Consider how you might use both Deep and Wide together to reach a new prospect.

# HOW TO MAKE A GREETING CARD

Print personalized, professional greeting cards from your PC

Contact campaigns often require multiple touch points with a target executive and their staff. Greeting cards are an excellent format for thanking helpful assistants, prompting stalled responses, and more. Using simple page-editing software, you can produce professional-grade greeting cards that deliver a powerful impression.

> **WHAT YOU'LL NEED:** Page-editing software (I use Adobe InDesign), laser printer capable of running letter-size bright-white cover stock (Kromekote 12-point C1S recommended), rotary trimmer (Rotatrim MasterCut II 15"), Handi-Scor scoring machine, burnishing tool, and A7 outer envelopes.

Greeting cards are powerful tools for Contact Marketers to create a connection, cement favor with a friendly assistant, or prompt a stalled sale.

The steps, materials, and equipment shown will help you produce a highly professional card. But you still have to make it compelling and relevant to the recipient. The best way to do that is to feature something personalized on the front panel.

I use cartoons with personalized captions, but unless you have extensive experience with them, you'll find they are tricky to work with. Still, you can create compelling themes with a recipient's profile picture, a photo of their building, or perhaps some other image they've posted to social media. Envato (https://elements.envato.com/add-ons) offers an extensive collection of Photoshop action sets—scripts added to the program that allow you to convert any photograph into an oil painting, caricature, comic book art, double exposure, and much more, producing an effect that will amaze and delight any recipient.

Use the rear panel to brand your card with your logo and contact information. Cards are most personal and effective when the message inside and the addressing of the outer envelope are written by hand.

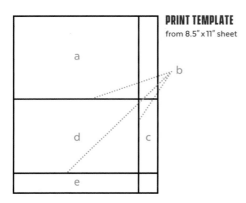

**1.** Create template with front (d) and rear (a) panels nested in upper left corner of page, with 1.5" trim area on side (c) and 1" bottom trim area (e). Do not print trim and fold marks (b).

**2.** Template should show art for the front panel (d) right side up and rear panel upside down (a). Again, trim and fold lines are for reference only and should not be printed on card.

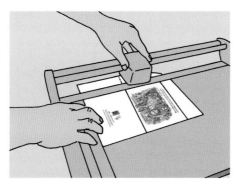

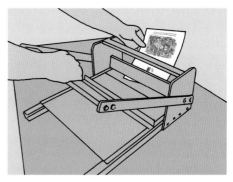

**3.** Place printed card in rotary trimmer short side up (shown), align against bottom stop at the 7" mark, and trim. Then place card long side up and trim to 10".

**4.** Place trimmed card faceup in Handi-Scor machine (adjust card stop on machine to score exactly halfway down, minus $\frac{1}{32}$"). Press handle and remove.

**5.** Use score to form crease in card, then use burnishing tool to flatten folded card.

**6.** Card is ready to be written and sent. Use hand-addressed A7 envelope with stamp; include handwritten note inside for best effect.

# DIGGING REALLY DEEP

The final story in this chapter explores a level of personalization that goes beyond mailing lists and profile scrapes. It's in the Deep category, but the approach is like that of an investigative news report—requiring research and constant observation. It's a time-consuming process, but it just might be the approach you need for one of your hard-to-reach prospects.

## CASE STUDY
## Deep Personalization in Action

**BACKGROUND:** Mikey Pawell, a business development rep for DocSend, is an elite sniper when it comes to making connections and closing deals on LinkedIn. He keeps a constant watch on his top accounts, looking for posts or other indicators of an opening to connect and talk business. Like a soldier, he waits patiently for opportunities to respond to in-the-moment triggers with sniper-shot precision. Each outreach quickly goes from online signals to offline contact pieces, always personalized to the targeted executive and their immediate circumstances.

And Zach Barney happened to be in the crosshairs.

When Barney, who heads inside sales for the eastern United States for Nearmap, bemoaned on social media the lack of healthy food in the office around the holidays, Mikey Pawell was listening.

**CHALLENGES:** In a sense, every business is in DocSend's target market. The document management platform helps companies distribute content, track readership, and gather insights that help them sell. It can work for any company, but Pawell has learned that conversations about document handling must be carefully timed, as his ideal prospects are usually deeply occupied with selling rather than making their process easier. For him, it's all about the timing—and the personal approach.

**CAMPAIGN SPECIFICS:** Pawell's technique is to watch for posts and pictures on social media, and to search for details most people might overlook, or, in Barney's case, a desire or need he could meet that would get the prospect's attention.

Pawell's response to Barney's comment about the lack of healthy food in the company lunchroom was met the next day with the delivery of a large box stuffed with fruits and vegetables. The delivery came eighteen hours after Barney's post first appeared on LinkedIn. By transitioning offline and striking quickly, Pawell's personalized gift made an enormous impact.

When the gift box arrived, Barney was so impressed that he launched a second post. It showed a photograph of the gift box with the contents splayed across the table and was accompanied by a rave about the swift initiative demonstrated by Pawell's gift. The post went viral and a deep initial connection was made.

Barney's response, of course, was to connect and listen to Pawell's pitch. "Of course I'm going to take a meeting with him," Barney said. "It shows that he's paying attention and making extra effort just to have a conversation with me."

**RESULTS:** Pawell's precision aim has paid off many times already. In Barney's case, the well-timed box of produce produced our favorite kind of reaction as Contact Marketers. Barney immediately loved the way Pawell was thinking and welcomed his contact. Moreover, Pawell's actions inspired a robust surge of evangelism on social media.

The social evangelism shown by the recipients in both stories is significant and valuable. For Pawell, it leads to more conversations with people who are eager to connect and certainly open to having a conversation about document management. Or, I suspect, anything else Pawell might have to say.

Zach Barney

### A BOX OF PRODUCE OPENED THE RIGHT DOOR

*Mikey Pawell uses watchful waiting in his social selling routine. When he spots an opening, he springs to action, sending gifts of personal interest to prospects. He did precisely that for Zach Barney, who had complained of the lack of healthy food options in the company's cafeteria. The next day, Pawell had a box of produce delivered and the conversation was on.*

**KEY TAKEAWAY:** We've seen throughout these personalization case studies that you must prepare. Through Pawell's creative efforts we see once more the power and purpose of Contact Marketing—and personalization—in action. Each time one of Pawell's gifts arrive, the recipients are astounded, and certainly impressed. The way DocSend treats its outreach mission is a reflection of how DocSend operates in general. We must always remember, every time we reach out to someone for contact, it's an audition. It shows prospects who we are and how we think.

---

## VARIATION

Pawell has used this approach many times. In one case, he found a photo of a prospect in his office. By enlarging the view, Pawell spotted a tiny detail, a logo sticker on the billboard behind the prospect. It was the logo of an obscure brand of gourmet coffee, which he recognized as being an important marker. Shortly thereafter, the prospect was stunned to discover he had received a pound of his favorite brand of coffee. Not many people had ever heard of it, and it left him wondering, "How could Pawell have known about this?"

---

# PUTTING IT ALL TOGETHER

What a blessing it is to be able to incorporate a target executive's personal details, interests, passions, and trigger events in our contact campaign efforts. Personalization is one of the most useful tools we have as Contact Marketers, to engage in ways that instantly build interest and rapport with people we don't yet know.

Personalization's continuing evolution is making it an even more powerful tool for Contact Marketers. As the stories in this chapter show, in its new Wide and Deep forms, along with new tools to scrape profiles and discover reliable contact details, personalization is the central driver of the remarkable results Contact Marketing is producing. There would be no stories of 100 percent response rates without it.

# WIDE VS. DEEP

Wide personalization is data driven. It is entirely reliant on accurate data. Without it, the campaign will crash, as recipients read much more than a simple error into the misspelling of their names. It becomes a damning exposé on your ability to heed details and deliver solid results.

Deep personalization has its own challenges. It requires detailed research for each targeted executive to identify markers that will define each outreach effort. Detailed research is a meticulous operation that takes time, making Deep personalization a slow process.

As the following chart shows, both Wide and Deep personalization campaigns are highly positive and can reach response rates of up to 100 percent. Wide personalization lists scalability and brand control as huge advantages. However, new AI applications (see chapter twelve) and simple controls can mitigate scalability and branding issues, making Deep personalization an equally powerful approach to create prized connections with valuable prospects.

*Wide vs. Deep Personalization*

|  | **WIDE PERSONALIZATION** | **DEEP PERSONALIZATION** |
|---|---|---|
| **Scalability** | Unlimited | Nonexistent |
| **Brand Control** | Absolute | Nonexistent |
| **Impression** | Highly positive | Highly positive |
| **Effectiveness** | Up to 100% | Up to 100% |
| **Case Study Examples** | Lee Hamilton's cartoon-style renderings<br><br>Dom Steinmann's falcon glove campaign<br><br>Engagio's bobblehead campaign (both Deep and Wide) | Insurance company's BigBoard mailing<br><br>Engagio's bobblehead campaign (both Deep and Wide)<br><br>Mikey Pawell's LinkedIn-inspired healthy food gift |

## Critical Next Steps

> **OBJECTIVE:** Use personalization to go wider and deeper in your Contact Marketing campaigns.

### Step 1. Take time to understand and test Wide and Deep personalization.

Both are quite useful, but they are not the same thing. The better you understand them, the better they will serve your campaign. Be careful not to impose the rules of one on the other, as it may kill the effect you're after. Remember, Wide personalization is the application of readily available data in a uniform way across an audience. Deep personalization is the application of individualized research findings to produce unique outreach elements, one by one. Requiring a Wide personalization campaign to incorporate profile scrapes defeats scalability and possibly brand unity. Using skeletal list data to squeeze out thinly relevant gifts will also compromise results.

### Step 2. Use Wide personalization to unify brand/message and scale outreach.

Wide personalization campaign elements require specialized skills to create. These should be advertising-grade pieces that clearly integrate your outreach message and brand, forming a powerful, audacious presentation that causes people to react. If you can afford it, hire an agency to help you keep things straight and expertly hone your message.

### Step 3. Adopt Deep personalization to enable decentralized Contact Marketing from the field.

Deep personalization is enabling a lot of people to break through without big budgets, which is incredibly useful across the business spectrum. Field reps can use it to connect with valuable prospects without summoning the marketing department. Same for independents, who pay all their own marketing expenses and have no access to agency help. Consider developing standardized packaging and guidelines for correspondence, and drill those with your team.

# POINTS TO REMEMBER

✔ The nature of personalization is changing. There are now two forms, Wide and Deep.

✔ Deep personalization is based on performing deep research on a prospect and fashioning a customized gift or other form of contact campaign to connect.

✔ Wide personalization is based on using data from a list to apply personal details to the same contact device.

✔ Both forms of personalization produce powerful results; neither is incorrect nor inappropriate for Contact Marketing campaigns.

✔ The potential disadvantages of Deep personalization are loss of brand control and lack of scalability.

✔ An advantage of Deep personalization is that it gives any member of a team a way to easily put the power of Contact Marketing to work in their sales efforts.

✔ The potential disadvantages of Wide personalization are mistakes due to quality of data input and lack of exclusivity.

✔ Two advantages of Wide personalization are that it gives the organization complete control of its brand and that it can easily scale to any size audience.

✔ It is possible to mix attributes of Deep and Wide personalization, as was the case in the Engagio bobblehead doll campaign. Everybody got the same thing, but Engagio used individual profile scrapes and each piece was individually carved to look like each target contact.

✔ While the Deep and Wide approaches can sometimes be successfully merged, be careful not to impose the logic of one form on the other.

✔ Personalization is a feature of many campaign success stories throughout this book. It should be integrated into your contact campaigns wherever possible.

# CHAPTER 5

# GIFT GIVING AND JEWEL BOXING

"What's in the box?"

That's always the question when a gift shows up. What could it *possibly* be? An unopened gift box represents unlimited potential. Anything could be in there. The right box can magnify the spectacle of the gift tenfold, maybe more. It makes whatever's inside irresistibly intriguing and unimaginably exciting.

That's the effect of jewel boxing. It makes whatever's inside—virtually anything—seem jewel-like. It is an amplifier of the desired effect to be generated by the contact device within. The right box is the first impression that leads to connections that are critical to the growth of your business.

Boxes come in all shapes, sizes, designs, and materials. There are coarse, industrial materials like corrugated cardboard; finely crafted boxes made of wood, veneers, plastics, and metal; and works of pure fantasy made of cardboard, paper, and other materials. Boxes and containers can be plain, tastefully branded, or utterly fanciful. There are boxes with windows and locking hasps that allow the recipient to glimpse what's there but require them to make contact to get inside.

Some boxes have integrated video screens with personalized messages, some have laser-etched logos and personalized details. Some form fanciful shapes with exotic folds. And some are simple purpose-designed cardboard boxes adorned with blunt artwork and stark black ink. Even a brown paper bag can evoke a deep sense of irony if something valuable and astonishing is inside.

> *We must always be thinking about how we can extend the practice of gift giving in our bids for important meetings.*

Once the box's secrets are released, a whole world of possibility springs from the gift within. In the previous chapter, we looked at how personalization has expanded to Deep and Wide dimensions. In the Deep form, profile scrapes reveal personal markers that define an individualized portrait of each targeted contact. These details equip us as Contact Marketers to deliver powerful experiences to open doors.

Wide personalization has its place, too. Do I really need to know the name of your dog before I send you a cartoon about your great success in business? Do I need to know which are your favorite cities in Europe to send a beautiful set of engraved knives for your kitchen? Both approaches have produced extraordinarily strong results, and they're based on simple name-and-address data and the expectation of a strong fit between the services offered and the needs of the recipient. It's one-size-fits-all, but the fit is significant and nearly unbeatable.

We must always be thinking about how we can extend the practice of gift giving in our bids for important meetings. How can we stretch it even further, how can we create new uses, experiences, and outcomes?

We can turn to virtually any scientific or artistic discipline to find new material. 3-D printing might offer interesting possibilities, allowing us to produce stunning gift items that couldn't exist any way other than through layer-by-layer, additive printing. It is also used to produce impossibly intricate confections and other food items. Wouldn't it be fascinating to send a 3-D printed chocolate sculpture as a gift, literally giving the prospect a taste of the future?

Experiences are also given as wildly appreciated gifts. Robert Smith sends his clients to racing school or aloft in a Soviet-era MiG jet fighter. Richard Branson will soon be sending tourists into space. Could that be used in a Contact Marketing campaign? Closer to the ground, there seem to be endless possibilities for classes, events, and thrills.

It's often said of gifts that "it's the thought that counts." For Contact Marketers, it is the concept that counts. How does the gift address the recipient's interests, needs, or wants while advancing your strategy? The right concept shows the recipient who you are and how you think. It says you're paying attention. And it makes connecting with you irresistible.

# GIFT GIVING

## Suspense-Building Gifts

It seems there are endless ways to express strategy through gifts, but there are certainly examples that stand out. John Ruhlin is the author of the best-selling book *Giftology* and a master of the art of strategic gift giving. His stories of highly imaginative gift campaigns flow unimpeded, one after another.

In one, he builds intrigue by having a tailor reach out to a targeted CEO's office, announcing she is being sent to fit the executive for a set of custom shirts. The sender is never revealed as the appointment is set and measurements taken. The CEO will surely try to pry details from the tailor about the sender, but the secret is always kept. "I don't know who is paying for these, I only know I've been sent to make some shirts."

When the shirts arrive with John's business card placed atop the clothier's box, the CEO just has to reach out. It's irresistible. John's gift campaigns always involve the highest quality, in the gift, presentation, and follow-up. These elements are particularly evident in this next story.

## CASE STUDY
# John Ruhlin's Knife Campaign

**BACKGROUND:** John Ruhlin strongly believes in giving an experience along with any gift. In this example, he takes the experience to a new extreme, incorporating a multitouch element in its presentation. He knows that top executives are often hardened to the advances and requests of sales reps, so he cleverly includes their *spouses* in the campaign as influencers.

**CHALLENGES:** The campaign brief calls for reaching the CEOs of Fortune 250 companies. These executives are in great demand and fiercely guarded by their administrative staff. No one gets through unless they're known, famous, or from one of the other Fortune 250 companies. The challenge is to navigate the hazardous path not only to get a few minutes on the phone with them, but to get them properly engaged for a sale or high-level referral. It's a perilous place, where contact rates are low and the stakes are high. One sale can not only create a wildly high ROI but can also change the trajectory of the Contact Marketer's business overnight.

**CAMPAIGN SPECIFICS:** Ruhlin's campaign involves the gifting of knives. A set, really, of fine Cutco knives, with the recipient's name or company logo laser-etched on each blade. But Ruhlin doesn't send the whole thing all at once. He turns it into a drip campaign, with the block and a single knife arriving first, followed by subsequent pieces in the set arriving separately, a week or so apart. Each new installment arrives in beautiful silver wrapping with a handwritten note.

This is strategic gift giving. Each new component renews the target contacts' excitement and builds their sense of expectation for the next installment. Their spouses look forward to each piece as well. As the set builds in their kitchen, they start asking, "So when are you going to do business with this person?" The campaign cleverly turns spouses and life partners into leverage points to make contact and do business.

**RESULTS:** Ruhlin reports that of forty-nine CEOs targeted so far in his knife campaign, thirty-eight connected, twelve agreed to meetings, and six became clients. The total spend on the campaign was $60,000, the estimated haul $750,000, for an ROI of 1,200 percent.

**KEY TAKEAWAY:** Ruhlin shows us that effective gift giving isn't really about the gift at all. It is about the experience, the audition, and the demonstration of the giver's competence and value as a potential partner in the contact's success. The prospects immediately know Ruhlin will approach any task with creativity, audacity, and great effectiveness. In the end, what else matters to a buyer?

John Ruhlin/Giftology

**JOHN RUHLIN'S SHARP SERIAL KNIFE CAMPAIGN**

*Giftology author John Ruhlin understands the importance of involving spouses as influencers in his contact campaigns. His campaign starts with a single Cutco knife in a countertop storage block. A week later, another knife arrives, and the next week, another. It doesn't take long for spouses to ask, "So when are you doing business with this person?"*

## Artful Expressions

While Ruhlin's approach is a brilliant example of a one-size-fits-all approach to personalization, Kenny Madden is a true believer in Deep personalization. Before Madden ever became involved in sales, he was educated in Britain as a fine artist and painter. As any Contact Marketer might expect, the combination has served him well. But it wasn't until about ten years ago that he realized sales and fine art had any sort of useful intersection.

Working as a sales development rep, he noticed his colleague had gotten an unusual out-of-office message from a prospect. It said he would be out for the next two weeks collecting rocks on Mars. Inspiration and mischief struck all at once. "I told my colleague, 'Send him a copy of Andy Weir's *The Martian*,'" he explained, "'and add a Post-it note that says life on Mars can get a little lonely this time of year.'"

Madden's hunch paid off. Upon his return, the prospect called and asked for a meeting, which produced an immediate $28,000 deal. And it got him thinking, "What if I can inject into my approach something that could only come from me? I wonder what sort of response I could get."

## CASE STUDY
# Kenny Madden's Business Expressionism Campaign

**BACKGROUND:** After initial success with a colleague's campaign, Kenny Madden, the fine artist turned sales rep, wondered if the art he'd been trained to create might open doors to some of his top accounts. He decided to run a test of his own.

**CHALLENGES:** Madden had three important accounts yet to be activated. All three were startups based in the Flatiron Building in Manhattan. The structure is an architectural icon, so Madden figured the CEOs would probably have a personal attachment to their noteworthy place of business. His challenge was to use those facts to produce a campaign that would help him gain access and win business.

**CAMPAIGN SPECIFICS:** Madden produced three slightly different original paintings of the building, each with handwritten Post-it notes about some sort of event tied to their businesses. One referenced a quote in *Forbes*, another quoted comments made on a social media post. There was no request for a meeting in any of the three packages he sent. This might seem counterintuitive, but Madden explains his rationale: "When you don't ask for anything, but lead with something people really care about, amazing things happen." And they certainly did.

**RESULTS:** All three CEOs responded, two with emails, the third through the company's chief marketing officer, who was asked to reach out to see what Madden's company does. The result was $180,000 worth of immediate business and an additional $480,000 in the pipeline—a yield of potentially more than half a million dollars in business from three paintings and a few Post-it notes. Setting aside the value of Madden's talents and work on the three paintings and estimating $500 for materials and shipping costs, that was a 36,000 percent return initially and a 132,000 percent ROI overall.

**KEY TAKEAWAY:** Madden calls all of this "Business Expressionism," the use of a personally generated object, usually some form of art, in an outreach effort to a

Kenny Madden

### KENNY MADDEN'S "BUSINESS EXPRESSIONISM"

*Kenny Madden was torn between his love of fine art painting and a career in sales, until he realized how powerful they could be together. That's when he invented what he calls "Business Expressionism," the use of handmade art to deliver something of personal value to the recipient, resulting in a multitude of high-level meetings.*

critically important potential client. He uses his formal paintings to open doors, but Madden quickly discovered that it's not about the production value. It's about the personal value of the sentiment. This is why even his quickly drawn Post-it notes yield a return. So a key takeaway is that art opens doors, but it's art *plus* the personal touch that makes the difference.

But do you have to be an artist yourself? At one of his earlier posts, Madden was working with a sales team that was fascinated with his stories, but one by one they lamented, "We're not artists. How can we do this, too?" His response was brilliant. He asked, "What is it you do that you can't *not* do every day?" He explained that creating art was his "can't not do," and asked the reps each to take personal stock.

One woman spoke up. "I like to knit." That was all Madden needed. "Okay, knit something for one of your top prospects." The timing was perfect. She had two accounts that had just inked a strategic partnership together. So she knitted a scarf for her target contact featuring the combined logos and colors of the two companies. A week later, a letter arrived from the company's CEO, thanking her for the scarf. "What do I do now?" she asked. "You just wait," Madden replied. A month later, she got a call that led to a $160,000 deal. She now incorporates knitting into everything she does.

The overall lessons of his campaigns are obvious. Madden's approach reminds us that we're not buyers and sellers; we're people. When we do something special for a stranger, with a simple acknowledgment of something important happening in their lives, we humanize ourselves. And when that happens between two people who should be doing business together, the results can be powerful.

It's also important to register Madden's advice: Send your gift and be patient. Resist the temptation to pounce and pitch. If something is meant to happen, it will. If it isn't, consider the fact that you've done something worthwhile for another person as your reward. There are plenty of deals out there.

It's also important to remember that while we're not all artists, we all have our own "can't-not-do" that will help us stand out to our accounts and prospects. These are the things that make us unique. For me, it's drawing cartoons. For Madden, it's painting. For you, it might be knitting or cooking or taking photographs. Take stock, find your own "can't not do," and start giving your gift to the world. It will respond with more than a few gifts of its own.

## VARIATION

Sometimes Madden's art and handwritten notes combine into cleverly disarming Post-it note drawings. They're often simple graphs with an x- and y-axis, an upward trend, and two variables. One of his favorites depicts "You" on the vertical axis and "Me" on the horizontal, with the trend line curving skyward. What a wonderful sentiment and a simple way to melt the ice.

## Sweet Interruptions

If Kenny Madden's approach is laid-back, Rick Tobin's is even more so. I first learned of Tobin's surprising campaign while speaking at an event in Florida. I asked the audience, "Does anyone have their own can't-fail method for breaking through to important contacts?" Tobin raised his hand. He started by saying, "You'll probably think this is foolish, but . . ." and then he unleashed an amazing story.

## CASE STUDY
# Rick Tobin's Cupcake Campaign

**BACKGROUND:** Rick Tobin is a successful commercial real estate broker in the Fort Lauderdale–Miami area. He does what most successful brokers do in their markets: He networks in the community. He's active on social media. And he is always on the hunt for new prospects. Those come to his attention through referrals, local business articles, and industry events. Once he identifies a prospect, he uses good old-fashioned follow-up and perseverance to open relationships that lead to sales and referrals. At least that's the plan.

> *What was the ROI? Divide $200,000 by the cost of a cupcake and multiply by a hundred. I get 5 million percent.*

**CHALLENGES:** One prospect in particular was being quite resistant to Tobin's approach. Tobin had been trying to reach him for months. Week after week, month after month, he would call but was always told the fellow was out of the office, out of town—essentially, anything to get rid of the call. Tobin tried everything he could think of. He desperately needed to interrupt the negative pattern. Then one day, inspiration struck.

**CAMPAIGN SPECIFICS:** Tobin discovered the prospect's birthday was coming up the next day, so he whipped up a plan. That following day, he visited the local bakery and bought a cupcake decorated with a birthday candle. Then he headed straight for the prospect's office and checked in with the receptionist. "This is for Bob," he explained. She opened the box and her expression changed from a skeptical frown to a radiant smile. "Hold on," she said, and suddenly the prospect appeared and invited Tobin to join him in his office.

**RESULTS:** In that first conversation, Bob apologized for being difficult to reach and asked Tobin to explain what he does. The net result was an immediate $200,000 deal. We can appreciate this wasn't simply a "Thanks for the cupcake, here's a $200K deal" kind of exchange. The prospect was aware of Tobin's persistence and respected it. But it certainly was the pattern interrupt needed to turn everything around. Contact Marketing campaigns are micro-focused. They can be a campaign targeting as few as one person. So in this instance, the contact rate was 100 percent. And what was the ROI? Divide $200,000 by the cost of the cupcake and multiply by a hundred. I get 5 million percent.

**KEY TAKEAWAY:** You don't have to spend a lot to use Contact Marketing tactics and win big orders. As Tobin's story demonstrates, the value is in the concept and execution. Not the price of the object used to break through.

Cupcake by DisplayFakeFoods.com

**RICK TOBIN'S
$200,000 CUPCAKE**

*When he found it impossible to reach one particular prospect, Rick Tobin noticed the fellow's birthday was quickly approaching. On the special day, Tobin stopped by with a cupcake decorated with birthday trimmings. The prospect was so moved by the gesture, he rewarded Tobin's perseverance with an immediate $200,000 deal—and a 5 million percent ROI on his cupcake purchase.*

## Gifts as Rewards

Tobin's modest little cupcake campaign actually set a new record. It was the most profitable contact campaign I'd found (at least until the Orabrush story came along, see chapter ten), edging out Rick Bennett's contact letter in *The Wall Street Journal* by 1.5 million percent. In that campaign, Bennett produced contact with Oracle founder and CEO Larry Ellison, resulting in a $350 million sale and a 3.5 million percent ROI (featured in *How to Get a Meeting with Anyone*).

As the two Ricks show, contact campaigns can address as few as a single target executive. Focused in that way, the outcomes are binary and extreme. It's either a 0 or 100 percent response rate, and if the value of the desired outcome is high enough, the ROI can be absurdly high. That's great, but it doesn't address the challenge facing most enterprise sales teams. Each rep is often tasked with connecting with a few hundred accounts. Multiply that by a few hundred sales reps and the scale of the challenge becomes quite large.

Kristin Gallucci's "California Gold Rush" campaign is a useful illustration of how Contact Marketing can address the need for contact at scale. It also broadens our definition of gift-giving strategy. Most gifts are given as a token of appreciation, as a gesture of friendship. But gifts can also be held back as a reward—the correct term is a "hold-back device"—for the prospect taking a desired reaction. We commonly see this approach in direct marketing campaigns, but not so much in the realm of corporate or sales-related gifting.

## CASE STUDY
## Kristin Gallucci's Stetson Hat Campaign

**BACKGROUND:** Gallucci and her partner wanted to win new clients for their B2B ad agency. With fresh award wins and new record-breaking campaigns for their existing clients, they felt the timing was right to step out and expand their roster in the financial services sector.

**CHALLENGES:** Financial services is a mature market filled with incumbent ad agency relationships. In order to compete, Gallucci's agency would need to demonstrate the value of its creative and strategic thinking. Moreover, it needed to quickly pare down its list of five thousand possible accounts to five hundred, and then quickly generate meetings from that core group.

**CAMPAIGN SPECIFICS:** The strategy was to use a multiwave, dimensional mail campaign. As each wave progressed, recipients were asked to respond in some way, signaling their intent to engage further. This approach produced a natural thinning of the list toward the desired core five hundred prospects.

Stetson

### KRISTIN GALLUCCI'S
### STETSON HAT CAMPAIGN

*Kristin Gallucci's agency pitch followed a California Gold Rush theme, offering to help recipients prospect for gold in their markets. The multiwave campaign included several mailed pieces, culminating with a note and a tape measure. Each targeted executive was asked to measure their head for a fitted Stetson hat, which was delivered in person to kick off their first meeting.*

The theme of the campaign was the "Gold Rush Days," suggesting the agency would help the financial institutions mine new gold in their markets. The first wave contained a miner's lamp, with appropriate messaging about lighting the way.

Next came a miner's pan with tiny nuggets of gold. The final wave arrived with a tape measure and a note, asking recipients to measure their heads for a custom-fitting of a fine Stetson cowboy hat. The executives were then asked to forward their information and commit to meeting with agency representatives, where the hat would be presented as the final gift of the campaign.

**RESULTS:** Driving to the core five hundred on their list, the campaign produced a 73 percent meeting rate, with $2.4 million in immediate revenue against a cost of $180,000. Based on initial sales and the cost of the campaign, it generated a 1,300 percent ROI. That's interesting, but the numbers alone cannot measure the true effect of the effort. It generated 365 meetings, some of which became ongoing new relationships. Initial stats do not take into account the lifetime value of those relationships.

**KEY TAKEAWAY:** The campaign combined many tactics, including a modified version of the half-of-a-gift tactic described in *How to Get a Meeting with Anyone*. That is, after sending two gifts in a series, recipients were sent a tape measure to specify their hat size so they could receive the final gift. But the final gift only came when the prospect agreed to meet with one of Gallucci's reps. The tape measure is also an involvement device. It made the process fun, to measure your head in order to gain the prize. All of this surely had recipients thinking, "I love the way you think," which is precisely what you want when selling advertising agency services.

The multiwave structure of the campaign, using three successive dimensional mail efforts, is also interesting from a Contact Marketing perspective. It incorporates elements of a persistence campaign, building interest and ultimately response when the final effort arrived. It humanized each of the reps to their top accounts and made it fun to agree to meet. It set the tone for the establishment of a valuable set of new relationships that will generate revenue for years to come.

The campaign incorporated other significant elements. By starting with a list of five thousand and allowing recipients to self-select, Gallucci's team was able to identify the core 10 percent of the group who were actually worth their time and effort to secure meetings. Moreover, each wave of the campaign progressively solidified the positive impressions needed among the core group to move a sale forward. The multiwave approach became an efficient way for the agency to find its own nuggets of gold in the list, allowing it to focus its attention where the impact would be greatest.

I suspect everyone would love to have a Stetson hat, even if you aren't a cowboy or cowgirl. It's just one of those things you'd like to be able to pull out and wear when life literally takes you on a rodeo ride.

## Giving Experiences

All gifts incorporate experiences, but not all gifts are physical things. Robert Smith thinks the experience itself should be the gift. His contact campaigns are highly personalized, based on profile scrapes and Deep personalization. While the gift itself is a custom-tailored experience, its presentation has to take some physical form. So Robert produces what he calls "Theme Boxes," often using converted cigar humidors as the vehicle.

## CASE STUDY
## Robert Smith's Theme Box Campaigns

**BACKGROUND:** Smith's promotion agency, Axcelerate, often is tasked with creating connections with top CEOs around the world. His go-to method for creating those connections is a "Theme Box," containing an experience of a lifetime as the gift.

**CHALLENGES:** Smith targeted two Fortune 50 companies he was interested in approaching for agency work. He could get general information about the CEOs of the companies, but wanted to dig deeper and, of course, break through with great impact. The challenge would be reaching such highly protected contacts.

**CAMPAIGN SPECIFICS:** As Smith researched the two CEOs for contact, he discovered one was a Formula One racing buff and the other an aviation enthusiast. So he formulated Theme Boxes for each using fine cigar humidors. Inside, he mounted a high-quality scale wooden model of a Formula One car to the base of the box.

   Atop the model were two tickets to the Skip Barber Racing School. Smith created a similar box for the aviation enthusiast, this time attaching a scale model of a Korean War–era MiG-15 at the base of the box. The main gift was a ticket for a ride in an actual MiG fighter in Reno.

**RESULTS:** Both CEOs welcomed contact and were thrilled with the approach. Smith says his Theme Boxes are meant to send recipients on a trip of a lifetime, and they always result in contact.

**KEY TAKEAWAY:** Theme Boxes are meant for big, bold bids for contact with extremely high-value executives and prospects.

Custom box by Rob Hetler; MiG experience by MiGFlug

**EXPERIENCE OF A LIFETIME IN EVERY BOX**

*Using Deep personalization and imagination, Robert Smith's Axcelerate agency produces Theme Boxes to gain a CEO's attention. Here, a MiG jet fighter theme plays out with a fine wooden scale model of the jet, MiGFlug voucher to ride in the Korean War-era MiG-15, aviator sunglasses, and more.*

## VARIATION

Theme Boxes can express virtually any theme, so the experiences within can be anything. But the experiences must be spectacular and tied to research gleaned from profile scrapes and more. Imagine a football jersey and two tickets to the Super Bowl, or a scale model of Virgin Galactic's SpaceShipOne with a ticket to go to outer space.

# HOW TO MAKE A CUSTOM BOX
(Like they do at the UPS Store)

Contact campaigns require careful attention to detail to achieve a level of polish that opens important doors. That includes outer packaging. Shipping boxes come in many shapes and sizes, but when you're sending something that doesn't fit the standard range, it can be useful to produce your own custom box in any size you need.

*WHAT YOU'LL NEED:* Large sheet of corrugated cardboard, large ruler or tape measure, pencil, perforation wheel, box cutter, roll of 2" packing tape, and a large, flat surface safe for cutting.

No one knows if it was Oscar Wilde or Will Rogers who first said it, but it is certainly true that we never get a second chance to make a first impression. In any Contact Marketing campaign involving sending something tangible, the outer packaging is the first thing the prospect will see. So it had better be good.

Packing anything for shipment usually involves some form of corrugated cardboard box. That's a lucky coincidence because the brown kraft, industrial look of corrugated cardboard seems to provide the perfect backdrop to embellish the looks of whatever is inside. I use custom-printed corrugated packaging for all my cartoon contact pieces, which makes it look like they're coming from a cartoon art gallery. It makes the whole presentation irresistible, as people are constantly drawn to the packages, asking what's inside. Which is precisely the effect we want.

If you don't have custom packaging, making your own is simple enough, and it will allow you to lend an impressive, bespoke quality to your Contact Marketing campaign.

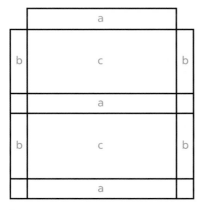

**1.** Box should have a spine and two end flaps (a), four side flaps (b) and two side panels (c).

**2.** Measure pieces to be enclosed, adding 3″ to all dimensions. Contact device shown measures 25″ long, 12″ tall, and 1.5″ thick, so the folded custom box in this case should measure 28″ × 15″ × 4.5″.

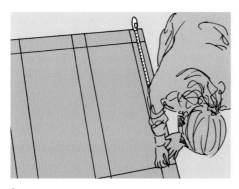

**3.** Using a large ruler or tape, measure and draw grid shown in diagram above. In this case, the flattened box should measure 37″ × 43.5″.

**4.** Trace over measured grid lines with perforation wheel. Remove corners as shown in diagram in step one.

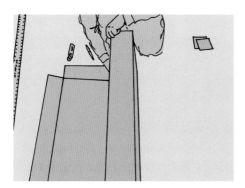

**5.** Starting at the bottom of the box, tuck in low corners and close the box in a rolling motion.

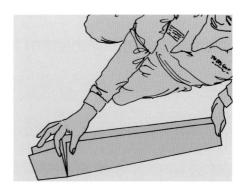

**6.** Check fit of corners and flaps, wrap contact piece in bubble wrap, and close and tape box with packing tape.

# JEWEL BOXING: NOW LET'S PUT IT IN A BOX

Robert Smith's Theme Boxes are interesting not only for their ability to create critical connections but in the way they bring focus to the box itself. The whole thing—the wooden box, the scale model at the base, and extras—are all wrappings. The real gift is the experience of a lifetime the box opens up—living out the lifelong dream of flying in a jet fighter or taking racing lessons. The rest is what I would certainly term "jewel boxing."

I use jewel boxing when I send cartoons. The outer packaging is a custom-designed carrier printed with a collage of cartoon art in a mezzotint screen, making the package look like something from a cartoon art gallery. They attract an embarrassing amount of attention in public, but that is precisely the effect I want. The box is a big part of why the cartoon contact piece is so effective.

> *The box is a big part of why the cartoon contact piece is so effective.*

While all eyes have been glued to digital screens in recent years, boxes and outer packaging have been undergoing their own remarkable digital transformations. Even lowly brown corrugated boxes can now be personalized, serialized, and even launch their own digital experiences triggered by coding embedded within the printed graphics. Digitization has also changed the way logos and other graphics are applied to virtually any substrate, using vectored graphics and lasers to etch or cut intricate designs.

## The Corrugated Cardboard Box

What an elegant design corrugated cardboard is. Those wavy sheets of coarse brown kraft paper sandwiched between two flat layers create a protective crush zone and a lightweight, sturdy material for containing things. Big things. Little things. Heavy things. Really, just about anything.

Nearly everything we order online arrives in some form of corrugated box. Double- and triple-wall corrugated cardboard is stiff and strong enough to suitably contain anything from kitchen appliances to heavy industrial machinery.

Designers are also drawn to corrugated cardboard, and I'm no exception. The contrast of the blunt, rough industrial nature of cardboard against any smooth white surface and bright colors is dramatic. Corrugated cardboard can easily accept printing, providing a broad palette for designers.

The wavy portion, or "flute," comes in five single-wall variations, ranging from A-flute (5 mm) to G-flute (0.5 mm), with many combinations of double- and triple-wall versions for heavy-duty shipping. For most applications in contact campaigns, B-flute (3 mm) and E-flute (1.5 mm) are just right for rigid packaging, and single-sided corrugated sheet makes an elegant solution for flexible or rolled designs.

B-flute cardboard produces rugged industrial shipping enclosures, while E-flute produces much finer boxes that accept direct printing without distortion between flutes. E-flute is my favorite all-around packaging material for my cartoon contact campaign pieces. It makes an elegantly counterintuitive outer package that can look quite stunning, while remaining stout enough to handle the rigors of shipping.

The corrugation process allows for flexibility to print direct to substrate (directly onto the already-formed sheet of corrugated material) or to assemble the board using preprinted four-color sheets. It's highly versatile, very useful stuff. None of this is particularly new.

But lately, corrugated cardboard has gone digital. Large computer-aided design (CAD) tables precisely map out, score, and cut cardboard, while equally large flatbed printers apply graphics directly to the cardboard. While this production process started as a method of prototyping, it has become the accepted low-volume production method for corrugated packaging.

Along with other advances, the new digital platform allows for true personalization of each printed piece and the inclusion of new digital watermarking technology, making every box one of a kind. HP's Link Technology, for example, can embed into any image a digital watermark that acts like a QR code, yet is imperceptible to the human eye. Treasury Wine Estates has developed a similar technology that launches augmented reality experiences from its own image-recognition mobile app that could easily work from a cardboard box as well (see more in chapter twelve).

This link technology opens all sorts of possibilities for our contact campaigns. The recipient could, for example, simply point their smartphone at the box and launch an overlay of you stepping in front of the box, explaining why you're sending the gift and reaching out. Or the image could be linked to a personalized landing page that offers something of value to the recipient while setting a tracking pixel for retargeting in a persistence campaign. Or launch an email, text, or video message, or offer some sort of incentive for further engagement.

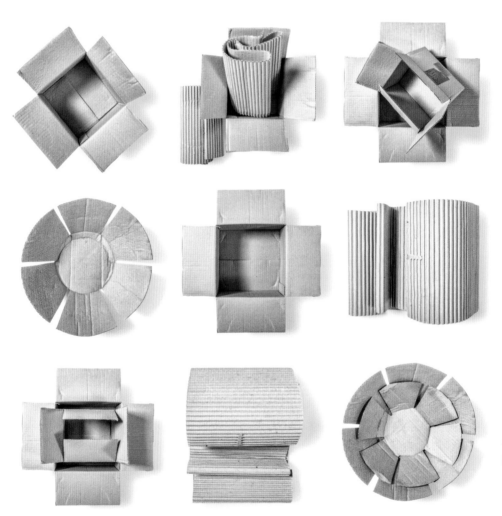

iStock

### CORRUGATED CARDBOARD PACKAGING

*The rough, industrial ethos of brown kraft corrugated cardboard can form surprisingly elegant packaging for virtually any gift or visual metaphor. Affordability and toughness combine with a paper surface that easily accepts printed graphics to produce the perfect jewel boxing platform for Contact Marketing campaigns.*

"Corrugated packaging has become mainstream, part of our digital lives," BoxMaker's director of marketing and communications Katy Hart explains, "but it's still just as functional and cost effective as it ever was." I would add, it makes what was once simply a coarse, commercial shipping material into a crucial element for our contact campaigns. It imparts an invaluable visual impact to help us create instant connections with important contacts.

## CASE STUDY
# Jewel Boxing My Own Cartoon Campaigns

**BACKGROUND:** I enjoy a powerful advantage as both a marketer and one of *The Wall Street Journal*'s cartoonists. And as you must know by now, I use my cartoons to break through to people I should never be able to reach. The cartoons have worked well for many years, but I am always looking for ways to improve the effectiveness of those campaigns.

**CHALLENGES:** Cartoons already get more than their share of attention. In editorial readership surveys, they're almost always the best read and remembered part of magazines and other publications. Still, when they're shipped, they have to be boxed, and boxes don't have that same visual impact—or can they? That was the goal when redesigning the carrier for my cartoon contact campaigns, which was originally produced in plain, unprinted corrugated material. The challenge was to create a new version of the outer packaging that would have the same visual impact as the cartoon piece inside, and to test for any effect that might have on response to the campaign.

**CAMPAIGN SPECIFICS:** The test and regular packaging are both used to ship my BigBoard contact device: an 18″ × 24″ foam core board with a personalized cartoon on one side and a branded message from the sender to the recipient on the reverse. The two versions—plain and printed—were tested head-to-head to see if one had more effect than the other. The artwork for the printed version was a collage of cartoon art at very large scale, then reduced to a coarse black mezzotint pattern.

**RESULTS:** The test revealed that the printed outer packaging outperformed the plain version by roughly 10 percent. In the context of Contact Marketing, where response rates can soar as high as 100 percent, that may not seem like much, but it was a significant addition to an already-high contact rate. I have seen the effect of the packaging whenever I show up somewhere to ship a BigBoard.

It attracts an overwhelming amount of attention, prompting many to ask questions. What is it? What's it for? Where did you get it?

**A PRINT FROM A CARTOON ART GALLERY**

*Part of the BigBoards' allure is the corrugated outer packaging that makes it look like it came straight from a cartoon art gallery. 5" × 7" greeting card shown for scale.*

**KEY TAKEAWAY:** Sending a gift in distinctive packaging gives it a powerful advantage—when it arrives, everybody knows about it. I once sent a BigBoard to the president of a company I wanted to do business with. We already knew each other, but our initiative together had stalled. I sent the piece to revive the contact and move the deal along. When I called to inquire if the piece was received, the receptionist already knew all about it. She explained the president had been carrying it around the office, showing it off. But she first noticed it because of the packaging it came in.

## Custom Wood Boxes

The industrial ethos of corrugated cardboard is nice, but what if you want to step it up a bit? Consider moving up to a custom wood enclosure.

Barry Mills knows a lot about the power of fine wooden boxes to enhance marketing results. As CEO and owner of Kelowna-based Wood Gift Box in British Columbia, he has seen the effect firsthand. "Premium wooden boxes tend to make products look good and sell even better," he said. "You take a middle-priced wine, put it in the right box, and you'll increase revenue well beyond the cost of the packaging. That's the power of packaging done well."

Mills's operation focuses on producing relatively short runs of beautifully finished wooden boxes with finely detailed but understated branding using laser-etching technology. The results are impressive, as you can see from the accompanying photographs. The boxes are such fine pieces of work themselves; it's easy to imagine recipients holding on to them for years.

## CASE STUDY
# Custom Wooden Boxes Launch Syrup Brand

**BACKGROUND:** A small maple syrup producer wanted to graduate from being a local provider to a national brand. In essence, its owners wanted to use a small contact campaign to greatly expand its footprint and scale—fast.

**CHALLENGES:** Once a company is typecast, it's hard to shake the impression. In this case, the company was known as a supplier of a superior syrup product, but a boutique operation not capable of fulfilling large orders. The reputation was severely hampering the owners' aspirations to grow the company into a national brand.

**CAMPAIGN SPECIFICS:** The solution was to deliver samples of the company's product to national retail buyers in custom wooden boxes with its logo laser-engraved on the top panel. The boxes made the product look like it was already a premium national brand, which helped the buyers move beyond their preconceptions of the company.

**RESULTS:** The boxes made the product look like a superstar brand. As a result, the company secured the meetings and deals it needed, and it made the leap.

Boxes by WoodGiftBox.com

### FINE WOODEN BOXES MAKE ANYTHING LOOK GRAND

*Wooden enclosures come in a variety of types, including boxes with hinged tops, sliding panels—even padlocked lids with windows to tease the contents inside.*

**KEY TAKEAWAY:** The customized box made the small maple producer look the part, thus helping it become the national brand the owners hoped it could be. First impressions matter.

Mills's company works with marketers all over the world, but one commission stands out above the rest. When the final Harry Potter movie was released, the producers wanted to make a grand gesture to the cast, crew, and top pop culture influencers. So they had Mills's team produce boxes for copies of Master Potter's magic wand from the movie. It was a parting gift that was eagerly received—and coveted—in no small part because of the box it came in.

To say fine wooden enclosures create a bit of magic might not be far off. But what if you want to create an even bigger impression?

## High-Fashion Packaging

At the other end of the scale from corrugated cardboard is high-fashion packaging, which often takes form as whimsical, intricate, fantasy-like enclosures. Eight-sided boxes that close at the top with a circular fan of flaps, impossibly complex pleated bags, prism-shaped boxes that twist thirty degrees from bottom to top, or double-ended boxes that screw together. These enclosures are usually made of stiff cover stock, and as the accompanying diagrams show, they are impossible feats of paper engineering somehow made possible.

These high-fashion containers are the work of design wizards like Evelio Mattos, creative director of packaging and branding at Phoenix-based Design Packaging Inc. The company produces packaging for a long list of luxury brands and elite fashion and cosmetics clients. But wouldn't you know it—it is a Contact Marketer, too. Some of its most fascinating work comes in the form of influencer packages, utterly whimsical pieces sent to social media influencers, designed to cultivate social media buzz for their clients.

## CASE STUDY
## Social Media Influencer Campaign

**BACKGROUND:** When companies launch new products, they must maximize the impact in traditional and social media. Publicists push the stories to the press, but a separate strategy is needed to generate buzz on social media platforms. To meet that need, marketers are using social media influencer campaigns. The objective is to inspire the recipients to post about the launch to their vast followings, creating instant positive impressions and goodwill.

**CHALLENGES:** A large branded-goods company was launching a new baby product and wanted to magnify the reach on social media. Millions of new moms are active on Instagram, Facebook, and Pinterest. The challenge was to connect with all of them by reaching out to the top influencers in the new-motherhood interest segment.

**CAMPAIGN SPECIFICS:** Designer Evelio Mattos devised a campaign device that would provide a layered unveiling of the launch story. The package arrived swathed in soft wrapping. Inside, there was a short blurb about the product, a comment from the founder, and a brief statement of why there was a need for the product.

Designed with deep interactivity in mind, the intricate box included heat-sensitive ink, so the story progressed as recipients handled the piece. By pulling a lever, a smaller box emerged, and secret compartments opened and panels popped out at the pull of a ribbon. All these devices revealed hashtags the company wanted recipients to share, eventually culminating in a request to take photos, pose with the product, and post it all to their followers.

**RESULTS:** Evelio says it's hard to track direct results from influencer campaigns, but the company could immediately see a jump in posts about the launch product and uses of the launch hashtags. Ultimately, he says, "When you send one hundred boxes to micro-influencers, you suddenly have a huge splash, which is just what we got and what the client wanted."

### FREE BOOK OF BOX DESIGNS BY EVELIO MATTOS

*Designer Evelio Mattos shares some of his most elaborate designs for boxes created for fashion, retail, and marketing missions in his e-book,* Packaging & Dielines. *The designs are stunning and the price is right: It's free.*

Evelio Mattos/Design Packaging

### HOW IMPOSSIBLY INTRICATE BOXES ARE MADE

Packaging & Dielines *reveals how boxes with seemingly impossible designs and facets are made. Shown here, the dieline plan for spiral-shaped box top and bottom pieces that twist onto one another to form a sealed enclosure.*

Evelio Mattos/Design Packaging

Evelio Mattos/Design Packaging

## THE BOX ALONE MAKES AN ASTONISHING IMPRESSION

*Evelio Mattos's spiral box is a prime example of the jewel boxing effect in action. Whatever might be inside is made all the more dramatic and impressive by the box itself.*

**KEY TAKEAWAY:** Audacity is always a key goal in our contact campaigns. We want recipients continually asking, "How did you do that?" We want them asking their marketing department heads, "Why aren't we doing something like this?" In Evelio Mattos's designs, we see there is no limit to the level of imagination and production value that can be expressed with outer packaging.

# SAY THANK YOU

Whether a gift is store-bought or handmade, expensive or not, a simple or grand gesture, the proper response is to thank the person who sent it. People used to write thank-you notes and cards, but it's become a dying art. Lori Richardson, president of Score More Sales and author of *She Sells, She Leads*, sees that as a strategic blunder. She says thank-you cards are not only good manners; they are a requirement for establishing critically important relationships in business.

Consider what a thank-you card is. It's a handwritten note, inscribed personally by the sender, expressing their gratitude for something someone has done. It's a kindness in response to someone else's kindness. Thank-you cards are a gift themselves that not only express appreciation but also demonstrate the quality of one's character. They are a secret weapon in our auditions for business from prospective accounts.

> *Thank-you cards are a gift themselves.*

Lori recalls the story of a young man she met when he was first starting out in sales. At an event a few years later, he reintroduced himself and gave her his card. That led to a later conversation, which led to Lori buying his service. What surprised her was that she never received any expression of appreciation from the rep.

Determined to show him the importance of the gesture, she sent a box of thank-you cards with her own note, advising him to always recognize the value of a handwritten card. She sent another card to the rep's CEO, praising him for the good job he'd done following up on her business. After all that, there was still no note of thanks in return.

It's probably not possible to measure the results of a lifetime's worth of sending thank-you cards. But it's easy to see that it has a positive effect. So here's a question: Could a box of thank-you cards be used as a contact campaign itself? I believe it can, particularly if the cards mean something to the recipient. The solution would be to personalize the cards, so each time they're used, the contacts send a piece of themselves. And as we know, the more personal the gift, the more likely you will have the impact you seek.

**THE GREATEST GIFT YOU CAN GIVE IS GRATITUDE**

*When Score More Sales president Lori Richardson is shown a kindness, she always returns the favor with a handwritten thank-you card. It's not just a nice gesture, it is an important show of respect that defines the sender's character and opens the door to more business.*

iStock

# PUTTING IT ALL TOGETHER

We've seen some fascinating approaches to gift giving. John Ruhlin showed how gifts can be given in sequence to build a cumulatively stronger impression while injecting a robust persistence element into the campaign. He also showed that influencers aren't just colleagues at the office. They can also be senior executives, assistants, industry peers, even spouses.

Kenny Madden inspires us to give something of ourselves in our gifts, something utterly unique and personal to bridge the divide. And he inspires us to trust the magnetism of our contact gifts. Send the gift and wait. Don't say anything about what you do, your company, or what you want. Let them come to you.

Rick Tobin showed us how something as simple as a cupcake can humanize us and create a connection with important prospects while setting a new ROI record. Kristin Gallucci took us on a completely different sort of journey, cleverly combining elements of persistence, natural selection, multimodal communication, and cumulative impressions to produce a campaign that changed her agency's scale. And Robert Smith showed us that gifts aren't just things; they're experiences. Sometimes the best gifts are just that—an experience of a lifetime that can very easily open the door to a lot more success and greater scale.

We've seen that packaging itself can be the gift. Corrugated boxes and enclosures give us a broad palette of options for creating custom pieces that project quality and intrigue, well beyond what their rough, inexpensive nature might suggest. I told you about my own use of jewel boxing, turning my contact pieces into objects that look like they're coming from an art gallery. And in the process, the campaign gets a boost. We looked at other enclosures made of handcrafted, laser-etched wood and ornate, fanciful box designs that are sure to create an impression.

And finally, Lori Richardson tied it all together by reminding us that the act of saying "Thank you" can also be a gift. You can even weaponize thank-you cards as your own contact piece. So how does this all tie together, and how can you put it to use in your own campaigns?

# Critical Next Steps

> **OBJECTIVE:** Try different gift-giving approaches and packaging to make a powerful first impression on your prospects.

### Step 1. Experiment with process.

Gifts can be given all at once, or they can be drawn out into incremental deliveries. They can target a single recipient or include a group of decision makers and influencers. They can be split into two gifts. They can be anonymous and mysterious. Experiment with all these options and with the integration of other outreach elements (phone calls, social media touches, emails, cards, letters, etc.), test and record them, and form them into a process that can be distributed, learned, and repeated to produce predictable outcomes.

### Step 2. Box and gift are components of one unit; give both equal attention.

The gifts you give should be full of imagination, personality, and value. The same goes for the packaging you send them in. Don't rely on the fading tug of a FedEx, UPS, or USPS urgent envelope or box to break through. Develop your own unique packaging (or have it developed for you) that is similarly infused with imagination, personality, and value.

### Step 3. Be audacious, be outrageous, but be smart.

Gifts and packaging are an opportunity to demonstrate the quality and impact of your thinking and the value of your proposed involvement with the recipient's business. This is your chance to go wild, to deliver something unexpected and delightful. It's a time for boundless imagination, but it's also a time for disciplined thinking. Everything must operate efficiently to open doors, foster relationships, and move sales through their cycle.

# POINTS TO REMEMBER

✔ A fine box can make anything look more impressive. Use that effect in your gift campaigns.

✔ There are options today for boxes made of corrugated cardboard, wood, metal, and plastic, with laser-engraved details that make any contact campaign even more impressive.

✔ Deep personalization can be applied to gift giving by researching the prospect's personal details, passions, and needs and finding a gift that addresses those markers.

✔ Sometimes gifts can be physical objects, sometimes they can be experiences represented by those objects.

✔ It's best to define a gift-giving process, especially in the case of Deep personalization and one-off gifts, to protect your brand and keep your messaging on target.

✔ The monetary value of the gift isn't as important as the thought—or concept—behind it. Remember Rick Tobin's $200,000 deal from a four-dollar cupcake.

✔ Gifts can be given in one step, over a series of steps, or as a reward for taking a desired action.

✔ Consider including influencers close to the target executive in your campaign. They can change the outcome greatly.

✔ Ideally, gifts should be something uniquely from you—in Kenny Madden's words, discover your "can't not do," the things you do that make you uniquely the person you are.

✔ Consider sending a gift without a request for contact or anything else. You might be surprised at the response it generates.

✔ Pay at least as much creative attention to the outer packaging as you do to the gift itself.

✔ Always say "Thank you" when someone does you a kindness. You never know how it might come back around.

# CHAPTER 6

# VISUAL METAPHORS

Visual metaphors are not what you'd typically think of as a business gift. They're not a fruit basket, a pen, or a logo-plastered set of golf balls. They are not the deeply considered gifts that come from thorough research on individual traits and interests. In fact, they're really not much of a gift at all, although they present like one.

Instead, they are purely an object meant to communicate a message, to dramatically illustrate a problem or risk the target executive faces, or a solution they may have not considered. Visual metaphors can employ a hybridized use of Wide or Deep personalization, if personalization is involved at all. They operate under assumptions across the target audience but can also be triggered by specific events.

Almost any object can serve as a visual metaphor. A pencil, a toy, spilled food. A discarded shard of roofing material, a scale model, a block of wood. In some ways, they are a lot like the cartoons I use in my own contact campaigns. The humor of the cartoon always defines a theme for the letter copy that accompanies it; a visual metaphor does the same.

Just like cartoons, visual metaphors can bring a smile to the faces of the toughest recipients. They can melt away the natural resistance important people have to being contacted. Their days are filled with meetings, commitments, and deadlines. Their inboxes are stuffed with more messages than they can possibly digest. Their social media feeds are stuffed with even more tugs for attention.

# VISUAL CUES

But as you're about to read, visual metaphors provide a unique opportunity to break patterns of heads-down, endless servitude to our mobile devices and computer screens. Visual metaphors are tangible objects; they're a refreshing change from our everyday digital lives.

My research for this book has resulted in the accumulation of many curious objects, some of which can be found on the table behind me in my studio. I see the business cards featured in the next chapter, "Pocket Campaigns," all of which incorporate visual metaphors as part of their appeal. Kevin Mitnick's lock-pick card is a vivid metaphor for the kinds of IT security breaches he helps his clients avoid. Remo Caminada's dentist card pairs with a sleeve with a die-cut tooth outline that cleverly demonstrates the value of dental care.

The table also houses a collection of what look like food disasters; a toppled, melting ice cream cone, a couple of spilled cups of coffee, a glass of spilled milk. Any one of these ultrarealistic fake-food items could be placed in an impressive box (see the previous chapter, "Gift Giving and Jewel Boxing") and presented as visual metaphors. The spilled glass of milk provides plenty of fodder for copywriters to talk about lost opportunities, risks, and their solutions for avoiding them.

Almost anything can serve as a visual metaphor, but for this chapter I have focused on three examples. You'll read about (and see) Dan Waldschmidt's impressive campaign using swords (which I described in *How to Get a Meeting with Anyone* but include with photography here). And you'll read about a block of wood and a miniature set of dining room furniture as door-opening devices. I have also included several more suggestions for visual metaphor items from the Museum of Modern Art, Apple, and your local toy stores. From these, you will see simple patterns emerge, as well as demonstrations of the incredible power of visual metaphors as contact devices.

# DAN WALDSCHMIDT'S SWORD CAMPAIGN

Dan Waldschmidt has the most amazing method for connecting with his most qualified prospects. As the author of one of the world's most popular sales blogs and the best-selling book *Edgy Conversations*, and an ultra-marathoner (he regularly runs hundred-mile races—and *wins*), Waldschmidt's personal brand is all about knife-edge, ultra-competitiveness. But his business isn't what you'd expect: He isn't a sales trainer; he is a top-ranked turnaround specialist. Waldschmidt's mission is to help companies who have found themselves in trouble. That most often surfaces in the form of missed earnings estimates, as reported to investors and stock exchanges.

And when that news hits the business media, Waldschmidt is there, waiting to run his campaign. As soon as he spots a missed-earnings-estimate story, assuming the company's circumstances fit his parameters, he commissions a full-size sword from the prop maker who made the swords for the movie *Gladiator*.

These are beautiful works of art, finely detailed and utterly authentic to the Roman period. Each sword is full sized, with a handcrafted leather handle and hand-forged blade. And on the blade the target CEO's name is engraved, along with the inscription, "If you're not all in you're not in at all."

The swords are placed in a beautiful wooden box with a handwritten note that reads, "Business is war and I noticed you just lost a battle recently. I just wanted you to know, if you ever need a few extra hands in battle, we've got your back." There are no logos or other elements of corporate identity, just a simple handwritten note from Waldschmidt.

At first it would appear there is no branding in his approach, but it's just the opposite. Waldschmidt's brand personality is perfectly conveyed by the contact piece itself. He is ready to go to war, ready to do battle, ready to compete at the highest level on your behalf. He intends to win, and you, as the recipient of his contact device, will win as a result.

While the sword is a gift, it's also much more. It is a physical display of the value and quality of thinking Waldschmidt intends to employ on the recipient's behalf. He explains, "There are four qualities for any successful personal brand. You must be extreme, disciplined, give lots of value, and be human."

He believes too much in business is based on logic, but feelings trump price and quality. The challenge is finding a way to create positive feelings immediately with someone you don't yet know.

## CASE STUDY
# Sword as a Visual Metaphor

**BACKGROUND:** As a successful sales thought leader and turnaround specialist, Dan Waldschmidt has developed a surprisingly effective process for connecting with CEOs of distressed companies. Waldschmidt's turnaround services are expensive; each commission is worth $1 million and up.

**CHALLENGES:** When a company has to announce a missed earnings estimate to its Wall Street backers, it is an incredibly stressful time for the CEO. A missed earnings estimate means their vision for the company is failing. They are under immense pressure to create a plan to change the company's fortunes. During this time of intense work, the last thing the CEO wants to do is take a sales call.

### DAN WALDSCHMIDT'S
### ASTOUNDING SWORD CAMPAIGN

*When Dan Waldschmidt executes a contact campaign, it's a demonstration of the same audacious thinking that makes him so effective as a top turnaround specialist. Each effort costs $1,000, the campaign generates a near 100 percent response, and each engagement is worth at least $1 million. Now, isn't that the sort of person you'd want leading a turnaround at your company?*

Sword courtesy of Dan Waldschmidt

**CAMPAIGN SPECIFICS:** Waldschmidt's process includes thirteen scripted steps, which his team uses to spring into action as soon as the news story hits. The story appears, a sword is ordered with a personalized inscription, it's sent with a handwritten note, and Waldschmidt follows up two days after it arrives.

**RESULTS:** So far, Waldschmidt has sent two hundred units, and all but four CEOs connected, resulting in eighty-three deals, for a 98 percent response rate and a 41 percent conversion. With each deal worth at least $1 million, Waldschmidt spent $200,000 to generate more than $80 million, yielding a 40,000 percent ROI.

**KEY TAKEAWAY:** Waldschmidt's sword campaign is a classic example of visual metaphors in action, demonstrating their incredible power to immediately plant a point of agreement in the recipient's mind about the need to connect. The sword is a direct representation of the value he brings to his turnaround engagements. And the recipient immediately gets it.

There is the metaphor itself—the sword—but there is also the quality of Waldschmidt's execution. He didn't send a cheap little toy; he commissioned a collector piece and had it engraved with the recipient's name. He "jewel-boxed" it in a fine wooden box and included a handwritten note. The recipient gets a direct view of how Dan's mind works, particularly of how he'll approach the challenges ahead for the recipient's business.

# ONE MAN'S TRASH, ANOTHER MAN'S TREASURE

Waldschmidt's sword campaign was a huge success, but does that mean a visual metaphor should cost $1,000 per copy to work? Not at all. In fact, it can literally be a piece of junk, as long as it breaks through and supports the theme of your message.

Imagine you're in the commercial roofing business. You're anxious to break through to the property owners and managers in your area. You could spend a lot of money on digital and print media ads, have slick brochures printed up, and have, of course, very respectable business cards produced for your team of reps. Still, if you really want to leap past your competitors, you'll need to take a shortcut to establish relationships with important buyers. You can try doing what everybody else does—or you can think like a Contact Marketer.

Imagine further that your contact campaign might consist of a chunk of fouled roofing material presented in a fine wooden box. The accompanying note could explain that this small sample of failed roofing material is an example of the problems that may already exist on their rooftops—problems you'd like to help them avoid. It's a scrap, a piece of junk really, but it quickly tells the story of what's actually happening on thousands of rooftops right now, and recipients know it deserves their attention.

## CASE STUDY
## A Simple Block of Wood

**BACKGROUND:** InsurAtlanta owner and founder Howard Silvermintz recently connected with one of his favorite new authors (me) on LinkedIn, but he wanted to cement the contact with an offline exchange.

**CHALLENGES:** Like many authors, I'm quite open about making connections on LinkedIn, especially with people who introduce themselves with the words "I read your book . . ." The problem is, after a brief exchange of a few sentences, it's hard to remember whom I've connected with. As explained in greater detail in chapter ten, LinkedIn connections must be followed up with more interaction, particularly off-platform, in forms other than digital messaging. Otherwise, they're quickly forgotten.

**CAMPAIGN SPECIFICS:** Silvermintz's solution was to send a block of wood through the mail. Literally. No paper wrapper. No jewel box. No packaging at all. He just grabbed a 4" × 6" scrap of plywood, wrote my name and address on it, added postage and a return address label to the upper corner, and sent it off through the mail. On the back, Howard included a quick note with his phone number, asking to connect.

**RESULTS:** You're seeing the results right here. I hear a lot of contact campaign stories, and many of them are quite amazing. But only the best of them end up in my books. When I received it, I admired the audacity of addressing a scrap of wood, slapping some postage on it, and sending it to make a connection. I also admire the spirit of turning almost anything into a visual metaphor—and of spending almost nothing to make it happen.

*Wood courtesy of Howard Silvermintz*

**EVEN A BLOCK OF WOOD CAN BE A BRILLIANT VISUAL METAPHOR**

*Anything can serve as a visual metaphor, even a lowly scrap of wood. With a little imagination and some postage, it becomes a surprisingly audacious device for breaking through.*

**KEY TAKEAWAY:** Howard Silvermintz's marvelous block of wood arrests our sensibilities. It says, "I want to get in touch, and I'm willing to take risks to do it. It's that important." It's the kind of approach that easily inspires you to respond, "Man, I love the way you think."

---

## VARIATION

Copy themes are wonderfully malleable. Just about any object you might want to use can be made to deliver a powerful message. Look around your desk. A pencil could be a visual metaphor for drawing up plans for anything. And before you commit your plans to ink, we should talk. An eraser could remind a potential contact that, while some things can easily be erased, there are other things that cannot. A fine pair of scissors not only makes a useful gift, they're easily used as a metaphor for cutting anything—waste, expenses, taxes, whatever.

---

# SHOW AND TELL

Visual metaphors can represent value you hope to introduce to a prospect's business or perhaps a risk they face that you can help minimize. In the following example, the metaphor was a miniature version of what the prospect sells: furniture. Using a scaled-down model of the prospect's product is a smart idea. It's an object of affinity. It's something the prospect will appreciate and keep in their office. It's also a great way to gain their attention.

That was the thought process behind this next contact campaign to reach large furniture retailers, to sell a sales-training package worth millions of dollars. It started with a miniature wooden dining table and chairs mounted to a baseboard. The table was meant to get the prospect's attention. A USB memory stick was placed on the tabletop to open a conversation, with a plug-and-play video of the rep speaking into the camera to the recipient, explaining his reason for reaching out. The miniature furniture display was accompanied with a set of case studies demonstrating the effectiveness of the company's training methods.

As with any visual metaphor, the item sets the theme for the opening conversation. This one was about not leaving money on the table with every sales transaction in the retailer's stores. It's a well-targeted message, reinforced by the visual metaphor, topped off with a compelling use of video.

## CASE STUDY
# Miniature Furniture Campaign

**BACKGROUND:** A well-known sales and success training company targeted a contact campaign to the top twenty furniture retail chains in the United States.

**CHALLENGES:** Top management at the twenty largest US furniture retailers are surprisingly difficult to reach (see another story about one of these contacts in chapter two). The contact campaign for this sales and success training company will need to overcome heavy resistance to connecting with unknown sales reps looking to pitch.

**CAMPAIGN SPECIFICS:** The campaign sourced dollhouse furniture for use as the visual metaphor, a visual representation of potential growth in the furniture market, with the theme "There's still a lot of room for growth." Company representatives expected the miniature furniture to capture attention and hearts, leading recipients to treat the pieces as functional art on their desks. Ultimately, the point of the campaign was to capture attention and create positive disposition toward the company and its reps.

**RESULTS:** Of the twenty accounts targeted, over half responded within the first three weeks. Three bought in immediately, producing a half-million-dollar bounty. The company expects the entire haul to be $6 to $7 million. Cost of the campaign: $500. If they top out at $7 million, that's a 1.4 million percent ROI.

This special video presentation was made for you less than 48 hours ago.

THIS IS WHAT WE BRING TO THE
**TABLE**

**MINIATURE FURNITURE SPURS GIANT GROWTH**

*Although the marketer used dollhouse furniture, there was nothing small about this campaign, which generated $500,000 worth of new business. Sent to a handful of furniture store owners, the campaign included the miniature table and chair set, plus a USB memory stick containing a personalized video.*

**KEY TAKEAWAY:** This is a forceful example of the power of a visual metaphor to engage a prospect. Many of the recipients remarked that it was the best outreach piece they'd ever seen. They were impressed with the way the rep presented himself and his offer of value.

When we reach out to prospective clients, they're watching and noticing which of us is earning their respect, perhaps even their admiration. They notice how we choose to present ourselves, how we solve problems, whether we respect their time, and if we've done our research. Visual metaphors give us the perfect vehicle to open conversations that lead to profitable relationships.

# PUTTING IT ALL TOGETHER

Visual metaphors can be anything, since every physical object has an identity and purpose that can be spun into a message. In this chapter's examples, we see how a sword was used to communicate the values of fighting fierce battles to help the client win the war of survival and business competition. A block of wood was used as a visual metaphor to communicate the solid thinking of the sender. And miniature doll furniture conveyed the sender's vision for substantial growth in the retail furniture market.

All these examples show that visual metaphors release a bit of magic when they're used to reinforce a central point. *I will fight for you. My ideas are solid. I see enormous growth potential for you.*

Visual metaphors are a form of gift, but a slightly odd one. No one is sitting around waiting to receive a sword, a block of wood, or a set of dollhouse furniture. While few would put such items on their wish list, these visual metaphors illustrate their points magnificently.

When we examined gift giving in the previous chapter, I noted that the gifts were enhanced through the use of Wide or Deep personalization. Does the same thing apply for visual metaphors? Not so much. Dan Waldschmidt includes personalization when he engraves the name of the targeted CEO on the blade of the sword, but he clearly didn't research the prospect's favorite activities, interests, and recent life events—other than the missed earnings report. It's clear that Dan does not need to know the name of a CEO's dog when he's delivering his message.

Personalization can have an application, and it should always be considered as a possible enhancement to the campaign, but it is not a necessary component of visual metaphor–based campaigns.

Jewel boxing can have a highly positive effect with a visual metaphor component. In fact, I would say it could be a critical element for these campaigns. Dan Waldschmidt's swords are greatly enhanced by the packaging. Remember, jewel boxing is about presenting whatever's inside as though it is itself a jewel. Sending a failed bit of roofing material in a beautiful wooden box says it's something valuable because it shows us something important, though it may be just a piece of trash in another context.

*Visual metaphors are not gifts. They are truths translated into physical form.*

If you're planning to use a visual metaphor in your own campaign, take the time to search for something perfectly suited to telling your story, demonstrating a problem you can solve, or illustrating a vision. The world is full of unusual stuff, and there are great sources for things that defy logic or belief.

# Critical Next Steps

> **OBJECTIVE:** Use a visual metaphor to stand out and deliver a key message to a prospect.

### Step 1. Project a message, challenge, or issue—but not your brand.

Almost anything can serve as a visual metaphor, but not everything should. Before you choose an object, choose a message, a problem, or a challenge that your metaphor should represent. It should have nothing to do with your brand. It is purely to illustrate a concern you will help your prospects solve. Your metaphor should have recipients nodding in agreement with a big smile on their faces. That will never happen if you make the fatal mistake of portraying your brand as a metaphor. Ask yourself, What major pain points can I solve for the prospect? How can I show those visually?

### Step 2. Create an inventory of visual metaphors for your campaign.

Visual metaphors are not gifts. They are truths translated into physical form. Just like a cartoon, some resonate better than others. The idea is to gather possibilities, then be brutally selective with each concept. And although not required, it's helpful if the concept puts something truly unique and fascinating in the hands of your targeted executives. As you brainstorm, make sure the items are easily sourced. Your logo should *never* appear on any visual metaphor item.

### Step 3. Put it in a box.

As you source visual metaphor items for your campaign, pay equal attention to the packaging you'll use to send it. It should be distinctive, even a bit outrageous itself, but always in support of the metaphor concept within. The box you send is the first impression you'll make. Please refer to chapter five for more discussion of "jewel boxing."

# POINTS TO REMEMBER

✔ Visual metaphors are powerful devices that present like a gift but don't require the same amount of individual research.

✔ Almost anything can serve as a visual metaphor: a pen, piece of wood, sword, scale models, fake food spills . . . anything.

✔ Items to be used as visual metaphors must be fascinating and illustrate a central point.

✔ Almost any object can be fascinating in the right context; it's your job to build that context into your campaign.

✔ Even though visual metaphor items are not something a person might hope to receive, they can be nonetheless powerful, illustrative, and enthusiastically received.

✔ The right visual metaphor item can remain in the prospect's office for years.

✔ Personalization can be a factor, but it does not seem to carry as much critical importance as with other kinds of gifts.

✔ Like cartoons, visual metaphors should bring a smile to recipients' faces.

✔ The goal is always to leave the recipient saying, "I love the way you think. Let's meet."

# CHAPTER 7

# POCKET CAMPAIGNS

The exchange of business cards is a universal ritual. In every country, in every culture, they are meant to convey the status of the person dispensing the card. When we hand out our cards, we want people to be impressed.

So we have them printed on extra-thick specialty paper stocks with sandwiched color layers, funky fibers, and glossy finishes. Card printers invite us to include foil stamping and embossing to make our logos stand out and convey the impression that we have achieved some sort of lofty standard. Our titles are similarly gold plated and inflated. Some stretch on for two or three lines, as though the reader will be impressed by word count alone. Similarly, 90 percent of the titles containing the words "Chief" and "Officer" should never exist.

If our business cards were meant to impress, it's not working. Attitudes are changing quickly about business cards. Many people have simply eliminated them from their contact repertoire. When they connect, their mobile phones are now their card dispensers. It's simple enough to trade contact details right there on the spot. Others simply say, "Let's connect on LinkedIn right now," and the link is made.

But if you rely on tapping phones together to convey contact info, what happens when your new contact forgets your name and those details are lost forever in their address book? No lasting impression made there. Connecting on LinkedIn isn't much better. It fails to register for long.

I recently ran an impromptu poll on LinkedIn in which I asked about business card usage. Half the commenters said they'd gone completely digital, calling business cards "wasteful." I think it's far more wasteful to miss any opportunity to make a lasting impression with everyone you meet. Why hold back?

# A NEW BREED OF CALLING CARDS

What we need is a new paradigm for our business cards. What we need are pocket-sized Contact Marketing campaigns—Pocket Campaigns—that we can hand out to share our contact details but also to provide an item that creates entirely new business opportunities. Our cards should not be saddled with positioning us as false royalty. They should be helping us do more business.

> *Our cards should not be saddled with positioning us as false royalty. They should be helping us do more business.*

"Pocket Campaign" is a term I coined after researching business cards for this book. I wanted to know what makes some cards stand out so much from the rest, and how we could put those lessons to use in Contact Marketing.

If you google "World's Coolest Business Cards," you'll find the same group of cards over and over. There's James A. W. Mahon's cleverly perforated business card for his divorce practice. Internet security expert Kevin Mitnick's etched metal lock-pick tool set. Terry Miller's metal card for his bike repair shop that doubles as a multitool for emergency repairs. Dr. Anita Wehrle Lechmann's interactive molar card that makes it seem fun to go to the dentist. And then there is fitness trainer Poul Nielsen's card, printed on a stretchy sheet of rubber, that achieves something I have never seen before. It generates a staggering response rate, ROI—and new business. And that response is *multiples of 100 percent.*

These cards represent an entirely different strategy for the exchange of contact information. Their mission is to playfully convey what the cardholder does, how they create value, and how well they do it. Ironically, by virtue of being the kind of person who would have such a card, these impress all the more.

Note: The cards in the following examples are not Pocket Campaigns, but they are the inspiration that led to the new campaign form. As you read through the chapter, you'll see the progression from amazing, involving business cards to a multilevel campaign that launches from your pocket, ties into an overarching persistence campaign, and produces response and ROI metrics.

# INTERACTIVE CARDS

## A Card That Steals the Show

Imagine having a card people find so fascinating, so desirable, they're willing to pay or climb over one another at a conference to get a copy. That's what happens when Kevin Mitnick hands out his business cards after delivering keynote speeches all around the world. So who is Kevin Mitnick and why are people so anxious to get ahold of his card?

Kevin has one of the most intriguing cards in the world, but his personal story is even more fascinating. If you've seen the movie *Takedown*, you already know part of that story. Kevin was an infamous hacker in the 1990s who served a five-year term in federal prison for computer crimes. But his is also a story of a remarkable turnaround. Upon release, he returned to his life as a prolific hacker, but this time he did so on retainer by Fortune 500 companies that pay to have him expose vulnerabilities in their IT systems. Today he is one of the world's leading authorities on internet security.

A man with a story like that ought to have a pretty solid business card. And he does. The card is made of chemically etched stainless steel and contains a set of lock-picking tools. You can actually pick a lock with his card. That makes it a powerful visual metaphor for what Kevin helps his clients prevent—break-ins—and a brilliant involvement device. You can't help but smile at his card and handle it endlessly.

## CASE STUDY
# Kevin Mitnick's Lock-Pick Cards

**BACKGROUND:** In the early 2000s, a notorious computer hacker is released from prison. Kevin Mitnick had been among the very first group of people to receive serious prison time for computer crimes.

**CHALLENGES:** Upon his release, Mitnick faced two serious challenges. First, his one and only skill remained hacking into computer systems, which is what led to his incarceration in the first place. What else could he do for a living? And second, how could he rebuild his reputation after having been branded a convicted felon? He needed to turn his hacking skills and infamous persona into something useful and positive, so Mitnick rebranded himself as the world's leading expert in computer crime—and how to prevent it.

**CAMPAIGN SPECIFICS:** Mitnick's reputation and notoriety had already received a boost with the release of *Takedown*, a Hollywood movie based on the illegal hacking and resulting imprisonment chapter of his story. To update it, Mitnick moved into public speaking, eventually giving addresses all over the world as the new IT security guru. Along the way, he realized he needed a business card that matched his bigger-than-life history of downfall and redemption as the guardian of corporate computer security. Seattle graphic designer Jeni Mattson took on the project and produced a card out of stainless steel, with cutouts revealing a miniature set of lock-picking tools. The card was meant to serve as a visual metaphor for what Mitnick does: helping clients avoid break-ins to their vital computer systems.

**RESULTS:** The movie and public speaking successfully cemented Mitnick's new image, helping him land several hundred Fortune 500 companies as clients. His new job? Hack his clients' computer systems and report his findings. Along the way, Mitnick's business cards have gained their own following and have added considerably to his internet fame. Today, Mitnick uses his lock-pick cards to open doors to all sorts of top accounts.

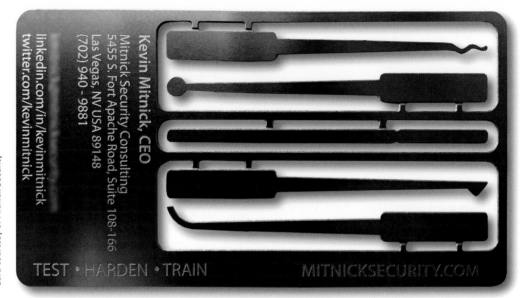

Card courtesy of Mitnick Security

### KEVIN MITNICK'S LOCK-PICK BUSINESS CARD

*After serving five years in federal prison for illegal hacking, Mitnick used his lock-pick card to crack the worldwide IT security market. The functional lock-pick set serves as a visual metaphor for the kinds of risks he helps his clients minimize, contain, and avoid.*

**KEY TAKEAWAY:** Kevin Mitnick's metal cards helped him achieve his rebranding mission post-prison. But they also help us to redefine the branding mission of business cards as Pocket Campaigns. In the photograph, you'll see none of the conventional trappings of branding are present on the card. There is no logo, there are no company colors. There are simply contact details and the lock-pick tool set. But the design and practical purpose of the card play the leading role in the branding value of the piece. The distinctive outline of the card itself has become Mitnick's logo. The functionality of the tools and the visual metaphor of the potential danger of the tools in the wrong hands are what cement his image as a category leader in IT security. Who else would have the audacity to have such a card?

But there is something else here, something most business cards never have. There is an implicit invitation to play, to interact, to detach the tools and see if they work (they do, see https://mitnicksecurity.com/shopping/kevin-mitnick-lock-pick-business-card for a video demonstration). The idea of having a card that is an interactive device will be a theme throughout the case studies in this chapter. It should also be a theme in our own Pocket Campaigns.

## A Card That Pops (Open)

While Kevin Mitnick's card has a sinister appeal and practical purpose, Ethan Goller's card is meant simply to surprise and delight. Goller is president of Structural Graphics, which has been producing brilliant pop-up paper sculptures for advertisers for decades. Some pieces spring to shape when freed from an envelope, others open whole new worlds when two pages are pulled apart in a magazine.

I have been an admirer of the company's work since my early career in direct marketing. Back then, I was creating campaigns for the major magazine publishers using personalized cartoons as a device to get attention and draw recipients into the mailing. My mailings worked—and set many records—because they entertained recipients into the envelope, rather than teasing.

> *It's all a direct result of his business card being more than just a business card.*

Structural Graphics did the same thing by cleverly integrating its pop-ups and pop-outs into mail pieces. In an industry overrun with teaser copy, fake checks, and other forms of manipulation, it seemed we were the only ones who lived the mantra "Entertain, don't tease." Today Structural Graphics continues to innovate, combining its elegant paper sculptures with embedded video and virtual reality (see more of the company's work in other sections of this book).

Of all the people interviewed for this section of the book, Goller is the one who uses his business card most like a Pocket Campaign. Let's take a look.

## CASE STUDY
# Ethan Goller's Pop-Up Business Cards

**BACKGROUND:** Goller works primarily with major advertising agencies located on Madison Avenue in New York. He spends a lot of time there, calling on clients and presenting new strategies and solutions.

**CHALLENGES:** Occasionally he discovers new agencies while calling on others. A contact strategy would be useful to make impromptu calls on the agency's creative director, but building security measures make that all but impossible. Even without security concerns, creative directors are busy, agencies are busy, and drop-in calls are highly discouraged.

## CAMPAIGN SPECIFICS:

When Goller notices a new agency on the building tenant/ floor listing, he makes a note of it. While waiting for his scheduled appointment to begin, he googles the agency to discover the identity of the creative director.

After his meeting, Goller proceeds to the other agency's lobby and checks in with the receptionist. He explains, "I was meeting with another agency in the building and thought I'd stop by while I'm still in the building. Does Georgia Daniels (creative director) have five minutes for me to introduce myself?" The receptionists are always ready to tell Goller to take a hike. But then he hands them his business card. It appears to be a simple two-panel folded card, but a paper sculpture pops out when opened.

**RESULTS:** As soon as the receptionists open and close it a few times, everything changes. "Hold on a second, let me see if I can get her down here." A few moments later, the meeting takes place. "I can't tell you how much business this has gotten me," Goller says. "Even the creative directors are impressed."

Card courtesy of Ethan Goller/Structural Graphics

### SOMETHING ALWAYS POPS UP

*When Structural Graphics president Ethan Goller presents his pop-up business card to introduce himself to new ad agency prospects, astonished receptionists always seem to play with the card and make sure he gets in.*

**KEY TAKEAWAY:** What's significant here is that the cardholder has stepped into a new realm with his business cards. Ethan Goller's fanciful cards provide the unusual advantage of allowing him to stop in unannounced, anywhere, and get a meeting with a high rate of success.

Goller's use of his card is hardly unusual. Stopping by a prospect's office and asking for a quick meeting is the essence of cold-calling in sales. What's different is the device Goller uses to completely change the dynamic of the interaction. The prospects and their receptionists are thrilled he stopped by. And it's all a direct result of his business card being more than just a business card. It is a visual metaphor and a miniature example of the unique solution he has to offer. His card is a prime example of a contact campaign that fits in his pocket.

Contact Marketing is often something done at a distance. We send campaign pieces across town, across the country, all around the world. We send email and use digital marketing with no concern for proximity. But Goller's simple drop-off of his business card, and the response it creates, shows us that Contact Marketing can also be conducted in person.

# A Card That Splits

Goller's business card enables him to drop in on prime prospects, but James A. W. Mahon's new clients simply walk through the front door. Finding prospective clients isn't a challenge, but when you're a divorce lawyer, making them comfortable talking about their possible split is. Lawyers are a serious bunch, a fact not lost on Mahon. When he decided to open a new family law practice at the Marshall & Company law firm in Yellowknife, he wanted a card that would make him seem more approachable. Divorce, after all, is a painful event. So why not ease the sting with a bit of levity?

In conversation with his friend Chris Hirsch, James mentioned his interest in having a card that would stand out in a creative way yet still inspire trust in his practice. If you mention something like this to Chris, things happen. The associate creative director for John St., a Toronto-based branding agency, Chris was in a unique position to help.

The result fit the criteria of Mahon's creative brief perfectly.

## CASE STUDY
# The Divorce Card That Splits Equitably

**BACKGROUND:** Canadian divorce lawyer James A. W. Mahon was setting up a new practice at a parent law firm and wanted a business card that would set new clients at ease with the divorce process.

**CHALLENGES:** When couples divorce, it's a difficult time for all. When Mahon considered ordering new business cards, he wanted something that would go beyond the simple conveyance of contact details to become a device to help ease his clients' anxiety.

**CAMPAIGN SPECIFICS:** Chris Hirsch, at the time an associate creative director with Toronto-based branding agency John St., created Mahon's card. It was printed in black ink on a classic laid cover stock, featured a single icon of a legal scale at the top, and laid out Mahon's name, title, and contact details in a sensible, conservative font.

It was like every other law firm card in existence, with one small but very important twist. Mahon's phone and fax numbers and his email address appeared in both lower corners of the card, and a perforation line divided the card in half.

The simple gesture of making his card equally divisible—with contact details duplicated on both remaining pieces— exactly mirrored the purpose of his divorce practice: to create a fair and equitable division, to make inconvenient sacrifices, all with a sympathetic smile. After all, life goes on, even after a divorce.

**THE CARD THAT ALMOST MAKES DIVORCE FUN**

*James Mahon's business cards, predivided in two, were designed to help his divorce clients cope with their situation through a bit of humor. The cards have also fielded countless referrals owing to their clever nature and the viral pass-along they inspire.*

Card courtesy of James A. W. Mahon

**RESULTS:** While Mahon's cards did provide a humorous relief to clients, the real success came from word of mouth via the internet. When the cards appeared in a few design competitions they went viral, and the attention still shows no signs of slowing down. As of this book's writing, it has been ten years since Mahon's card first appeared, long after he moved on from his original law firm. To this day, Marshall & Company is still peppered with calls asking for Mahon. As a contact device, the card has been remarkably successful.

**KEY TAKEAWAY:** The card does a brilliant job as an involvement device and as a visual metaphor for the service Mahon offers. His card demonstrates that even the most serious business sectors can make their contact outreaches engaging without losing their credibility. Ironically, they may gain far greater market validity by being the kind of firm that doesn't take itself too seriously and takes risks.

The card shows that Pocket Campaigns, indeed any Contact Marketing campaign, needn't be shockingly expensive. Sometimes simple but shrewd goes a long way. James Mahon's card was a standard, inexpensive business card with a clever twist and minimal added production cost from a single perforation cut.

# Poul Nielsen's Stretchy Card

Leonardo da Vinci once said, "Simplicity is the ultimate sophistication." Had he been alive today, I imagine da Vinci would have approved of Mahon's card for its simplicity and audacity. I think he would have appreciated Poul Nielsen's card as well, another Chris Hirsch design.

Nielsen and Hirsch met at a barbecue and struck up a conversation. Hirsch asked what Nielsen did for a living. He explained his passion for starting his own fitness training business. Hirsch asked if Nielsen would mind if he developed a business card for the fledgling business. Three weeks later, the "stretchy" card appeared.

Produced on a business card–sized sheet of gum rubber, the card is stretched on a jig before printing. Once the ink has dried, the card is removed and returns to its original shape. The result is a floppy card that is unreadable until the holder grasps both ends and stretches it. The action reveals Nielsen's name, the fact that he is a fitness trainer, and his phone number.

The best detail of all isn't printed on the card. It's the action of stretching it. You see, the very action of pulling on the card to read it means Nielsen already has you exercising. He is providing a sample of his training service, but also of his approach to fitness. He believes it should be fun, which is immediately conveyed by the card.

## CASE STUDY
# Poul Nielsen's "Stretchy" Business Card

**BACKGROUND:** Poul Nielsen wanted to start his own fitness training business. After a conversation with a designer at a barbecue, the fledgling business was launched with an innovative set of cards printed on rubber sheets.

**CHALLENGES:** Fitness training, like every other business, is a competitive market. Entrepreneurs must differentiate themselves in ways that are powerful but affordable.

**CAMPAIGN SPECIFICS:** The "stretchy" card was conceived by designer Chris Hirsch as a way to not only reveal Nielsen's contact details but also to provide a sample of his fun-loving approach to fitness. The hook is that the card is printed in a stretched state, leaving Nielsen's details scrunched together. Recipients must stretch the card to read it, creating a dramatic and fun reveal of Nielsen's identity. By stretching the card, recipients get a small sample of what it's like to work out with their new trainer.

**RESULTS:** Nielsen says every time he hands out a card, something extraordinary happens—he gains three to four new clients. Perhaps he hands one out at a pub. The recipient plays with it, reveling in the fact that Nielsen already has them working out just to read the card. They ask, "Can I keep this?" "Of course," Nielsen replies, and the trap is set.

The recipient then shows the card to everyone they know. "Hey, take a look at this," they'll say. And when each new recipient gives it a stretch, the comment "Look at that, he already has you exercising" gets them all laughing. And a number of those people give Nielsen a call to sign up. To be clear, this card does what no other card does: It generates sales, all on its own. It inspires evangelism, which drives multiples of 100 percent in response and in sales.

**KEY TAKEAWAY:** Pay attention to assertions throughout this book, particularly regarding the new Contact Marketing model, setting 100 percent as the new baseline for response and opening the possibility of going beyond a 100 percent response rate. Consider your own business cards. I'll do it right along with you. Mine have always stood out. Being a cartoonist, my cards have an unfair advantage. They include my cartoon art somewhere on the card and my

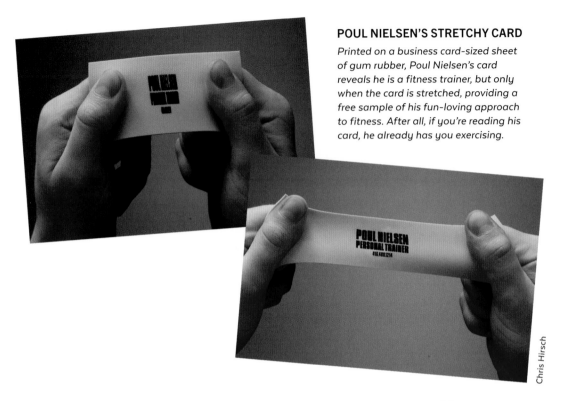

**POUL NIELSEN'S STRETCHY CARD**

*Printed on a business card-sized sheet of gum rubber, Poul Nielsen's card reveals he is a fitness trainer, but only when the card is stretched, providing a free sample of his fun-loving approach to fitness. After all, if you're reading his card, he already has you exercising.*

Chris Hirsch

cartoonist signature, making the recipient aware they're actually talking to one of *The Wall Street Journal*'s cartoonists. But my cards have never generated a single sale on their own. I am reasonably sure yours haven't, either.

All the business cards in this chapter have led to the inspiration of carrying Pocket Campaigns, rather than mere business cards. Nielsen's rubber cards should be a wake-up call for everyone carrying business cards, and especially for those who've "moved on" to guaranteed obscurity by tapping phones together, swapping digits, or whatever. Nielsen's card should inspire you to never let an opportunity like that pass through your fingers again.

## A Card for Big Smiles

We're not done. There are more stories I want to share so you can join the Pocket Campaign revolution. The next story is a truly inspiring example of the power of an engagement device in place of a business card.

Dentists' business cards are notoriously dull, which doesn't help much as most people think of the service they provide as one of the most unpleasant experiences in life. Swiss designer Remo Caminada had these thoughts in mind when asked to design a business card for Dr. Anita Wehrle Lechmann, whose office sits in the tiny village of Flims-Waldhaus, nestled in the Swiss Alps.

Caminada recalled his experiences as a child, when a visit to the dentist meant much pain and no fun. Drawing from his childhood experience, the designer decided Dr. Lechmann's business card should be involving and fun, and quickly demonstrate why it is so important to visit the dentist regularly. Most of all, he wanted the card to make people smile.

## CASE STUDY
# The Card That Makes It Fun to Visit the Dentist

**BACKGROUND:** Swiss dentist Dr. Anita Lechmann approached designer Remo Caminada about designing a new business card for her practice. She was willing to pay a lot not only for the design but also for the production on a per-piece basis. She wanted a breakthrough, something that made it fun to visit her practice, with none of the usual cartoonish renderings of a smiling tooth holding a toothbrush.

**CHALLENGES:** Caminada drew upon his unpleasant experiences at the dentist as a child. To meet the challenge, Caminada had to ask, "How can I make this card fun, but also, how can I demonstrate the reason behind visiting the dentist?"

**CAMPAIGN SPECIFICS:** His solution was to produce a two-piece card, consisting of the actual business card with a very special outer sleeve. That component was produced with C1S (coated one side) paper stock featuring a glossy, pearlescent white surface. The sleeve was assembled with the shiny surface inside and a die-cut outline of a molar cut into one side.

Placement of the tooth-shaped window and the lower portion of a telephone icon on the inner card were carefully coordinated. Thus, when the card was in the sleeve, the lower portion of the phone icon showed through the tooth-shaped window and looked like a cavity. When the card is removed, the cavity goes away and the tooth is restored to its natural pearly white beauty. The action of pulling the card in and out of the sleeve brilliantly illustrates the value of dental visits.

**RESULTS:** When the doctor first heard the five-dollar-per-piece cost for the cards, she wasn't fazed. Her faith was rewarded immediately by the first

**THE CARD SAYS AND SHOWS IT ALL**

*Why go to the dentist? Remo Caminada answered that question with a two-piece design for his client, Dr. Anita Wehrle Lechmann. When the card is in the sleeve, a black dot appears on the die-cut tooth. Removing the card erases the black dot and restores the tooth to pristine pearlescent perfection.*

+41 (0) 81 911 22 21

DR. ANITA WEHRLE LECHMANN eidg. dipl. Zahnärztin
Spezialausbildung in Parodontologie & Implantologie
contact@dentista-surslva.ch
Behandlung in der Zahnarztpraxis von Frau B. Welzel-Heinicke
Promenada 39, 7018 Flims Waldhaus

Card courtesy of Remo Caminada

example given out to a patient, which resulted in an immediate referral. She reports that patients have been fascinated with the cards, resulting in a constant stream of new patients; they inspire play and evangelism.

**KEY TAKEAWAY:** If a business card can make it fun to visit the dentist, it should inspire us to take a critical look at our own business cards—and the lack of strategy behind them. If we choose business cards based on the cheapest cost, we miss the point. Pocket Campaigns are an investment in generating new business, not simply handing out contact details. Viewed in this light, we see whole new concepts and strategies emerge that can change prospect behavior and change our results.

That the card produces new patient referrals on its own is not the normal function of a business card. It is, itself, a campaign that is producing a strong return on investment. It's also easy to see that the card delivers on the objective of every contact campaign, to elicit the reaction, "I love the way this person thinks."

# A Card That's a Quick Fix

This next story is not so much about a campaign, or even a business card. It's about a design exercise that creates an important impact on the Pocket Campaign strategy. At first, you've got to be thoroughly impressed that a bicycle mechanic would have a card like this. It was created for Terry Miller, owner of Broke Bike Alley bike repair in Fernie, British Columbia.

That the card was actually an agency design exercise actually makes it a bit more interesting. Created by Rethink Communications, the piece was produced to represent what it would look like if a bike shop owner were to invest in a big agency campaign. It answered the following question: If a small bike repair shop had an unlimited marketing budget, what would its business card look like and what would it do? Surprisingly, it's the reason why many of the cards that show up in "world's coolest business card" Google searches exist. It's a fascinating window into what business cards could become.

Design competitions are also a chance for agencies to flex their creative muscle, which results in some pretty fanciful solutions to questions no one asked about business cards. It would be easy to dismiss those designs as irrelevant. They're too expensive, too extreme for business cards. But not for Pocket Campaigns.

In Terry Miller's case, the brief was to create a solid metal business card that communicates the value and culture of his business. His quality of work and reputation are billet-solid. He truly cares about you as his client; he wants to make sure you're always covered, never caught in a jam out on the trail on your bike.

Most metal business cards are produced using laser or photochemical etching, made of stainless steel or aluminum sheets that are just half a millimeter thick. The Broke Bike Alley card was stamped from one-sixteenth-inch-thick stainless steel for strength and weight. And it's more than a business card. It is a sturdy multitool you keep in your wallet. Smart.

## CASE STUDY
# Broke Bike Alley Multitool Card

**BACKGROUND:** This was a campaign of a different kind, to win a design competition rather than new customers for a business. But we can easily imagine the thinking applied here working for our own businesses, providing a useful tool that always remains in the recipient's possession, always valued as a reassuring backup.

**CHALLENGES:** Since this is a competition among some of the most creative people in the world, the concepts must create great impact. In design competitions, the thrust isn't about making an affordable solution that fits the clients' budget or branding. It's about going all out in order to create something that will be memorable and astonishing.

**CAMPAIGN SPECIFICS:** Working within the confines of the standard 2" × 3½" business card format, Rethink's designers created a tool that covered most mishaps on the trail. There is a half-inch crescent wrench head; a multisized socket wrench to accommodate six commonly used bolt heads; a three-inch ruler along the top edge; an angled cutout forming a tire lever for replacing tires on rims; and a set of three spoke wrench heads for on-the-trail wheel adjustments. The Broke Bike Alley brand, Terry's name, and all contact information are stamped on the card as well. The result is a handy, useful tool. It's easy to imagine it becoming the must-have item among the local bicyclists, and from there, becoming a viral campaign for the repair shop.

**RESULTS:** The project was one of the winners in the competition, so for the agency, it was mission accomplished. The design has since gone on to achieve internet fame as one of the "world's coolest business cards," benefiting Rethink immeasurably. It has also made Terry Miller, who really only repairs bikes on the side, an internet celebrity. Years after the original competition, people continue to discover it online, and since it's a business card, too, Miller's full contact details remain on display. If he ever does decide to open his shop, the audience is there waiting, all over the world.

**KEY TAKEAWAY:** Holding on to Terry's card and keeping it with you at all times means you always have the tool you need to fix your bike. It also serves as

Card courtesy of Terry Miller and Rethink Communications

**YOU NEVER KNOW WHEN YOU'LL NEED IT**

*Terry Miller repairs bikes and does a darned good job of it. But what if your bike breaks down somewhere out on the trail? Miller extends the positive vibe with a business card that doubles as a multitool, for the times when he's not around to fix it himself.*

a constant reminder of where you got it. Clearly, this is not functioning like a normal business card. It's creating an unfair marketing advantage for Miller's business, the kind of advantage we all want as Contact Marketers.

# A NEW CAMPAIGN FORM

Pocket Campaigns start with a business card–sized involvement device. The piece must be an invitation to play, interact, or to put the device to use. We've just seen amazing examples of how some business cards do that already, but that's just the first step in a Pocket Campaign, which also involves a jump offer, jump page, tracking pixels, and a tie-in to a digital persistence campaign using retargeting ads. Let's see what that might look like in actual practice.

Industrial designer and Zootility founder Nate Barr has created an ideal engagement device for a Pocket Campaign, something he calls the "WildCard." Composed of two elements of millimeter-thick stainless steel, the whimsical credit-card-sized piece serves as a survival tool that fits easily in a wallet. The prominent feature is the knife blade, which nests safely in the frame of the piece, but can rotate into position for use as a cutting tool. The WildCard also has various cutouts and stampings that serve as a bottle opener, nail puller, two screwdrivers, and a stubby ruler. The multiple uses make it a useful tool and an irresistible play toy a recipient should keep for years.

One interesting design option, as shown in the illustration, is to add a sleeve to the WildCard, which completes the branding of the piece for the campaign. In our illustrated example, the sleeve features a fictional campaigner's logo and contact details, and on the back includes a link leading to a jump page with a video to explain how the tool works. The purpose of the landing page is also to set a tracking pixel, triggering an ongoing retargeting persistence campaign (which I talk about in chapter nine, "Digital Marketing"). Any Pocket Campaign recipient becomes part of the

> *Pocket Campaigns are an investment in generating new business, not simply handing out contact details.*

overall Contact Marketing program as soon as they visit the jump page and the tracking pixel is set.

From the recipients' perspective, it feels like they have received one of the coolest business cards they've ever seen. It's so fascinating, it occupies their top-of-mind thoughts for a while, compelling them to show it off. The linked video giving directions for use of the device makes sense, creating a seamless jump from the engagement device to a highly professional digital experience. Then

iStock (template)

### POCKET CAMPAIGN AT A GLANCE

*A Pocket Campaign launches like any other business card. But it's actually an engagement device that leads to a jump page that sets a tracking pixel and places recipients in your retargeting persistence campaign. Pocket Campaigns produce a response rate, sales, and ROI—something business cards could never do.*

suddenly, ads for the company seem to be everywhere, providing reinforcement of the initial contact and creating a positive impression of the company and its stature. Those impressions continue indefinitely, as the persistence retargeting ads pop up wherever the person goes on the web, making it very easy for the rep to follow up, cement the relationship, and generate new business.

From the users' perspective, they're still handing out "cards," but these do something their old cards did not. They're providing automated follow-up, creating relationships, and ultimately incremental sales. The rep hardly has to do anything other than exchange "cards," register the recipient into the campaign, and follow up occasionally. When they do, they'll find the prospects have been "warmed up," with new sales opportunities waiting to be claimed.

Finally, from the marketer's perspective, they will have to adjust their thinking about business cards. No longer an incidental, business cards will have been replaced with a campaign that produces a response rate, new business, and ROI. Unlike business cards, Pocket Campaigns should be in a constant test/ rollout regime, allowing the marketer to justify their expenditures with new revenue, while the campaign is constantly updated, tested, and maximized.

## Pocket Campaign's Five-Step Process

Business cards are a single-step process. You hand them out and you're done. Pocket Campaigns follow a five-step process.

### Step 1. Launch campaign.

Hand out the Pocket Campaign engagement device like you would any other business card. The recipient will perceive the difference right away based on the strength of concept anchoring your campaign and the string of steps that follow.

### Step 2. Create immediate engagement.

Use a campaign engagement device that prompts recipients to play, interact, and share. Devices can be kinetic, use sleeves, pop-ups, miniature samples or visual metaphors, live samples, and more. Above all, the engagement devices must be utterly audacious, clever, and somehow useful.

**WILDCARD REIMAGINED AS A POCKET CAMPAIGN**

*Zootility's WildCard is shown here, reimagined as a Pocket Campaign. It is presented to qualified prospects as a branded involvement device, drawing recipients to a jump page to view video directions for using the tool. The site generates a tracking pixel, triggering a digital persistence campaign, with ads for the marketer suddenly appearing wherever the recipient ventures on the web.*

### Step 3. Initiate digital component.

Use a QR code, image recognition technology, or simple URL on the engagement device to pull recipient to the jump page, which should be coded to set tracking pixels. Use some form of compelling value to create 100 percent compliance with the jump offer. Possibilities include directions for using the engagement device, a free gift such as a book or report, or signing up for critically useful content. The jump offer should <u>not be promotional</u>. It should only provide irresistible value, unrelated to your business goals.

### Step 4. Activate persistence campaign.

If you're already operating a persistence element within your Contact Marketing program, Pocket Campaign recipients will simply be activated into the persistence campaign like any other target executive or account. While the persistence campaign runs, reps will still monitor and follow up.

### Step 5. Test and evaluate.

Unlike any business card program, new tests of engagement and persistence elements should occur at regular intervals to constantly hone the effectiveness of the campaign and maximize response and ROI.

# PUTTING IT ALL TOGETHER

The designers of the cards highlighted in this section started with the mission of creating something that expressed their clients' personalities and value in a way that was engaging and created empathy. They didn't expect to inspire an entirely new campaign category.

But that is exactly what has happened. Each of the cards went well beyond the simple exchange of contact information and entered the realm of Contact Marketing. Each is a visual metaphor, an invitation to play and engage with the person dispensing the device.

The engagement devices are prohibitively expensive compared to traditional business cards, reaching as high as tens of dollars per piece. Does this remind you of other forms of Contact Marketing? It should. We already know the value of spending what it takes to break through to our most important accounts and prospects. To a Contact Marketer, a device that costs a few dollars, if it produces critical connections and new customers, is an irresistible bargain.

---

**Pocket Campaign:** A highly engaging business card–sized contact campaign that launches from the presenter's pocket and, through a series of steps, enrolls recipients in a digital persistence campaign that results in measurable response rates, trackable sales, and ROI.

---

The launch of a Pocket Campaign will look and feel like the exchange of any business card. You'll get a business card in return, and the recipient won't know what just happened, although they may experience an acute case of envy.

In the definition above, I reference "a highly engaging, business card–sized contact campaign that launches from the presenter's pocket." Let's take a look at how that can take form in the following list of Pocket Campaign engagement device types.

**KINETIC:** Recipient is encouraged to move or act upon elements of the device in order to create an action. Examples might be a card with a camera lens–like aperture and with a handle that rotates, making an iris open and close, or a pull tab that reveals information within. The object is to serve as a visual metaphor for what you do. If you're a photographer, the iris concept should reveal something extraordinary and surprising. The pull tab shouldn't simply be used to reveal your name and title; it should open a surprising world of drama and wonder, in contrast to a stark outer surface. I once saw a comedian's card that was a flip-book showing his face with various exaggerated expressions. The act of flipping the book quickly was hilarious, as you watched his face change rapidly from one expression to another. This, too, is an example of a kinetic Pocket Campaign engagement device.

**SLEEVED:** Consisting of an outer sleeve and an inner card or set of cards, this category relies on the interplay of removing the card and seeing something surprising. Remo Caminada's dentist card in this chapter is a powerful example of creating clever interaction between the two elements, at first showing a dulled tooth with a cavity, then transforming it into a healthy, glossy tooth. Sleeves can contain multiple cards as well, perhaps serving as a miniature portfolio for photographers and artists. A set of cards meant to be given away by recipients can turn the Pocket Campaign into a referral-generation device.

**POP-UP:** Most pop-up cards are composed of two sections that fold over like a greeting card. The action of opening the two folded panels erects a folded paper sculpture within. Ethan Goller's Structural Graphics card in this chapter is one example. More can be spotted on, for example, Pinterest; the variety of paper pop-up sculptures and elements can be breathtaking. Some can be a reverse-fold tab that depicts a simply drawn three-dimensional chair against a stark white wall, while others issue forth birds, dragons, and entire exotic locales. Pop-ups don't just exist in a fully open and deployed state, so keep that in mind in your design brief: What should it look like when closed? When opened? How can the opening action also show some aspect of how your solutions work?

**MINIATURE:** Some products or services present well in miniature, forming dramatic pocket-sized metaphors of what the presenter does or a problem he solves. A violin teacher might use a die-cut photo of the actual instrument, with her contact details, as an engagement device. A malpractice insurance rep could use a business card–sized X-ray of a chest with scissors left in after a surgery. Flow Yoga, a Vancouver yoga studio, uses miniature rolled-up blue foam yoga mats as their cards. The Urban General Store uses tiny shopping bags as their business cards.

**TOOL:** Kevin Mitnick's lock-pick card, Broke Bike Alley's multitool card, and the Zootility WildCard are all part of this category. They're devastatingly clever and provide unexpected utility while serving as powerful visual metaphors for what the presenter does. Kevin Mitnick helps his clients defeat nefarious hackers intent on breaking into computer systems, and Terry Miller's bike repair card gives recipients real value tied to keeping their bicycles in top shape. In the previous fictional campaign, the WildCard serves as visual metaphor for Mike Blacksmith's home inspection service, as the tool would certainly come in handy for new homeowners.

**ACTION:** Some engagement devices playfully invite recipients to perform a simple action, leaving them both delighted and enlightened. Poul Nielsen's stretchy cards are an example of playful action triggering an excited response. Poul's cards invite action, and that action serves as a free sample of his fitness training.

**LIVE SAMPLE:** Some Pocket Campaigns can simply be live samples to be handed out in order to demonstrate a service or product. Imagine a roofer with business card–sized pieces of fouled roofing material as a Pocket Campaign. Let building owners see how bad it can be up there, and remind them to service and replace their roof surfaces.

**DATA-DRIVEN:** An interesting newer development is the integration of memory drives in business card–sized devices. The drives can contain data, videos, presentations, or other useful files, or presented empty as a handy storage tool. Imagine a cloud storage services company using the device, with the message, "Here's some free storage space. If you'd like more, use this link to get another fifty gigabytes. My treat."

**REMEMBER, THESE ARE NOT BUSINESS CARDS:** The place to search for a campaign device is not with one of the many printers who sell cheap business cards in bulk. Not even the ones that sell expensive cards, including etched metal and carbon fiber. Your search starts with items that match one of the descriptions above, for an engagement device that fascinates recipients and leads them toward the web portion of the campaign.

**COMPELLING NEXT STEP:** To work properly, Pocket Campaigns must fascinate the recipient, evoke a playful or inquisitive response, and drive them to follow a link. There should be an offer of further value integrated into the pocket device. In the WildCard example above, the printed sleeve includes a link leading to a video that shows how to use the tool. My own Pocket Campaign folds out to become a mini portfolio of my cartoons from *The Wall Street Journal*, and includes an offer of a hand-signed giclée print of one of my cartoons if they visit the jump page.

**WEB COMPONENT:** The Pocket Campaign web component is simply a jump page that sets a tracking pixel. As soon as the recipient visits the page, that action is completed, but the page should certainly do more. In the WildCard example, I imagined setting up a landing page that contains a video to explain how to use the tool and links to the marketer's main site. If the offer is for something to be sent to the recipient, the page can open with a pop-up window to collect their details.

**THE PRICE OF GREATNESS:** Your Pocket Campaign adds an entirely new ability to generate business. I describe them as a replacement for business cards, but they're really a full-fledged campaign. So you should expect them to cost more than plain old business cards. Keep in mind, this is a contact campaign handed out in place of cards, but its purpose is to generate new revenues.

# Critical Next Steps

*OBJECTIVE:* Use Pocket Campaigns to drive new clients to your business.

### Step 1. Choose an engagement device format and make it extraordinary.

When you pull one of these out of your pocket, the device must be a surprising invitation to play or take action that captivates the recipient's imagination. Use the categories on the preceding pages to create a Pocket Campaign device that draws people to hold it, examine it, wonder how it was created or produced, play with it, and show it off. And critically, it must drive them to somehow want more.

### Step 2. Formulate an irresistible "jump" offer.

Pocket Campaigns require recipients to take a second step, to visit a jump page where a tracking pixel is set. You'll want 100 percent compliance with this step, so there must be an irresistible offer pulling them to the page. In the earlier example of the WildCard pocket tool, the sleeve includes a link to view an instructional video showing how to use the tool. It's not a promotional offer, just one of pure value. Visit this page to learn how the tool works. Similarly, you must formulate your own irresistible offer to lead recipients to a landing page, set a pixel, and enter the digital persistence element of your campaign.

### Step 3. Adjust your thinking.

Contact Marketing presents a challenge to every marketer because everyone is used to thinking in terms of super-low costs per unit. But that doesn't work here. With Pocket Campaigns, the challenge is to see past what cheap business cards cost and *focus on the value of the business you're pursuing.* Expect to spend as much as ten dollars per unit for a Pocket Campaign device, maybe more, and consider it a cheap investment for the expected return.

# POINTS TO REMEMBER

✔ Pocket Campaigns are inspired by collections of the coolest business cards in the world.

✔ The best business cards are not just cards. They're engagement devices that go well beyond company branding and the simple exchange of contact details.

✔ Pocket Campaigns are launched with an engagement device that is handed out like a business card.

✔ Unlike business cards, Pocket Campaigns lead to a program of ongoing, automated engagement that creates relationships and results in new business.

✔ Also unlike business cards, Pocket Campaigns are a true marketing campaign with measurable metrics for response, conversion, and ROI.

✔ Like any other marketing program, and totally unlike business cards, Pocket Campaigns should be optimized over time with an A/B split test/rollout regime.

✔ Like all other Contact Marketing campaign pieces, the object of the Pocket Campaign is to have recipients saying, "I love the way you think."

✔ Poul Nielsen's "stretchy" card shows us our campaigns can generate multiples of 100 percent response if they inspire evangelism.

✔ In handing out a business card, there is a one-step process—you hand it out and you're done. With Pocket Campaigns, there are five components: launch, engagement, digital, persistence, and evaluation.

✔ There are a number of engagement device types you can tap for your campaign, including kinetic, sleeved, pop-up, miniature, tool, action, live, sample, and data-driven. Can you think of others?

# CHAPTER 8

# UNSOLICITED PROPOSALS

In order to lead, executives need insights into the markets, trends, and world around them. Reliable, relevant insights are the ultimate gift to a C-suite executive, making them perhaps the ultimate contact device, too. But where do they come from? And if you have valuable insights to offer, how do you use them to break through?

Top consultants make millions of dollars helping C-level executives understand the forces shaping the way ahead. The best of them can actually predict the future with great accuracy. How do they do it? Obviously, they're not clairvoyants reading tarot cards or tea leaves. But they do have a crystal ball.

That is, they have cultivated the ability to look at current conditions and find patterns and overlooked details that can lead to disruptive future trends. When combined with individualized research to relate those to a particular company's

> "
> *Our goal as Contact Marketers is to always leave the people we contact thinking, "I love the way you think."*
> "

standing, those insights become profoundly valuable. We've seen in previous chapters the great advantage Deep personalization can bring to a campaign. It shows you're engaged, paying attention, and focused on providing value. Unsolicited proposals may be the utmost expression of Deep personalization in action.

Unsolicited proposals have the power to elevate you to trusted-adviser status with your top accounts. Each of the stories ahead examines different takes on a similar theme, starting with an assessment of the current situation that leads to a reveal of an important statement of insight. The insight is then extrapolated and given future meaning. An "if-then" statement examines the implications for the company if the prediction is correct. It all leads to a proposed set of next steps, including the ability to "take" a meeting at a given time rather than ask for one.

All the Contact Marketers featured in this section have devised clever formats to capitalize on their insights to get meetings. Assistants welcome them; targeted executives gladly take their calls. Their proposals gain viral pass-along within the company, providing the marketer with real-time insights as to who's paying attention to what, even giving the Contact Marketer the ability to identify the eventual buying committee.

Our goal as Contact Marketers is to always leave the people we contact thinking, "I love the way you think." Actionable insights that help top executives see into the future, identify an immediate opportunity to increase revenue, reduce risk, increase efficiency, or create an unfair advantage in their marketplace do just that. They leave our most important accounts and prospects loving and trusting the way we think—and wanting more.

## SETTING YOUR UNSOLICITED PROPOSAL STRATEGY

Sending a proposal to someone you don't know and have never worked with certainly is an audacious move. If its underpinnings of research and unique insight aren't precisely aligned, the effort won't have credibility, and you won't get in. Here are some questions to consider as you venture out with unsolicited proposals:

### What do you want them to do?

As a result of receiving or seeing the proposal, what is the desired reaction or action, other than getting the meeting?

### Who is your buying committee?

In most forms of Contact Marketing, you discover relevant stakeholders as you go along. But the meeting request takes a different form with unsolicited proposals; *you* set the meeting time and list of people who should attend. Discovery of their identities will be an important part of your preproposal strategy.

### Where will you research?

What sources will you use to gain a thorough image of the company, its people, and product/service/solution?

### What is your bold insight?

Your proposal must contain at least one bold statement of future opportunity for the prospect. It must come from your understanding of the industry, market, the prospect's company, and what is about to change. If you have no bold insight to offer, consider using a different contact strategy.

### What are your delivery options?

Who is the target audience and where can they be found? Are they all in the same office or spread around the world in different locations? Knowing who your audience is and where they are will determine how you will accomplish delivery.

# CURTIS BROOKS'S STORYBOARDS

If you're thinking this is a complex, difficult process, you're right. It is. You're about to become more of an expert on your prospects' businesses than they are, at least about the one issue or opportunity you want to advance. It's not easy, but as you're about to read, there are formats and tools that will make the process easier than you'd expect.

I first learned about the unsolicited-proposal contact approach from Curtis Brooks. He contacted me a month after *How to Get a Meeting with Anyone* was released, saying he had the ultimate method for breaking through to the C-suite. After talking for a few minutes, I had to agree. He really did have a method that was quite powerful.

Brooks runs the Magis Group, a company he cofounded after perfecting the use of unsolicited proposals to open doors. His proposals are always based on identifying a key strategic change the target company must make based on emerging factors in its market. The purpose is always to identify an opportunity to bolster the company's position within a five-year window.

"C-level executives are not looking to have you provide a solution," Brooks explains. "They're desperate to know what their business will look like in five years." He says they're always looking for the big picture, and his goal is to provide a set of topics for conversations that will help them see the changes they need to make. "Clients like to think of these unsolicited proposals as campaigns," he says, "but they're really change programs."

The Magis Group trains executive sales teams to produce and use their unsolicited-proposal method to reach the top levels of their top accounts. Brooks says there are two critical ingredients for success with the method: proficiency and mindset. Reps are trained to identify relevant factors, generate insights, and produce proposals in a specific format. But the reps must also take on the mindset of a C-level executive themselves. "They can't show any sign of submissiveness to the executive," he says, "and they must think in terms of *taking* a meeting rather than asking for one."

The results of the campaigns are in line with the best of Contact Marketing, with response rates approaching 100 percent in some markets. Brooks says he doesn't always get the assumptions supporting the proposal quite right, but executives are always willing to offer guidance in order to move forward.

## CASE STUDY
# Magis Group Unsolicited Proposal

**BACKGROUND:** Magis clients are often Fortune or Global 1000 companies, seeking an audience with other companies of similar stature. Others are smaller companies looking to step into bigger arenas.

**CHALLENGES:** Fortune 1000 and Global 1000 companies have deep defenses to keep unknown sales reps from unknown companies out. Top executives at these companies are always highly sought after, which makes them particularly difficult to reach from the outside. Clearly, a foolproof method for breaking through is needed.

**CAMPAIGN SPECIFICS:** Magis Group proposals take form as a nine-page storyboard, starting with a statement of the problem, then emerging factors, limiting factors, and an examination of alternatives. The proposal then moves on to summarize the opportunity, an "Imagine if you could . . ." summary of specific outcomes, and finally, a defined date and time the meeting should take place, along with a list of who should attend.

### UNSOLICITED PROPOSALS OPEN DOORS

*The Magis Group cofounder Curtis Brooks combines educated assumptions with an acute sense of design and a honed format to open doors to the C-suite. Part of his secret is not to merely ask for a meeting, but to take a meeting.*

Proposals are sent via email, with hard copies sent via overnight delivery. The idea is to create a paper trail over the course of the contact program, which can be three to nine months in duration. The proposals suggest a change program, but they also act as an identity campaign for the sender. They are meant to change the impression of the sender in the executive's mind to a more strategic entity.

Brooks has developed a specific format for unsolicited proposals. They are always nine pages long and they read more like infographics than proposals, which makes for an exceptionally quick study. One interesting feature is how the logos change in the upper corners of the pages. At first, the sender's logo appears at the top, but gradually through the seven-page layout, the two companies' logos appear at opposite top corners of the page, then on the last page it's the target company's logo alone. Brooks says this helps the executives start to see the bold promise of the proposal as their own.

**RESULTS:** Brooks reports that response rates to his own unsolicited proposals hover at the 100 percent mark. Magis is not in the business of creating the proposals for their clients but of training client sales teams to produce them in-house. Their response rates measure slightly lower. The expense involved in the campaigns is limited almost entirely to the cost of salaried time used to research and produce the proposals.

**KEY TAKEAWAY:** Brooks cautions that unsolicited proposals are not meant to be a presentation of value or a solution but an invitation to have a high-level conversation about a future opportunity. In this scenario, to offer a solution would be presumptuous. The only goal is to provide a "preemptive call-to-action story" that positions you as a strategic source of insight and opens doors to executive suites. The research you do on your target accounts and the time, effort, and creativity you put into your storyboard help you take the meeting.

# THE POWER OF INFOGRAPHICS

One secret to the Magis Group cofounder Curtis Brooks's success is that he makes his proposals more like picture books than written theses. They're inviting and easy to read, because they look a lot like infographics. Which invites the question: What if the unsolicited proposal were produced fully as a single-panel infographic? What effect might it have as an unsolicited proposal? Infographic specialist Brian Wallace says infographics are his own idea of the ultimate contact maker that can cross platforms and live indefinitely on the web and in social media.

Infographics are those fascinating illustrated stories-at-a-glance originally found in magazines, to simplify complex topics in a way that makes the information easy to absorb. They typically tell a story with a sequence of cascading points illustrated with graphs, maps, and geometrically styled icons and groupings.

Wallace, who produces infographics for major media outlets and commercial clients, explains, "These pieces can be out there five or ten years and continue to resurface, especially on social media." As Contact Marketers, we recognize the power of infographics as an opportunity to start an important conversation, too.

To create an infographic, Wallace begins with thorough research. "Infographics aren't just pretty designs," he explains. "They are the end product of a lot of exploration and investigation." From there, information is grouped and serialized, then finally committed to design.

Wallace believes the right infographic transcends language and makes you unforgettable. As a method for transmitting an unsolicited proposal, an infographic conveys instant stature and credibility, simply through the quality of the presentation and findings. It might be unusual to think of an infographic as a contact piece, but we should recalibrate our thinking. This is a device that can easily go viral and remain on station for years.

For unsolicited proposals to break through to our C-suite targets, they must be astonishing in content and presentation. An infographic can give us precisely that edge while being potentially viral online and even in the press. That's a unique combination among the tools we have available as Contact Marketers.

If part of our mission is to cause the impetus for a sale to spread throughout the target organization, a device that is meant to go viral could be a very good thing. It's easy to imagine the unsolicited proposal in infographic form being passed around among stakeholders, if not an entire department or the entire organization.

Following Curtis Brooks's advice that a paper trail should be associated with the campaign, imagine the effect of producing the infographic as a physical piece, perhaps mounted to half-inch foam board. Whatever form it takes, it's desirable to have insights that will help the target executive see into the future.

## CASE STUDY
# Infographic Lands NBA Player $64 Million Contract

**BACKGROUND:** Tobias Harris is an NBA player, considered to be one of the best small power forwards in the league. But Harris felt his contract terms hadn't kept up with his on-the-court performance.

**CHALLENGES:** Tobias Harris became a free agent after getting traded to the Orlando Magic. As his rebounds, blocked shots, and three-point stats soared, his pay did not. He wanted a new contract, with the Magic or with another team in the league. In order to force the point, he contracted Wallace's company to produce an infographic that would make his case, both to NBA management teams throughout the league and directly with his fan base.

**CAMPAIGN SPECIFICS:** An infographic was produced showing details of Harris's performance in the league since being drafted. It depicted his rapid improvement, encouraging fans to demand their team pick up the free agent. But it also gave any front-office crew the necessary stats to pitch a trade to team owners. The main goal was to circulate the infographic on the web and social media, to force Harris's current employer to make a far more lucrative offer to keep him in Orlando.

### INFOGRAPHIC HELPS WIN $64 MILLION NBA CONTRACT

*Tobias Harris's prospects to become one of the NBA's top-paid players soared when his team released this infographic touting his bona fides as a future league star. Essentially a proposal to make a trade for the free agent, the infographic achieved viral pass-along on social media and among key NBA executives, netting a new contract worth $64 million.*

Courtesy of Brian Wallace

**RESULTS:** The campaign was an enormous success. The infographic went viral and put great pressure on the Orlando Magic to step up and offer Harris a multiyear contract worth $64 million.

**KEY TAKEAWAY:** Smith's infographic for Harris demonstrates yet another way unsolicited proposals can enter the mindset of our target executives. The infographic wasn't sent discreetly to the team executives; it was distributed broadly to the fans. As an NBA player, Harris is a public figure, so pushing visibility of the infographic across social media made sense. But if the same tactic were used to reach executives, give thought to who the "fans" are here. For corporate contact approaches, stakeholders surely could apply pressure if they are inspired by what they see in the infographic.

# PITCHING THE FUTURE

## Personal Letters with Insights and Impressions

When you're trying to deliver value, most experts point to insights, knowledge, and business intelligence as their currency. *Whale Hunting* coauthor Tom Searcy sees it differently. He thinks the only thing of true value is a portal to the future.

If you imagine yourself as the CEO of a company, how much of a strategic advantage would it be to know the future trends and issues in your space? Before any of your competitors have a clue? What would that be worth?

It would be priceless.

Still, you don't just show up and say, "Hey, I know the future. Wanna see?" That's not the way Tom does it, either. He turns his meeting request into a series of messages sent through the mail. This means his prospect has something tangible (thus, of greater value); the request is not just another email in the executive's overcrowded inbox. Providing something tangible means it's more likely to get read.

Seeing into the future is quite a claim, but Tom has it reduced to a process that often leads

> *Contact Marketers know that uncrowded channels give them a far better chance of standing out. You do not stand out by doing what everyone else does.*

to startling conclusions. He starts by looking for unusual trends, anomalies in the quiet, stable patterns of business as usual. He has found those can often point to disruptive developments that can be extrapolated into the future.

## CASE STUDY
# The Future as a Contact Device

**BACKGROUND:** As a best-selling author and top sales/strategy consultant, Tom Searcy tailors his consulting services to large companies with large budgets and sales teams.

**CHALLENGES:** To sell his services, Searcy is required to foster contact at the highest levels, usually with the CEOs at some of the most difficult companies in the world to penetrate. Though he had coauthored *Whale Hunting*, a very successful book about making large sales, he recognized it wasn't enough to simply send a copy and hope for the best. He needed a much stronger reason for making contact and engaging in business together.

**CAMPAIGN SPECIFICS:** Searcy spends much of his time researching, reading, and watching for quirky stories or facts that call for greater attention. This often leads to discovery of future trends. For instance, he once noticed a sudden uptick in new installments of landline phones. At a time when everyone was dropping their old home phone lines for smartphones, he was intrigued. It led Searcy to an interesting discovery: that landlines were necessary in order to receive the popular cable television industry bundle of internet services with cable TV.

Then he extrapolated. Where will the convergence of cable television and internet services lead? How will they combine to create new opportunities for businesses to engage with consumers? And how does all that relate to the installed base of so many landline phones? For Searcy, it led to the discovery of an important new advertising platform that no one else even knew existed, involving pushing messages through television sets.

Once he identifies an emerging trend, Searcy uses an ingeniously simple, audacious method for outreach. He divides the insights into bite-sized installments and sends them as letters through the US Postal Service. The regular cadence doubles as an awareness tactic and a perseverance campaign. It hooks the executive because, as Searcy only reveals one piece of the future at a time, there's always more to learn.

The uninitiated will call that "old-school" because it's sent through the mail, but I just call it brilliant thinking. Who else sends personal letters through the mail these days? Contact Marketers know that uncrowded channels give them a far better chance of standing out. You do not stand out by doing what everyone else does.

**RESULTS:** Though a long process, Searcy's personalized approach has paid off handsomely. He now counts as clients nearly two-fifths of the Fortune 500 companies, helping them close on more than $5 billion in new sales. AT&T, 3M, Disney, Chase Bank, and Apple are among his clients. His method of telling the future in increments, through regular installments in the mail, is how all these companies became his clients.

**KEY TAKEAWAY:** Extrapolation, like divining the future itself, is based on supposition. No one can actually tell the future, but with some thoughtful work we can find micro-trends that might lead somewhere, and we can follow the trail. Where they'll actually lead is unknowable until we get there. But when you're able to present a case supported by facts and analysis, you are providing insights no one else has. And when those insights are broken into a series of segments, and those segments are delivered across set points on a time line, they become potent tools for opening doors, which leads to significant sales. Searcy should know. What he sells are million-dollar consulting engagements.

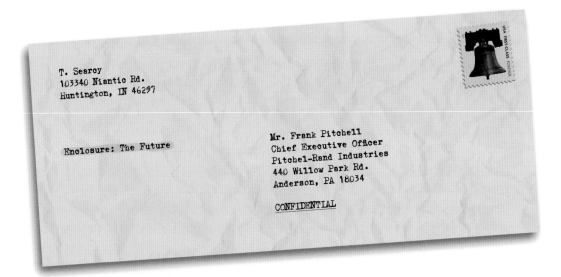

**A PLAIN WHITE ENVELOPE WITH THE FUTURE ENCLOSED**

*Tom Searcy cleverly delivers insights about future trends in a form every top executive can relate to—a standard typed executive letter in a plain white envelope. And then he sends it through the mail. With a stamp. Some may cry, "That's so old-school!" but Searcy clearly understands the difference between stale, old ideas and the crafty use of uncrowded channels to stand out.*

## Curious Minds Want to Know

I admire Searcy's contrarian approach. He's using a nearly deserted channel (the USPS) to deliver insights only he has (the future), to create a position in the marketplace no one else has (as one of the premier business strategy consultants in the world). But *Sales Manager Survival Guide* author David Brock has an even simpler approach to unsolicited proposals. He simply uses publicly available information to craft a basic "Did you realize . . . ?" statement.

## CASE STUDY
# Using Publicly Available Information

**BACKGROUND:** Author David Brock wanted to connect with the CFO of a large, publicly held grocery chain to propose a sale of his company's services.

**CHALLENGES:** C-suite executives are notoriously difficult to reach, but the problem multiplies exponentially with the size of the company. The grocery chain Brock had in mind was one of the biggest in the United States, which meant the challenge of breaking through would be formidable.

**CAMPAIGN SPECIFICS:** Before approaching the CFO, Brock studied sources of industry statistics and discovered an interesting fact about the average fresh-food loss across the industry. He then factored that against the company's annual revenue. The figure he computed was $13 billion of waste, which dwarfed the company's net annual earnings of $3 billion.

  Using those data points, he led his outreach to the CFO with a "Did you realize . . . ?" statement: "Did you realize you're paying your suppliers $13 billion every year for a product that ends up in dumpsters behind your stores? And if you cut down on that spoilage by 10 percent, you could add another $1 billion to your earnings?" The CFO responded, "How did you come up with that?" And the meeting was on.

**RESULTS:** The purpose of Brock's highly informal unsolicited proposal was to open a conversation with a difficult-to-reach C-level executive. And it worked brilliantly. With very little research, and almost no campaign, he was able to compose a valuable insight that prompted the question "How would you do that?" Once the prospect asked that question, he was engaged, curious, and ready to have a conversation that led to a sale.

**KEY TAKEAWAY:** Brock's approach was simple but effective. He spent a total of thirty minutes looking up a few stats, and then applied them to the numbers found in the company's annual report. Thus, his approach represents the other extreme in using unsolicited proposals to get meetings—the cost is zero. It doesn't take weeks or months to prepare. It's just a simple insight applied to the target company's current circumstances.

This is unsolicited proposals reduced to its most basic form. Do some quick research, discover a trend or fact that might be a concern, explore it, and extrapolate. If there is substance, reach out and have a meeting. Performing that basic research has never been easier with company websites, web search, and now, helpful tools infused with artificial intelligence (which we'll look at more in chapter twelve of this book).

# DELIVERING YOUR PROPOSAL

We've looked at the content of unsolicited proposals, but what about the delivery of the proposal itself? Are there tools to make the delivery of an unsolicited proposal even more productive?

You could send your PDF or PowerPoint deck as an attachment to email and follow up with a hard copy. That gets the digital file there quickly . . . But how will you know who's read it and to whom it was passed? Doesn't that simply become a black hole in your contact process? DocSend cofounder Dave Koslow says the practice of attaching files to email is an utterly broken system. He explains, "When you have to ask someone, 'Hey, did you get a chance to look at that thing I sent you?' you're starting off on the wrong foot."

Koslow says it's an awkward exchange that doesn't have to be. "Either the person did read it and feels you should have trusted them to read it," he explains, "or the person didn't read it and they either lie or own up to it and feel bad." The solution is what Koslow built—a web-based link-hosting platform that not only delivers the attachments but also gathers valuable intel for the user.

When an attachment is delivered via a DocSend link, it allows the user to see real-time stats for email opens/views, and document views and duration of views, down to the page level. It also tracks forwarding, giving the sender a direct account of who's viewing the proposal. What can we do with that as

Contact Marketers? Based on page-view metrics, we can see which parts of the proposal most capture the prospect's attention. And by tracking who is seeing the document, we get to discover who the influencers are.

Koslow says the resulting data can change the course of a sale dramatically. He recalls the experience of one user, who sent a proposal with the intention of talking about one aspect of their service, only to discover from the page-view metric that the prospect was interested in a completely different part of their offering. When the rep called to follow up, it was a simple transition to focus on the part that had already caught the prospect's attention.

Gathering intel is useful, but having greater control over digital files is important, too. I use PDFs a lot, and one of my biggest concerns is that the files can live on forever, completely beyond my control. The DocSend platform solves that issue, too, giving the user the ability to kill off files, limit who gets access, control downloads, protect content with watermarks, and more.

## CASE STUDY
# Sitetracker Uses DocSend to Open Accounts

**BACKGROUND:** Sitetracker VP of Marketing Brett Chester was looking for a way to reinforce his company's content marketing program.

**CHALLENGES:** Sitetracker supports its sales team with a robust content marketing program, but the company had no idea which subjects were generating interest and which clients were interested. The company also wanted better control of its documents, particularly the ability to remotely kill off PDF files, which otherwise live on indefinitely.

**CAMPAIGN SPECIFICS:** New content documents were optimized for the DocSend platform, keeping separate subjects on separate pages. The platform tracks reads by page, giving Chester the ability to see which subjects are generating interest at each account. Sitetracker reps also set up "Spaces," the DocSend term for living collections of documents for any given recipient, as a persistence campaign, to keep prospects engaged.

**RESULTS:** Chester discovered DocSend was transforming his content program into a robust account intel platform. Suddenly, the company had real-time metrics showing its reps which documents, and which pages of those

Courtesy of DocSend

## ATTACHMENTS AS INTEL SOURCES

*When you include an important attachment in an email—perhaps a proposal—it would be helpful to know if your prospect ever read it. Even better if you could see who else has read it, how long they spent on each page, and get a sense of their reaction. Shown here, DocSend's platform displays read/duration data for sent documents.*

documents, were being read—features of the platform that have allowed the sales team to focus on the issues of greatest interest at each account. The platform also delivered an unexpected new advantage by showing exactly *who* was reading each of those documents and pages, allowing Chester's team to better identify the stakeholders and influencers. As a result, Chester says the productivity of the sales team is booming.

**KEY TAKEAWAY:** Sending unsolicited proposals—or documents of any kind—is now an important part of the unsolicited proposal contact strategy. Rather than being a petty detail in the campaign, delivery of documents can now double as an intel-gathering resource. Sending an unsolicited proposal as a PDF or slide deck now helps you see who the stakeholders are and which portions of the document have captured their attention. A document management system like DocSend is a must-have for any unsolicited-proposal campaign.

# PUTTING IT ALL TOGETHER

Deep personalization, new tools to deliver and control documents, and a new set of engagement strategies make unsolicited proposals a strong contender for

Contact Marketing tests and funding. The easy availability of research data from social media, web search, company websites, and AI tools (which you'll read about in chapter twelve), makes it easy to weaponize insights into killer contact campaigns.

Curtis Brooks shows us that complex subjects and solutions can be distilled to nine-page PDFs that quickly convey an unsolicited proposal that is easy to read and tempting to pass along to influencers. Brian Wallace takes the idea of condensing a complex proposal even further, turning it into a device that ignites massive viral pass-along, with the potential of reaching millions of influencers and instigating desired outcomes.

Meanwhile, Tom Searcy and David Brock show us unsolicited proposals needn't be complex or overwrought. In Searcy's case, it's all about being curious, watching for trends, and in particular, small items that can lead to great disruptions within the next five years. His strategy of releasing those insights piecemeal, over the course of several physically mailed letters, are a sure way into even the biggest companies' C-suites. That approach has led to millions of dollars' worth of consulting fees for Searcy and billions of dollars in new business for his clients.

Brock's even simpler approach shows us anyone can do this. The secret is being involved in your prospects' industries, watching for simple changes, trends, or stats, and assessing what those might mean for their businesses. It's surprising how many insights can be drawn from that simple process. And even more striking how easily those can help us win important meetings.

## Critical Next Steps

> **OBJECTIVE:** Use unsolicited proposals to gain the trust, and business, of new clients.

### Step 1. Do your research.

Sending out unsolicited proposals really is Deep personalization in its most extreme form. To pull it off, you need to put yourself in a position to know more about a certain aspect of the prospect's business than they do. Read articles and annual reports. Do the same with the top three competitors of your prospect. Take the time to understand the market forces, the prospect's strategy, and where you see potent opportunities or significant risks. That should be the focus of your proposal.

### Step 2. Choose a format and delivery method.

Several formats have been discussed in this chapter, including slide decks, storyboards, infographics, even good old-fashioned executive letters. If you send the proposals as an email attachment, use a document management platform to track and measure engagement. And back up every electronic send with a printed copy, sent through the mail or via overnight courier.

### Step 3. Make it all about them, never about you.

You'll want to catalog quotes by the CEO and senior staff, particularly about where the company is heading and the challenges and opportunities they're excited to conquer. Sprinkle those throughout the proposal to keep their attention and their heads nodding in agreement. The final result should be a document that invites further discussion and causes a great stir of excitement within the target organization. It should *not* be a pitch for your product or service disguised as a proposal.

# POINTS TO REMEMBER

✔ In order to lead, executives need insights into the markets, trends, and world around them. Those insights can become a treasured gift to a C-level executive.

✔ Unsolicited proposals may be the ultimate expression of Deep personalization.

✔ Unsolicited proposals must center around a bold new insight, perhaps even a glimpse into the future.

✔ Unsolicited proposals shouldn't be long-winded documents; they should be presented in a format that makes it simple to digest complex thoughts quickly.

✔ The documents should transcend language with word pictures that can be easily shared and understood.

✔ Unsolicited proposals should not offer a solution. Instead they should be an invitation to have a high-level conversation.

✔ Use multiple modes of communication to transmit your proposal. Supplement digital files with hard copies.

✔ Discover and involve all stakeholders. That may be limited to buying committee members but could go so far as including competitors, even fan bases and social media hordes.

✔ If the influencer audience is broad enough, consider using an actual infographic as the proposal format and put it out on social media. Info-graphics can achieve viral pass-along and remain on the internet for years.

✔ Top executives' greatest interest is seeing into the future. Use your curiosity and powers of deduction to create a vision you can deliver, preferably in increments.

✔ Even simple, publicly available information from industry publications and company websites is enough to find insights that will open doors.

✔ Use a document-serving platform to control your proposals, gather real-time viewership data, and learn who's on the buying committee.

# PART 3

## TECH'S
## TOOLBOX

# CHAPTER 9

# DIGITAL MARKETING

Digital marketing is a broad and generic category of marketing. It addresses essentially anything on a screen. But behind the screen there is magic. As Contact Marketers, we're always looking for ways to create connections. And we're always looking to create magic.

We often think of digital marketing as a macro solution. Search optimization and pay-per-click are how we call the world to our websites. Digital marketing creates global reach in an instant.

But digital marketing is also a platform of extraordinarily targeted reach. Ads on Facebook and LinkedIn already narrow the target substantially. Still, as Contact Marketers we must constantly innovate and repurpose what already exists.

There are already forms of digital advertising that are getting us to the point of being able to target individuals, but much of what is there still requires the slightly off-kilter approach of a mad-scientist Contact Marketer. You will see that in the stories that follow, starting with Alec Brownstein's ingenious use of common pay-per-click advertising to make a handful of life-changing connections.

# ALEC BROWNSTEIN'S GOOGLE ADS

Alec Brownstein is a creative guy. He's held posts with several top-ten advertising agencies, won top awards, and serves today as vice president of creative and global executive creative director for Dollar Shave Club. But when he started out, he was a copywriter in New York, stuck in a job he didn't like.

He needed a change.

Inspiration came in the realization that most people—particularly those with, shall we say, "healthy" egos—tend to google their names to see what's been written or said about themselves. Alec used that to formulate a simple digital campaign to connect with the creative directors of seven of the top ten New York–based agencies.

## CASE STUDY
## Using Paid Search Ads to Reach Specific VIP Prospects

**BACKGROUND:** Alec Brownstein was dissatisfied with his post as a copywriter at a small Manhattan agency. He wanted more. He wanted to land his next job with one of the top ten agencies in the big city. But how?

**CHALLENGES:** No one in Manhattan is easy to reach, especially someone important, and especially someone in media or advertising—like the creative directors at the top agencies on Madison Avenue. Adding to the challenge, whatever Brownstein did would have to impress the creative directors creatively. And of all the people in the world, these people would be the hardest to impress on that basis.

**CAMPAIGN SPECIFICS:** Brownstein reasoned his target executives probably searched their names on Google more often than most people. His strategy was to use that to his advantage by bidding on the full names of his targeted contacts as search terms. Refining it further, Brownstein coupled those search

## GOOGLE ADS TARGETED TO CREATIVE DIRECTORS

*When ad copywriter Alec Brownstein decided he wanted a job with one of the top Manhattan-based ad agencies, he didn't fill out an online form or send a résumé. Instead he employed a simple Google Ads campaign, using the full names of seven creative directors as search terms. Every time they searched their own names, Alec's ad popped up, inviting them to hire him for his dream job.*

terms with the zip codes for each creative director's agency address. Since search terms like "Alan Reichenthal" in zip code 10028 were not in great demand by digital marketers, he felt reasonably confident bidding the lowest possible amount per click would still result in a dominant display of his ads.

The ads themselves were simple. Appearing at the head of all search results for each creative director was a text ad, saying, "Hey [creative director's name]: Gooooogling yourself is fun. Hiring me is fun, too." Each ad included a link to Brownstein's portfolio, where his best copywriting examples were on display.

**RESULTS:** Apparently, big agency creative directors do indeed search their own names, and do it quite frequently. Within weeks, Brownstein received messages from six of the seven creative directors targeted. Three of the six interviewed him, and one, at Young & Rubicam, hired Alec on the spot.

That amounts to an 86 percent response to the campaign and a 100 percent fulfillment of Brownstein's mission. He added important new contacts to his network and got the job he wanted. But there was more.

Brownstein's assumption about the bidding price for those esoteric search terms was correct. He paid a total of six bucks for the entire campaign. So let's have some fun: at a starting salary of, say, $120,000, that amounts to a 2 million percent ROI.

The campaign got Brownstein the job and then accomplished even more. His story went viral in the press and garnered nearly every award in the advertising industry, including a Clio.

**KEY TAKEAWAY:** This is a classic illustration of Contact Marketing in action. Brownstein bent the purpose of the Google Ads platform to his mission, targeting just seven very important people. That's not the way search advertising is supposed to work, but he made it work.

There are stories of Contact Marketers spending a lot per person to make a critical connection, as much as $10,000. That's perfectly in line with the Contact Marketing mission, if the business potential is equally high. But as Brownstein's campaign shows, it's not necessary to spend a lot to make great gains.

Brownstein's story tells us it's important to broaden our scope. He did that with our understanding of how paid search advertising works, that it can also be used to address singular people, not always a broad market. It also shows that Contact Marketing is not just for sales teams looking for a way to make important connections. The need to get meetings with important people is universal throughout the business world. And clearly, Contact Marketing belongs in the hands of job seekers as well.

# PUTTING GOOGLE ADS TO WORK

If Google Ads can help job seekers (and the rest of us) reach important contacts, can the Google Display Network be useful as well?

I sometimes have conversations with Contact Marketing clients about supporting the sales team beyond getting the initial meeting. Understandably, they want to reinforce the chances for a sale throughout the cycle. Digital marketing can help here, too, with a set of strategies that make use of retargeting (also known as remarketing). Retargeting works by setting a tracking pixel when someone visits a given site, then using that pixel when they visit other websites that participate in the Google Display Network, which reaches 90 percent of all people on the web. As the pixel is detected, the marketer's ads appear on virtually any site the tracked person visits.

You've already seen this in action. Let's say you visit the L.L.Bean site and browse for waterproof shoes. A tracking pixel is set and you go on your way. Then let's say you visit several news sites. If they're all participants in the Google Display Network (they are), you'll suddenly see L.L.Bean ads showing up on *The Wall Street Journal*, *The New York Times*, and other sites, perhaps even for the very shoes you were considering. This happens all over the web, all day long.

To make use of retargeting, you must have a website that sets tracking pixels as people visit your site (with appropriate opt-out controls). Once you have more than two hundred pixels set, you can set up an account with the Google Display Network and start running retargeting ads. But there are new alternatives that allow you to circumvent all that.

That's what Kate Blumberg, sales development and ABM team lead for a late-stage startup, counts on when she approaches an important account or prospect. She uses a service called Terminus to target specific people with her retargeting ads, even though they have never visited her company's site—and there is no tracking pixel.

## CASE STUDY
# Retargeting Ads Open New Doors

**BACKGROUND:** Producers of Hollywood movies do it. Publishers of blockbuster books do it. They run a slew of ads in the national media before launch to introduce their productions to the public, to create awareness and demand, and to encourage buying tickets or books. So why not do the same in advance of a sales call?

**CHALLENGES:** People have a natural tendency to avoid interacting with people they don't know. Running ads on *The New York Times*, *The Wall Street Journal*, CBS.com, and other sites visited by target executives would certainly create a positive impression, but how can it be done without buying an expensive national ad campaign?

**CAMPAIGN SPECIFICS:** Startup exec Kate Blumberg chose to use the account-based marketing platform Terminus to create the desired effect. Once an account contact has been identified, the service accesses third-party tracking pixels to start running retargeting ads. This makes virtually anyone accessible for digital display advertising.

The resulting experience for the target contact is that suddenly ads for Blumberg's company start popping up all over the web—on *The New York Times, The Wall Street Journal,* tiny sites, big sites, anywhere ads are displayed within the Google Display Network of more than two million sites. The impression is that Blumberg's company is huge, that it's a national advertiser and a major player. It's an impressive effect.

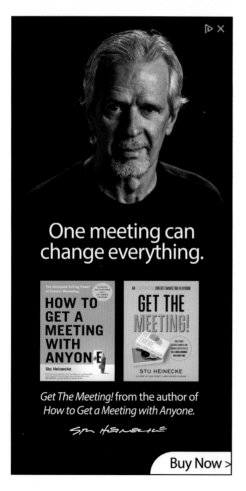

### INTRODUCE YOURSELF IN A MOST IMPRESSIVE WAY

*The point of retargeting ads in Contact Marketing is to introduce yourself in a most impressive way. In fact, if you see any of these ads while paging though* The Wall Street Journal, The New York Times, Forbes, *or any of more than two million sites on the Google Display Network, please expect my call shortly.*

**RESULTS:** The ads include a link to a personalized landing page that explains what her company stands for and what it can do for the contact. By the time Blumberg makes the first call, they're already impressed and certainly aware of her company. It becomes an easy connection. Moreover, the entire department knows about her company because they, too, have been seeing the ads "everywhere."

That "digital-surround" strategy is important in the current buying environment, where decisions are made by groups and departments, not just single decision makers. Once they make contact, Kate replaces the initial ads with new ones that create a persistence effect until a deal is concluded.

Blumberg is thrilled with the results of her retargeting campaign, with an ad-to-contact ratio hovering around 50 percent. When she adds a new target account to her campaign, she uses Marketo automation software to produce a new personalized landing page, requiring about thirty minutes start to finish. The 50 percent contact rate compares to 20 percent without the ads, so they are definitely paying off.

**KEY TAKEAWAY:** Digital marketing and, specifically, retargeting are giving Contact Marketers new tools to break through and keep the ball rolling on any given sale. Retargeting was out of reach for many, but new account-based marketing platforms like Terminus (RollWorks is another) now make it possible to target a single person or department with ads that open doors, create positive impressions, and help sales reps persist. These are important breakthroughs for Contact Marketers because we can now expand the mission from getting a meeting all the way through to supporting the sale itself.

# DISRUPTING WITH GEOFENCING

Another digital form begging to be part of the Contact Marketing mission is geofencing. It allows marketers to draw borders on maps and target only the people within the lines.

Geofencing is a disruptive technology, allowing marketers to do things they could never conceive of just a few years ago. A couple of examples:

- A car dealer draws a geofence around all the competing dealerships in its market. That gives the dealership access to all the people who've walked into its competitors' showrooms, people who are very likely to make an imminent car purchase. The dealer places ads for its own special offers, appearing on all the mobile devices held by those buyers, luring them away from its competitors.

- You're an exhibitor at an event, but the organizer won't release the list of attendees. Geofencing enables you to draw a fence around the exhibit hall, specify dates and times, and run ads to everyone there during the show. You don't even have to be an exhibitor to market to them.

So consider the possibilities for a Contact Marketer. If we can draw a fence around car dealerships and convention halls, we can certainly do the same around a target contact's office building. Propellant Media cofounder Justin Croxton explains, "Geofencing used to be the province of big-spend marketers, but it's now coming down in price so that anyone can put it to use." Croxton's agency specializes in serving SMB (small- and medium-sized business) clients with micro-budgets, which makes this the perfect opening for Contact Marketing missions.

Imagine geofencing the headquarters of a major account. Your ad starts showing up wherever the target contact surfs on the web and on any of more than six hundred thousand mobile apps they might use. Suddenly, you're everywhere, building awareness of your brand, but also creating the impression that you're a major advertiser. When your ad shows up on *The Wall Street Journal* or *The New York Times*, it has an impact. You're a big-time player, someone to know.

This is a similar approach to what Terminus uses, but geofencing allows you to target everyone at a prospect's company. If your prospect has been absorbing the impact of your ads before receiving your contact request, it's easy to imagine breaking through anywhere, anytime.

It's also easy to imagine the effect of continuing the campaign, creating digital persistence to support resulting deals throughout the sales cycle.

## TACTICAL EXAMPLE
# Using Geofencing to Corral an Entire Company

**TACTIC:** Use geofencing to raise awareness and interest at a particular company.

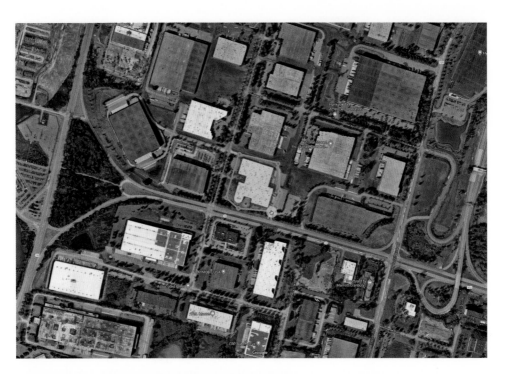

**GEOFENCING ADS TO REACH SPECIFIC LOCATIONS**

*Geofencing allows digital marketers to run ads only to people found in a specific location. It allows Contact Marketers to target a company's headquarters with their ads before reaching out to executives.*

**BACKGROUND:** An account has been targeted, contacts within the company have been identified, and the company address has been verified. The next step is outreach. But before you send anything, you decide to use geofencing to establish awareness of you and your company, making your prospect more open to your approach.

**CHALLENGES:** If the target company has more than one location, or if it is based in a building with other tenants, geofencing becomes more difficult. At minimum, a contact's actual location should be verified to properly target ads. In the case of multiple tenants at the target address, determine the benefits versus the costs of reaching all occupants of the building.

**CAMPAIGN SPECIFICS:** You produce ads in multiple sizes according to network-supplied specs, with a link target in mind. The primary purpose of the ads is to impress the contacts based on where they're seeing your ad, not necessarily to click a link. Still, clicking the link in the ad can bring respondents to a landing page that gives information, offers a report, or perhaps asks them to join a list. Actually, the offer and information on the page won't matter, at least for your purposes; the point in getting your prospect to the landing page is to set a tracking pixel to start serving retargeting ads to continue the ongoing persistence element of your program.

**RESULTS:** Because geofencing has proved to be effective, your results should be similar to those in the previous case study. Your prospect will be aware of who you are before your call and perceive your company as an important player in its field.

**WHAT TO KEEP IN MIND:** Whether the delivery method is geofencing or retargeting, the ads should be focused on creating an impression. That is, impressing the target executive with the mere presence of your ad on the pages of *The Wall Street Journal* or *Forbes* or other mainstream publications.

Reaching employees of a company's headquarters using geofencing is a similar approach to retargeting, but it's also quite different. Even though it focuses on a specific geographic area in a particular span of time, geofencing doesn't distinguish which of those people it hits. But it can create widespread coverage within a given organization, which can be an enormous plus.

The more team members, as a group, know about your brand, the more likely it is you'll break through to new business. Terminus does this, too, by matching third-party tracking pixels with names and email addresses of targeted executives. It then researches other influencers in the target contact's department and adds them to the campaign. That may be broad enough to sway decisions within a particular department, or it may not. Geofencing offers the option of hitting an entire cross-section of the company's employees, which may be a better fit for your Contact Marketing mission.

Better yet, why not use them both? If Contact Marketing is becoming a multimodal, multitouch solution, geofencing and retargeting together will ensure everyone who needs to be influenced before, during, and after the initial meeting will be thoroughly addressed.

# IT'S IN THE EMAIL

And then there's email. There are always outliers who make email work, but most often sales reps and targeted buyers are pretty frustrated by the whole thing.

It makes sense. On the sellers' side, email is cheap, and it can be (and usually is) automated—and in any case, it's often scripted, thus simple to use. On the buyers' side, there is just too much darned email cluttering their inboxes—probably because it's cheap, automated, and simple to use, and, therefore, a lazy substitute for making actual human-to-human connections.

Email can be effective, but mostly it's not. Sellers wonder why it isn't working. Buyers just wish it would stop. So let's take a look at how we can make our emails more effective and more welcome from the buyer's perspective.

When I'm asked by sales reps how they can make their emails more effective, I offer the following tips:

1. **KEEP IT SHORT.** I tell reps to cut the message length. Nobody's going to read pages' worth of words, especially if they don't know you. Ideally, an introductory email's message should be a dozen words or less. Sometimes more explanation is required, but never let it go beyond two *short* paragraphs. Make sure it contains obvious value derived from prior research. Keeping your email short shows respect for the recipient's time. It also forces you to get it right and get right to the point.

2. **TIME IT RIGHT.** I also point to advice about timing that I shared in *How to Get a Meeting with Anyone.* When I spoke with *High-Profit Prospecting* author Mark Hunter, he explained that the effectiveness of a prospecting email is directly tied to the time of day it's sent, even which day it's sent. If you want to reach a C-suite executive, Mark's advice is to send the email early Saturday morning or Sunday evening. On the weekends, there is no assistant to screen messages, and there are far fewer emails competing for the executive's time. Early Saturday morning makes sense because busy executives are often checking in before starting their weekends. And Sunday evenings work because they're often at their computers planning out their week ahead.

3. **INCLUDE VIDEO.** Beyond the basics of keeping it short and timing it right, there are a few things that could have a further positive effect on email engagement. One is to include video content. Vidyard (covered at length in chapter eleven) not only makes this exceptionally easy, it produces useful metrics to help you see who's engaging. The platform enables you to record personalized video messages right at your desk, making the outreach potentially more compelling and far more human.

4.  **USE DOCSEND FOR ATTACHMENTS.** Another powerful enhancement is to couple DocSend with emails. Covered in the previous chapter, DocSend is a cloud-based document management platform that allows you to include attachments that generate valuable intel as you infiltrate the targeted business. It reports in real time who opened the document and how long they spent on each page. It also shows whom the document has been forwarded to, allowing quick discovery of surrounding influencers and stakeholders.

5.  **ENGAGE THE RECIPIENT.** There are various ways to engage the email recipient. Video clips, mentioned previously, are one way. Another is including cartoons. I've written a lot about the use of cartoons in various marketing applications, and certainly in Contact Marketing campaigns. Not surprisingly, cartoons are also effective engagement devices in email.

## TACTICAL EXAMPLE
## Cartoons as Email Engagement Devices

**TACTIC:** Grab the attention of a prospect with an embedded cartoon in an email.

**BACKGROUND:** There is a client you're going to engage via email. You've followed the rule by keeping your content short and considered the best timing for sending it, but will you break through?

**CHALLENGES:** Email inboxes are completely overstuffed. If you're sending an email to someone you don't know, it's likely you'll never hear from them. They're already too busy dealing with the people they already know to divert attention to you. Something is needed to push through that steep resistance.

**CAMPAIGN SPECIFICS:** You can insert a cartoon device at the top of the page, which consists of a cartoon image with italicized text centered immediately below. The caption can be personalized, but the cartoon must reveal a point of agreement between you and the recipient in the humor. *Never jam your brand into the cartoon.* The subject line informs the recipient a cartoon is waiting within.

**RESULTS:** In countless tests, cartoon devices have tended to double open rates. That higher open rate tends to persist across multiple emails as well, making the cartoon device ideal for periodic drip campaign use.

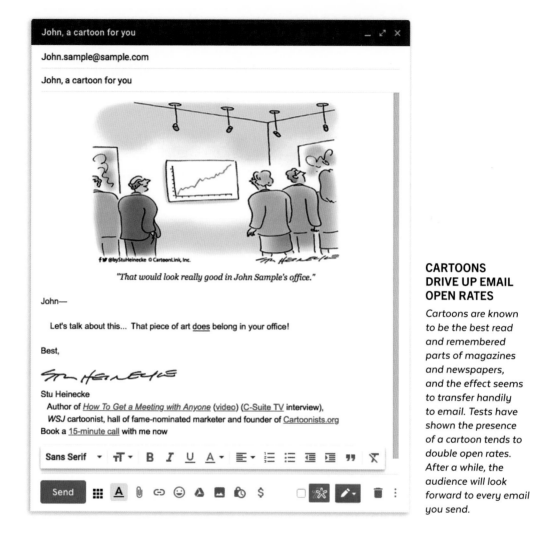

**CARTOONS DRIVE UP EMAIL OPEN RATES**

*Cartoons are known to be the best read and remembered parts of magazines and newspapers, and the effect seems to transfer handily to email. Tests have shown the presence of a cartoon tends to double open rates. After a while, the audience will look forward to every email you send.*

**WHAT TO KEEP IN MIND:** Email is a hopelessly overcrowded channel, and there are many better ways to stand out to your target contact. But email can still be effective. As you plan your use of email in your Contact Marketing outreach, be aware of the person on the other side. They don't want to be talked at with copy that is stupidly long, boring, and overblown. They especially don't want to be pitched. They want to be spoken to as a person, by someone who has taken the time to understand their needs.

With a few adjustments, you may find email can become more effective. It can be part of a multimodal strategy, but with emphasis on multiple modes of communication, not just one.

# PUTTING IT ALL TOGETHER

Contact Marketing will always be about skipping conventional thinking. It is contrarian in nature. When a form of marketing catches on and overheats, we look for another way to stand out. And when something becomes conventional, we look for a way to bend its purpose, turning it into something entirely new. That is what allows Contact Marketers to lead with astonishing results.

The tendency to lapse into conventional thinking certainly applies to digital marketing. Not long ago, digital was the disruptive technology of marketing. Today, it is utterly mainstream, filled with marketers wondering why they aren't standing out above the ever-increasing crowd.

The examples in this chapter are not the only digital options available to Contact Marketers to break through. Instead, they are a nucleus of an underlying thought. How can we make digital different? How can we use it to make individually targeted connections, even though the platforms were never meant for that purpose?

> *MacGyver would never use a coat hanger just to hang a coat.*

MacGyver would never use a coat hanger just to hang a coat. That spirit is evident in the way Alec Brownstein used Google Ads to connect with his dream job. Or in the way retargeting, the workhorse of e-commerce, has been rejigged to open specific doors. If MacGyver had access to geofencing, retargeting, or some of the email enhancements mentioned here, I'm sure he could have defused a good-sized bomb, even without the hanger.

## Critical Next Steps

*OBJECTIVE:* Make digital marketing work for you.

### Step 1. Digital marketing is persistence.

Retargeting, geofencing, and social media ads are now the core of the persistence module in Contact Marketing. Digital marketing is also the platform that converts Pocket Campaign engagements into new business. Use retargeting ad platforms to get your ads out to your contact targets. Set up a geofencing account to target specific buildings. Digital marketing can serve relentlessly as the core of your programmed persistence effort.

### Step 2. Repurpose, repurpose, repurpose.

Most digital marketers are looking for click-throughs and thousands of impressions. We're looking to influence one person at a time to take a meeting. *Their* response rates are measured in hundredths of a percentage point, *our* campaigns produce response rates as high as 100 percent. So we're not looking to use digital advertising in conventional ways. Alec Brownstein's brilliant use of Google Ads proves the point: He spent six dollars to reach seven people, seven critically important contacts. Our purpose is to bend conventional uses of digital marketing to create a one-to-one dialogue and a sense of inevitability that our proposed connection will take place.

### Step 3. Use digital media to discover buying committees.

Digital marketing and tools can also help us discover critical influencers and decision makers who affect purchasing decisions. Geofencing helps by targeting an entire building. Using tools like DocSend (chapter eight) and Vidyard (chapter eleven) allow us to see who's involved. By targeting the people around our primary contact, we are ensuring that our contact campaigns are influencing all the right people.

# POINTS TO REMEMBER

✔ Digital marketing, once the disruptive technology of marketing, is now mainstream and traditional.

✔ Most digital marketing tools must be repurposed to fit the one-at-a-time, high-value targeting of Contact Marketing.

✔ Alec Brownstein demonstrated the principle of repurposing with his brilliant Google Ads campaign, which he used to reach just seven key hiring contacts in midtown Manhattan.

✔ Retargeting ads can be used to create awareness and positive impressions before outreach, during contact, and throughout the sales cycle.

✔ Retargeting and geofencing are the key ingredients of the "persistence campaign" element that forms the new Contact Marketing model described in chapter thirteen of this book.

✔ Geofencing gives a medium-focus targeting ability to Contact Marketers, to address many of the employees of any company as long as they're all at the same address.

✔ Retargeting, document management, and embedded video platforms all give Contact Marketers tools to read engagement and discover key influencers and decision makers.

✔ Email is a hopelessly crowded platform, but it still can be used effectively.

✔ Always look for ways to bend the purpose of any digital or nondigital form of marketing—you just may end up with an incredible new tool no one else is using.

# CHAPTER 10

# SOCIAL MEDIA

When I speak of Contact Marketing and social media, I'm usually thinking of LinkedIn. You can make connections on Twitter, Instagram, and other social platforms, but LinkedIn is the place to hook up on a professional level.

On Pinterest, you can attract attention to a collection of images, a portfolio of work. It's possible to build enormous followings on YouTube. There certainly are important connections to be made on Twitter, and Facebook can be an interesting option for targeting specific people or companies. But none of these platforms can compete with LinkedIn for creating true business-to-business connections.

I think my experience is pretty typical. I'm not a millennial, so my social media usage centers around Facebook and LinkedIn. I have six or seven hundred Facebook friends. My connections are with family, old classmates, and some professional contacts.

LinkedIn is the space I reserve for business connections. Those are almost always inbound, often from people who have read my book and want to connect with the author. Others are a result of posts, either my own or from mentions in someone else's. All these connections are the result of exposure to my message: that anyone can get important meetings, and that those meetings can change their lives. The people who connect with me on LinkedIn constitute the core audience for my books, agency, consulting, training, and other services; thus, these contacts are critically important to me.

Meanwhile, on Facebook, old friends are posting memes of cute kitties doing silly things. My mom is there, too, posting about family, knitting, and church. Old classmates update their travelogues, share family milestones, and post pictures of what they're eating.

Several of my professional Facebook connections fail with utterly mistargeted live posts there about their success models. Facebook seems entirely too personal a place for get-rich-quick hustles, and talking about your business on Facebook often just makes you look obnoxious.

But if we look at Facebook as a marketing platform, rather than a place to gain leverage through posts, the view changes. Facebook ads can be useful in a Contact Marketing context. Even though it doesn't support targeting a handful of specific people, the platform offers a lot of control over targeting by audience and location. Let's look first at an astonishing story about using Facebook ads to make a critical connection with Walmart.

# FACEBOOK AD PENETRATES THE WALMART BUNKER

With 6,800 superstores in the United States and Canada, occupying more than a trillion square feet of retail space, selling everything from housewares and groceries to electronics, health aids, and sporting goods, Walmart is North America's largest brick-and-mortar retailer. Placement on its shelves almost guarantees explosive growth for any purveyor of consumer products. For that reason, the chain's vast purchasing department is so difficult to penetrate it's almost bunker-like.

That was the challenge faced by Orabrush, a tiny startup in Provo, Utah. The team consisted of Austin Craig and Jeffrey Harmon serving as the young marketing core, Jeff Davis as CEO, and Orabrush inventor and founder Dr. Robert Wagstaff. The fledgling company had already produced a strong online following and direct business through a series of clever YouTube videos. But the team's goal was to make Orabrush the best-selling tongue cleaner in the world. To do that, they needed to go beyond YouTube. They needed Walmart.

The team started like any other vendor knocking on Walmart's door. Fill out these forms, send us your sales and capacity numbers, tell us about your marketing, fax these other forms. It went on and on, so the Orabrush team decided to speed up the chain's slow-moving vendor intake process.

## CASE STUDY
# Orabrush Facebook Campaign

**BACKGROUND:** The Orabrush marketing team was having great success with YouTube videos to introduce its tongue cleaner product and push online sales. Its next conquest was getting on the shelves in all 6,800 Walmart stores across the United States and Canada.

**CHALLENGES:** The team had already gained a slight foothold in a handful of Walmart stores in Provo but felt the company's vendor intake process was leading nowhere. The team needed a way to recharge their bid. Adding to the difficulty, the Orabrush team had no idea who the actual decision makers were, and no clue whom to target in their outreach.

**CAMPAIGN SPECIFICS:** Facebook offers the ability to target by location, education, and employer. The Orabrush team used those markers to target people with college degrees in zip code 72716 who worked for Walmart, netting many of the company's top executives. The ad said, "Walmart employees have bad breath . . . Walmart needs to carry Orabrush! It will sell better than anything in your store." It also contained a link back to Orabrush, in case they wanted to reach out. Turns out, they did.

**RESULTS:** Within forty-eight hours, Davis says they heard from several Walmart executives who were asking to have the ad turned off. The executives were under the mistaken impression that the ad was running nationally, so when Davis explained how they targeted just Walmart headquarters, the tone of the call softened. "How did you do that?" they wondered.

Davis explained the team's digital media prowess at moving Orabrush product, and soon was put in touch with the buyer of dental products. She

### THE TWENTY-EIGHT-DOLLAR FACEBOOK AD THAT SET IT ALL OFF

*The Orabrush startup team was anxious to break through to the right buyer at Walmart, but how? Their solution was this twenty-eight-dollar ad targeted to Walmart headquarters, which resulted in a $1.47 million sale and ten-times jump in the valuation of the company, according to the company's CEO, Jeff Davis.*

asked, "Can you support an order for 737,000 units?" Davis replied, "Of course," and the company's standing immediately changed. At $1.47 million, the order itself represented an immediate 5.2 million percent ROI on the twenty-eight-dollar Facebook ad spend.

But the company's status also changed because it would now have product carried throughout the Walmart store network. Davis figures that single order multiplied the company's worth by a factor of ten, because other retailers and potential investors suddenly took the company far more seriously. Before long, Orabrush was available in thirty thousand stores in more than thirty countries in the Walmart, Target, Walgreens, CVS, Rite Aid, and Kroger chains.

And it was all set off by a twenty-eight-dollar ad run on Facebook for two days. At 5.2 million percent ROI from the order, plus an immediate 10X multiplier pushing the company's value from $2 million to $20 million, the Orabrush campaign is the new record holder for ROI from a Contact Marketing campaign—at 69,500,000 percent. One meeting truly can change everything.

**KEY TAKEAWAY:** This can have great application for Contact Marketers. Corporate buying is often done by committee, and without a clear picture of who the members are, it's difficult to move a sale forward. The story also confirms the effect mentioned in the previous chapter about targeting an entire headquarters with digital display ads. The Walmart executives perceived the Orabrush ad as a national campaign. It wasn't, but it had all the appearances of a much larger campaign, making the company seem much more impressive.

As Contact Marketers, we can use that effect to create the right environment for high-level connecting. This is not meant in a deceptive or misleading way, it's just the way people often perceive ads. When they see them in national news media or on big social media sites, the impression is always there. And it can help drive higher response to contact campaigns.

# LINKEDIN: BEST SOURCE FOR B2B LEADS

Facebook gives us interesting tools for reaching entire companies, but LinkedIn is the platform for reaching individual professional contacts. When you're targeting specific high-value business contacts, it's best to concentrate your efforts there.

A few facts: LinkedIn currently has over half a billion users. If it continues at the current rate, it'll reach a billion by 2025. It is the top channel for B2B content, but of the 590 million users, just three million post weekly content and only a million have published an article there. A massive 91 percent of marketing executives say LinkedIn is their best source of business content, while 45 percent of article readers are managers, directors, VPs, or C-level executives. Most telling, 80 percent of B2B leads come from LinkedIn versus 13 percent from Twitter and 7 percent from Facebook.[1]

> *You can think of LinkedIn as Contact Marketing's social media superhighway.*

You can think of LinkedIn as Contact Marketing's social media superhighway. The number of connections to be made there is staggering. Still, there are significant challenges.

When you're taking in thirty new contacts per day, it's impossible to remember who they are. If this is life on the social media freeway, the act of making a connection is like waving to someone as they speed past in the other direction. You'll wave, then move on to the next, and the next. Within sixty seconds, you won't remember any of them.

So, once you make those new connections, how do those new nodes in your network translate to business? Again, it's not as simple as it might seem.

---

[1] OmnicoreAgency.com, www.omnicoreagency.com/linkedin-statistics

Younger users who grew up on social media have an easy time making connections, but they aren't closing deals. Veteran sales reps, who are adept at creating relationships and closing deals, are finding time spent on social media to be more frustrating than helpful.

But there are people who are mining valuable business relationships and deals on LinkedIn. When you take a closer look, it's clear they are using strategies most of us are not. The most effective of those are based on either producing a constant stream of content drawing thousands of followers or using the platform to offer help to desired connections. In both cases, the trick is to transition quickly from the LinkedIn platform to other modes of communication.

Sending something tangible, like a card or letter through the mail, makes you stand out. Even sending an email or a simple direct message on LinkedIn helps.

Of course, there are strategies that don't work at all. Reps who request a connection and then immediately pitch are working against the grain of social media. When someone does that to me, I feel my trust has been violated and I immediately dump the connection. Others are sneaky and manipulative. You can usually spot those when they start a conversation with a generic request. Those, too, get dumped or blocked.

One recent connection asked if I would review his profile and offer feedback. I responded that I was not an expert in profile building and that he should ask someone else. When he replied, "That's OK, just take a look," I clearly smelled a ruse. The request made no sense, provided no value, and was an unwelcome, time-wasting distraction.

Some try another approach: "I'd like to talk with you to learn about your business and see how we might be able to help each other." Hmm. OK, so you know nothing about me, my business, or my book, but you want to get on the phone so I can tell you what I do and see what kind of opportunity that might produce? If you asked that of someone on your next elevator ride, what sort of response would you expect? "Uh, no thanks."

All these approaches are based in deception and manipulation. They usually stem from the misguided belief that "if I can connect with someone, even for a few seconds, I shouldn't waste the opportunity to pitch." Ironically, immediately pitching upon connecting is the surest way to waste any possible opportunity you might have. It's hardly the way any meaningful relationship should start.

## Producing Top-Notch Podcasts

To succeed on LinkedIn, you must find ways to stand out among half a billion members, all vying for attention but also looking for value. Podcaster James Carbary knows how to get people to respond and follow on LinkedIn. His philosophy on maximizing his LinkedIn potential is simple: Make a lot of content, post it daily, and generate mega-engagement.

The content he's referring to is his *B2B Growth* podcast. He releases one episode every day during the workweek. It's a consistent flow of thought leaders and marketing executives sharing their wisdom on what it takes to grow a business. James says it's important to produce daily content. High output might give the impression he's lax about quality, but as founder and CEO of Sweet Fish Media, Carbary offers full production services for podcasters, so the quality of each episode is top-notch.

But it's not enough to have a great stream of content; people also must be able to find it. For that, Carbary produced a unique innovation, tailored specifically to the LinkedIn platform.

Every weekday morning, as soon as an episode releases, James posts about it on LinkedIn. Each post comes in just under the 1,250-character limit, broken out into single-line paragraphs, written in a punchy style that gets readers excited. He does this to make the post intriguing, but also to maximize its readability on mobile devices. In the final line, he tells readers to find a link to the podcast in the first comment below the post.

That last line is critical to his strategy. He discovered a secret about the way LinkedIn boosts visibility of posts. The platform is built to detect organic engagement. When it sees a post getting ten or more comments in its first hour, the LinkedIn algorithm gives it more and more visibility across the platform.

> *To succeed on LinkedIn, you must find ways to stand out among half a billion members, all vying for attention but also looking for value.*

Placing the link to each podcast episode accomplishes two essential tasks. First, it keeps the original post clear of links. LinkedIn doesn't want embedded links taking traffic away from the platform, so when it spots those in a post, it becomes ineligible for a boost. Second, once one comment shows up, it starts a chain reaction leading to more comments, thus more viewership.

## CASE STUDY
# James Carbary's Daily Post Strategy

**BACKGROUND:** James Carbary's Sweet Fish Media produces podcasts, but Carbary himself uses his daily *B2B Growth* podcast to develop a following and to connect with his own high-value prospects as guests on his show. The podcast is both a content and Contact Marketing campaign that creates access to business leaders, authors, and company owners. These are Carbary's precise target audience for his podcast production services.

**CHALLENGES:** The biggest challenge of Carbary's podcast "campaign" is that it requires a deep commitment to producing a daily show, with unyielding consistency. The show has to happen every day, which means he must gather guests and conduct interviews every week. The unbending requirements of a daily show clash with the running of a business, particularly during travel. But Carbary says that, in many cases, a company's public relations department is happy to help make the necessary connections with target executives, as it is their job to find media opportunities.

**CAMPAIGN SPECIFICS:** Carbary's podcast is called *B2B Growth*. The name naturally attracts people in business who are responsible for producing growth. It runs daily, which means he is on the phone a lot, talking with company

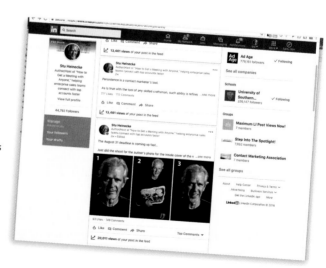

**DAILY POSTS GENERATE MEGA-ENGAGEMENT**

*The LinkedIn platform is designed to help users achieve business connections at scale. The system watches for posts of original content that gain quick engagement. Join an engagement group and it will help you get there faster. This is one of my recent posts, which generated twenty thousand views. Some attract hundreds of thousands, even millions, of views.*

leaders, thought leaders, and authors about getting their messages out and building audiences. It provides a natural segue to conversations about guests starting their own podcasts at the conclusion of each interview.

**RESULTS:** As a content strategy, Carbary's daily production of podcast interviews and posts on LinkedIn works superbly. *B2B Growth* is consistently ranked among the top twenty-five business podcasts on iTunes, averaging 1,500 downloads per episode and more than fifty thousand views of each post on LinkedIn. In the Contact Marketing role, the nine-hundred-plus episodes have also provided more than nine hundred sales conversations, making Sweet Fish now one of the largest producers of podcasts in the industry.

**KEY TAKEAWAY:** James Carbary's combined content and Contact Marketing strategy on LinkedIn has led to an amazing amount of engagement with marketing decision makers on the platform. It just works together. The more people he interviews, the more prospects he connects with. And the more shows he does, the more his reputation and reach grows, leading to more interviews, more connections, and more sales conversations.

# HABITS OF HIGHLY SUCCESSFUL LINKEDIN USERS

But what if that level of engagement could be multiplied? If even more people followed Carbary's daily posts and podcast interviews, wouldn't that also lead to more sales? Yes, it absolutely would. But *The 7 Habits of Highly Successful LinkedIn Users* author Dennis Brown says you don't even have to produce a podcast to make that happen.

Brown has an impressive LinkedIn story. He started three companies that were ranked among the Inc. 500 fastest-growing companies. One generated $80 million in revenue, another generated $20 million, and all of it came from LinkedIn connections. No marketing or advertising. Just LinkedIn connections.

If Carbary's daily content and boosted posts can help you reach a lot more of the right people on LinkedIn, Brown says you can amplify your reach even further. It's no coincidence the two know each other. In fact, it was through their collaboration that the engagement group strategy emerged. But Brown's version includes more options for gaining engagement.

## CASE STUDY
# Dennis Brown Model for Mega-Engagement

**BACKGROUND:** Dennis Brown has started three businesses that were all listed among the Inc. 500 fastest-growing companies. One produced $80 million in revenue; another produced $20 million. All three were built solely from connections made on LinkedIn.

**CHALLENGES:** Brown immediately realized that making connections on LinkedIn would propel his businesses quickly, but it all rested on his ability to reach people with his message. He discovered that automating his LinkedIn posts from Hootsuite depressed response. Ditto when he embedded video or art in the posts. Outbound links were especially damaging to his ability to virally spread his posts. His biggest challenge was finding the secret formula for consistent mega-engagement and converting resulting connections into new business.

**CAMPAIGN SPECIFICS:** After extensive trial and error, Brown focused on three steps for his engagement campaign. First was to create and post content that is "hyper focused and relevant to the audience," five days a week, and to keep it up with full consistency. His second step was to engage with influencers who were already attracting the audience he wanted. To do that, he followed them, engaged with their content, then followed up with personal connections on LinkedIn. The point was to tap into the followings of other thought leaders. And finally, Brown used engagement groups as multipliers.

> *Engagement groups are a collection of content creators who agree to amplify each other's posts with comments and Likes within minutes of the posting.*

Engagement groups are a collection of content creators who agree to amplify each other's posts with comments and Likes within minutes of the posting. Members are linked by ongoing direct messages that notify the group of each new post.

**RESULTS:** Brown's daily posts generate at least a hundred thousand views every week. Individual posts have produced as many as 230,000 views. LinkedIn tracks these results and compiles a dashboard, showing which companies, positions, and locations represent the largest engagement blocs. Aside from followers directly asking to connect, the dashboard results help Brown figure out which companies should be targeted for additional outreach. After all, they're clearly interested.

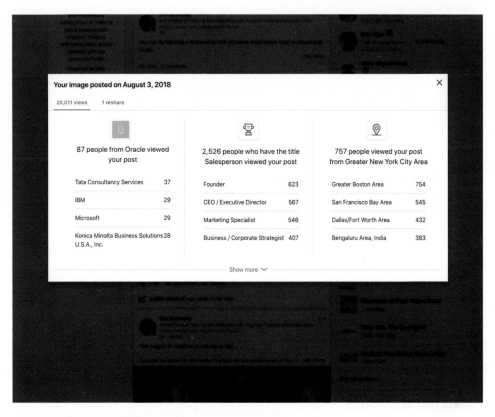

**THE FACE OF MEGA-ENGAGEMENT ON LINKEDIN**

*When a post gains traction, LinkedIn provides a direct window into what's happening with its engagement pane. In addition to total views, the three sections show the companies, types of executives, and cities that are generating the highest concentrations of interest in your message.*

**KEY TAKEAWAY:** Dennis Brown and James Carbary are collaborators, but they have distinct approaches to attaining mega-engagement. Carbary's method is based on releasing daily podcasts as the anchor feature of his LinkedIn posts. But that requires a serious amount of time and effort to secure interviews every single day of the week, every week, all year long.

Brown also has a podcast, but his interviews and episode posts are far less frequent. He still posts on LinkedIn daily, but his posts today are a mix of various kinds of content. Sometimes he lists his five favorite books and asks readers to list theirs. Other times he makes an assertion, lists the five most important factors, and asks if the audience agrees. He often lists and tags favorite influencers and asks readers for their favorites.

All these forms are designed to get people to respond and join in on the conversation. Tagging top influencers and authors often prompts their involvement, suddenly raising the quality of exchange and drawing in their followers.

As Brown says, "It's better to be the hunted than the hunter." Still, the prodigious level of engagement creates a measure of LinkedIn fame that easily allows him to reach out to virtually anyone and connect. Moreover, his reputation creates that reaction we're always striving for in our contact campaigns: "I love the way you think. Let's connect."

# USING LINKEDIN'S SALES NAVIGATOR

Brown's and Carbary's approaches are hybrids of content and Contact Marketing strategy. The focus is on generating a lot of engagement from a lot of people, with the worthwhile contacts self-selecting. But what if you have just a handful of top business contacts you already know you want to target?

Amanda Harkness suggests a rifle shot to Brown and Carbary's scattershot. She is like an assassin on LinkedIn, although there's nothing dangerous about her unless you happen to be a competitor. It is her sense of stealth, of patience, of doing her homework before making a move that expresses her true nature. If you're in her crosshairs, you will connect. And when you do, you'll be glad she reached out.

She says internet search makes it easy for buyers to get any information they want. Status sheets, data reports, and Gartner analytics all do a wonderful job informing market players, but their easy availability has made them ineffective tools for generating connections. Amanda's solution is to perform deep research into what the buyer is facing and how her company can help.

Her tools are LinkedIn Sales Navigator and information found on the target company's website. Navigator allows her to see what the prospects are liking and sharing on the LinkedIn platform. She can sometimes find information through the prospect's posts. She once found out about a prospect's dog because he wrote about it, and used that to open a conversation about their dogs, which led to a conversation about doing business. With Deep personalization, knowing about a target contact's dog, what they're posting, and watching what they're responding to on social media are precisely the kinds of insights that can create immediate personal connections.

On the company's site, she focuses on press releases. She might gather quotes from the CEO, saying something about initiatives the company has planned or in action. She looks for quotes from others in the target's industry that are relevant to what she wants to address for the buyer. She builds a dossier, a case for the two companies doing business together. And then she makes her move.

## CASE STUDY
# Sharpshooting on LinkedIn Navigator

**BACKGROUND:** Amanda Harkness is responsible for new business acquisition for Kony, an award-winning provider of mobile application development platform services. The company competes with industry giants.

**CHALLENGES:** The company's competitors include IBM, Salesforce, Adobe, Microsoft, SAP, and Oracle. Even though Gartner research places Kony in its Magic Quadrant for Mobile App Development Platforms, the company faces a steep uphill push against its better-known rivals. Going to market without the same level of brand awareness makes it tough to break through to top accounts.

**CAMPAIGN SPECIFICS:** Harkness uses a multimodal approach to her outreach efforts that starts first with background intel. She finds it particularly useful to archive recent quotes from a targeted company's CEO. LinkedIn Navigator (LinkedIn's sales tool that assists sales teams to build and nurture relationships on the network) is used extensively to monitor what the target contact is saying and doing and what their interests are.

Her process progresses with an email, then a phone call, then messaging through Navigator. All messaging revolves around what she has discovered about the target executive and company and how her company can help.

When she encounters objections, the previously gathered quotes from the CEO are used in sharpshooter fashion. Her responses always start, "But wait, your CEO has said . . ."

**RESULTS:** Harkness finds that her use of LinkedIn and Navigator give her a strong platform to stay in touch, monitor relevant activity, and ultimately break through. "Persistence is also a big part of this," she explains, "but you have to be creative with it. I once had to email a prospect forty times before she finally responded." Along the way, she was able to monitor the prospect for activity on Navigator.

**KEY TAKEAWAY:** Harkness not only uses LinkedIn and Navigator to take aim at prospects through their posts, she uses Navigator for alerts when they change jobs or receive a promotion. "The best source of meetings," she says, "is to find that person who was just promoted."

Her results come from being patient and thorough before ever reaching out. But they also come from a mindset that is a necessary ingredient for success in sales and in business. She starts with the conviction that she *will* connect, no matter what it takes.

# A SUPERHERO'S SUPER WEB OF CONNECTIONS

If Amanda Harkness is an assassin on LinkedIn, Nicolé Royer is Wonder Woman. Or maybe Spider-Woman. As with any superhero, Royer has her own specialized supernatural powers, spinning a web of deep connections and turning those into valuable new business and referrals. In other words, she's doing what a lot of us would like to be doing with our time spent on LinkedIn: making it productive.

Royer's underlying approach is surprisingly simple. She just wants to make meaningful connections. That doesn't necessarily mean selling anything, but it always involves getting to know the other person on a deeply human level. "Pretend like you're talking to a real person," she advises. "You wouldn't just come at them without introducing yourself and try to sell your product or service to them. You don't know them."

She says she likes making connections more than she likes selling, but that doesn't get in the way of generating business. In fact, quite the opposite. When she speaks to her LinkedIn connections, she's always looking for ways to facilitate solutions, while touching upon their interests and the events in their lives. The result is that she's helping a lot of people in ways that may never involve business, but surprisingly, they are often her richest source of referrals.

## CASE STUDY
## Nicolé Royer Creates Deep Web on LinkedIn

**BACKGROUND:** Nicolé Royer is a growth consultant, but really, she says, she's in the "people" business. Her livelihood depends upon having a robust network of company leaders, who either become direct clients or powerful referral sources.

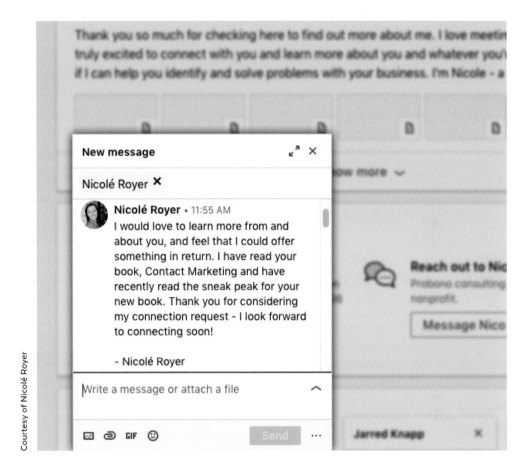

Courtesy of Nicolé Royer

### WEAPONIZING RELEVANCE AND ENGAGEMENT

*Nicolé Royer doesn't just ask you to connect on LinkedIn, she asks you to engage. She uses Deep personalization to prepare relevant messages and quickly digs into questions about how she can help. It's as if she already knows you, as shown in her message here when we first connected.*

**CHALLENGES:** Royer understands the law of reciprocity and she knows good things take time to build. She has discovered that reaching out to offer targeted assistance can open important doors, which has become the cornerstone of her LinkedIn contact strategy. Her biggest challenge is growing her network and reaping returns quickly.

**CAMPAIGN SPECIFICS:** Essentially, Royer's strategy could be likened to spinning a big, sticky web. She identifies target executives and thought leaders based on where they fit within her plan. Each contact is placed in her CRM (customer-relationship management) system and tracked. She then reaches out and asks three questions of each prospect: 1) Who is your ideal client? 2) What do you like to do for fun? and 3) What is your biggest problem? All her outreach efforts trace back to their answers to those questions.

That gives her plenty of reasons for sending a quick email with an article about something they'll find interesting. And nearly all her communication in those moments occurs outside the LinkedIn platform. "I step outside of LinkedIn as often as I can with my connections," she says, often sending as many as a hundred handwritten notes per month.

The notes get straight to the point because she still needs to bring the conversation around to talking business. To accomplish the transition, she plants nuggets of information during their correspondence, while in the handwritten notes, the tone changes to "Hey, I have an idea for you, can we chat about it?"

**RESULTS:** Royer's approach is unique in that it is based on cultivating relationships and in paying attention and adding value. Since she doesn't approach each interaction as a do-or-die sales situation, the interactions are relaxed and the person on the other end is grateful for her help. It doesn't go unrecognized that she is being selfless in offering solutions and suggestions that may never lead to doing business together.

As a result, Royer says she gets more business than she ever thought possible for her growth-strategy consulting and training practice. Her LinkedIn connections refer more deals than she can handle, and her business is thriving. It is a winning strategy that is organized, accountable, and flexible, all underpinned by her customer-relationship management program. This is the way to turn LinkedIn activity into productive activity.

**KEY TAKEAWAY:** So many of us are spending time on LinkedIn, wondering if it's justifiable. Sales management is wondering how to better monetize the team's use of LinkedIn or any social media. If it doesn't lead to results, then maybe it's better doing it the old way.

Royer's approach shows us it's not only possible to be profitable through LinkedIn; it's imperative that we put this unprecedented resource to work in our careers and for our businesses. Then give and be patient.

While it may be a soft approach, all the strategies in this chapter—really, the crux of Contact Marketing—are about making personal connections and eventually getting what we want. We are Contact Marketers, we're apex hunters.

But the hunt is nuanced and also involves enticing others to us; on LinkedIn we can't just search. We must also be found. We can find people we want to connect with through research, but by using the dynamism of LinkedIn, our strategy must also make us visible to the right people.

## TACTICAL EXAMPLE
# Making Your LinkedIn Profile Stand Out

**TACTIC:** Give your LinkedIn profile a makeover so it gets—and deserves—attention.

**BACKGROUND:** LinkedIn is a social media platform but also a search engine by professionals for professionals. At some point during your contact process, it is highly likely target executives will visit your profile to understand who you are and whether they should invest the effort to connect. Therefore, your profile should be optimized to express who you are and the value you can deliver.

**CHALLENGES:** Many of the people who view your profile are not looking for you specifically, they're looking for someone *like* you. Someone who solves the problems you do, perhaps someone with similar achievements or skills similar to your own. If they don't know you, your profile must grab their attention within seconds and create fascination and a desire to go further. Since most profiles amount to little more than a copy-and-pasted résumé, they can easily turn visitors off. "Not everyone is looking for new hires," notes LinkedIn branding specialist Donna Serdula. "Many are on LinkedIn to connect with partners, allies, and solution providers."

Your LinkedIn profile is a form of campaign. Some viewers may find it in a search, others will visit to get a sense of who you are. In both instances, each profile view can be thought of as a result of the campaign. If someone asks to connect or follows you, those are even stronger responses. Serdula advises engaging those visitors quickly. "When you get notification someone has visited your profile," she explains, "they're raising their hand. They're inviting further contact."

> *Your profile should be optimized to express who you are and the value you can deliver.*

**CAMPAIGN SPECIFICS:** According to Serdula, the ideal LinkedIn profile should tell the story of who you are and how you can help. It should also be written with a target audience in mind and strategically built around vital keywords. Just like SEO, the object is to show up at the top of the search on LinkedIn, clearly positioning yourself as someone they'll want to seek advice from and work with. Profile pictures must be clear, crisp, well lit, and professional. These are not glamour modeling headshots, they are your digital first impression. Dress and carry yourself as you would if meeting an important contact in person.

**BEFORE**

**AFTER**

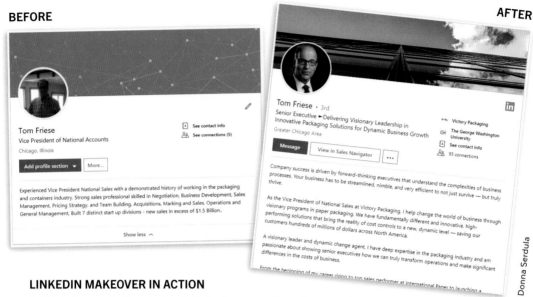

Donna Serdula

## LINKEDIN MAKEOVER IN ACTION

*In this before-and-after photo set, LinkedIn personal branding expert
Donna Serdula shows essential steps for creating a more inviting and invigorating profile page.
She says profile pages are where people come to check you out. It is your digital introduction. They
don't want to see your résumé, they want to meet you.*

**WHY IT'S NEEDED:** Imagine heading to a meeting with someone who can
   change the scale of your career, your life. You have your facts together, you've
   taken time to research their needs and initiatives. You have it nailed. Except for
   one thing. Your clothes haven't been washed for days. You haven't showered for
   a week. How do you suppose your appearance might affect the outcome of the
   meeting? Would the contact feel like they can trust their budget to you? Would
   you have any credibility at all in the contact's mind?

   Your LinkedIn profile is just as important. It tells people who you are—not by
   what you say, but by how you've implemented your brand. And they do check.
   It's probably the first place they look to see if you're legit. This is not a place to
   dump your résumé and call it done. They want a narrative that says you are one
   of the best at what you do and that you can expertly handle their challenges.

**WHAT TO KEEP IN MIND:** If you plan to use any concepts within this book, you
   need to have your profile in order. If you can't do it alone, get help.

# PUTTING IT ALL TOGETHER

We've just taken a very brief look at social media through a very narrow lens. We're only looking at how it can help us get top-level meetings. Social media is nearly as broad as the whole of our combined daily human existence, in which millions of people expose their fascinations, toxic politics, favorite animal tricks, and latest meals. It is a messy place.

But social media also gives us powerful tools to connect, be found, and to shape others' impressions of us and our enterprises. The tools center around posts, ads, and profiles, but there is also a culture to learn and observe. Social media is not the place to make a pitch, at least not in the traditional sense.

This is the place to introduce yourself through your thinking and leadership. The more you post and the more exposure it earns, the more followers you will attract. Some will become sales opportunities, but it is also in that intangible whirl of activity and influence that your own targeted contacts will get a sense of you.

Social media is where most connections take place today. It is part of the fabric of modern business life, and certainly of selling. If you're not on social media, get there now. If you are, you probably recognize the need to adopt new strategies to optimize your efforts.

LinkedIn is where you go to make professional connections. Surprisingly, Facebook and Instagram, while focused on personal relationships, are also good places to connect with professionals on a friend-to-friend level. Twitter is a place to blast thoughts and content to large audiences. Pinterest and Instagram are also great platforms to connect on a visual level, perhaps to share a portfolio of your work. But each platform requires a lot of daily attention to build and keep followings. Decide how much time you're willing to spend on a daily basis and stick to it. As a Contact Marketer, LinkedIn is the first place to concentrate your efforts.

Obviously, it makes sense to maximize the effectiveness of your social presence. As James Carbary and Dennis Brown demonstrate, there are ways to multiply that presence geometrically, by posting focused, thoughtful content daily and using engagement groups to immediately amplify your reach.

But social platforms are not posting boards; they are living, breathing communities. Many users are on throughout the day. They're already engaged. Nicolé

Royer and Amanda Harkness have shared with us how that constant presence can result in opening important doors with prospects. Their message is to engage on a human level and to quickly take the conversation offline. Making simple connections on LinkedIn alone has become an insignificant, unmemorable act. As Contact Marketers, we must create ways to make the most important connections far more significant and memorable with fresh content and deeper, off-platform engagement.

Donna Serdula reminds us we have personal brands within social media that are defined by our posts of original content and also by our profiles. An ideal profile opens doors and attracts new business, while a poorly executed one can block any attempt you make to connect with top accounts. Your LinkedIn profile is your digital handshake, your first impression. It is essential that you make it a good one. Your success as a Contact Marketer depends on it.

# Critical Next Steps

**OBJECTIVE:** Make your social media time, particularly on LinkedIn, productive.

### Step 1. Put LinkedIn first.

Facebook, Instagram, Twitter, and other social media platforms are great, particularly for certain audiences and missions. But if you sell to other businesses and if your needs revolve around connecting with other professionals, LinkedIn must become your primary focus for Contact Marketing uses of social media. Make sure your presence there is powerful, active, and optimized. Get your profile in shape, remembering it is your digital introduction, not a laundry list of everything you've ever done. Answer the question all visitors have: "Who are you and what can you do for me?"

### Step 2. Go beyond the platform.

Connecting on social media is so common, so frequent that it is no longer a significant interaction. You may have connected with someone, even had conversation, but it's not enough. They still don't know you and have formed no intention yet to do business. The key is to move significant connections off the platform. Take a call, meet for coffee, do an interview. Or send something. Otherwise, the connection will be meaningless.

### Step 3. Review often.

Social media can quickly become a burdensome waste of time. Evaluate the return on your efforts constantly and make adjustments. Otherwise, it can be like blowing on a pinwheel—a lot of flashy motion but zero movement toward your goals.

# POINTS TO REMEMBER

✔ Social media is a broad landscape, where connections can easily be made.

✔ LinkedIn and, to a lesser degree, Facebook, Twitter, and Instagram are the platforms to make professional connections.

✔ LinkedIn is like a search engine for professionals seeking to connect with other professionals.

✔ While social media can be a bonanza for making business connections, it is not the place to pitch.

✔ LinkedIn can be used as a springboard to create enormous reach and credibility as a thought leader, thereby positioning you as someone important to have as a connection.

✔ Producing daily content places you in the top 0.2 percent of members as a thought leadership source.

✔ Engagement groups can multiply reach by activating LinkedIn's mechanism for promoting posts to more members.

✔ Your profile is your digital handshake. It is a campaign that must be optimized to allow people to find you and decide you're someone of merit, someone worthy of further investment.

✔ Retargeting, geofencing, and social media ads help to open doors to important contacts, while creating a positive brand impression and familiarity.

✔ The culture of social media is based on mutual respect and selfless giving. Heeding that culture will open doors to important contacts.

✔ Immediately pitching after establishing a new connection is the surest way to get blocked. Engage, explore, and take the conversation off-platform. *Earn the right to pitch.*

# CHAPTER 11

# VIDEO

I believe video is the third level of literacy in modern life. The first is reading and writing. The second is digital literacy, being comfortable and capable with computers, smartphones, social media, and the core programs that magnify our productivity. Video is how we communicate with the world at large, how we create connections, how we humanize ourselves to others at scale.

Naturally, video has become a key tool for Contact Marketers in their outreach to critically important contacts. Also, quite naturally, video literacy is strongest among millennials, who have stepped into the workforce with considerable skills and great comfort with the medium. But really, video is for everyone. If you don't know how to use it, by all means, jump in and learn. It is one of the most important skills a Contact Marketer can have in the quest for scale-changing connections.

Throughout the practice of Contact Marketing, we are building experiences that demonstrate our ability to take on a challenge and deal with it in a particularly thoughtful way. We're showing the quality of our thinking and the thoroughness of our execution. We're showing prospects what it would be like to work with us and the kinds of results they can expect from that collaboration.

Video is the perfect platform to express all that and more. We can present a short movie, communicating everything a target contact needs to know about us, while addressing a critical issue in their workplace.

The formality or informality of the composition, the production values, the enhancements of music, animations, and other cues tell the potential contacts everything they need to know about your ability to conceive and execute an audacious plan.

The effective use of video in Contact Marketing seems to follow two courses. The video succeeds either from the creativity expressed within or the technology used to deliver it. Sometimes it's both.

In *How to Get a Meeting with Anyone*, I shared the story of one company's launch campaign that involved personalized videos delivered on iPads to just thirty high-value contacts. The campaign worked because the videos were personalized and well produced but also because of the technology used for delivery (the iPad had just been released and was still a novelty).

In the stories that follow, we'll take a look at examples of creative execution and delivery technologies used to create impact in contact outreach campaigns. Vidyard enables delivery of personalized videos embedded within emails. It's a platform custom-made for Contact Marketers, with real-time metrics showing who's watching the videos and how many times they've watched, allowing users to identify and connect with the most responsive recipients right away.

> " *Video is how we communicate with the world at large, how we create connections, how we humanize ourselves to others at scale.* "

If you want to deliver your videos in physical form, there are fantastic new formats for doing that. And they don't come close to the cost of an iPad. They can be mailed, sent by overnight courier, some even incorporate elements of jewel boxing discussed in chapter five.

Briefly delving into YouTube will showcase a variety of creative video styles. Some are stark and simple, shot on a smartphone in selfie fashion, while others are more stylized; some are crazy; others are scripted and care-fully produced. Some are professional; others are not. For Contact Marketing purposes, personality and the communication of relevant value in video are what opens doors. And there are no two better examples than Ryan O'Hara and Alex Perkins, who generate appointments using truly creative approaches to video.

Whether or not you're already comfortable creating and using video, the following stories will surely add to your literacy in this important mode of communication—and help you get meetings.

# PERSONALIZED VIDEOS IN EMAIL

Adding video to your Contact Marketing tool kit can be quite simple. One suggestion: Set up a free account on Vidyard and use the camera on your computer or mobile device to start sending personalized videos immediately. Or go all the way with an enterprise-level membership.

That's how you'll be able to record, upload, sequence clips, and embed them in email. It sounds simple enough, but before Vidyard appeared, there was no way to insert a video into the body of an email. Video files are too large to attach to an email, so the only way to include one was with a text link to YouTube or Vimeo—not very handy, and certainly not impressive.

The Vidyard platform is much more than a video-embedding platform, though. It is also a contact intelligence node like DocSend in chapter eight, allowing users to view metrics on video views, length of views, and the identity of each viewer. If the video is forwarded, the sender will see who's watching.

As Contact Marketers, we understand the value of real-time contact intel. It allows us to see who is engaging and what has their attention. It also allows us to discover who plays a role in purchase decisions, giving us an entirely unfair advantage over our competitors.

With the technical abilities to record on the spot and watch the metrics add up, it might seem like Vidyard is simply a platform, but it is also a vibrant, artistic movement. Vidyard understands that videos must be compelling or they won't create impact. As a Contact Marketing tool, that impact is all about creating a human-to-human connection.

To reinforce its commitment to video excellence, Vidyard hosts two annual competitions, the Video in Business Awards (www.vidyard.com/video-in-business-awards) and the Fast Forward virtual summit (www.vidyard.com/fast-forward) every year in October/November, honoring the best videos in outreach, customer service, and retention, and sharing best practices and educational sessions.

## A Video Message for You

Personalization is key to creating a human-to-human connection with an emailed video. Tyler Lessard, Vidyard's VP of marketing, says even the subject line "A video message for you" changes the impact of the email. "Of course people are going to open it," he says, adding, "and if they see the video is actually part of the personal correspondence, they'll fully engage." Most videos on the platform start with the sender smiling into the camera, with the recipient's name handwritten across a whiteboard in the shot.

Lessard says the messaging should always be personal. "Be yourself, don't try to be a news personality," he advises, "and make sure your video includes strong messaging, is customer-centric, and highlights value." He says users of the platform are seeing three to five times greater open rates, and when calls are booked with the video element, there is a higher attendance rate as well.

## CASE STUDY
# Video Embedded in Email Greatly Boosts Results

**BACKGROUND:** Lauren Wadsworth was a recent SDR hire for Dynamic Signal, a company providing a mobile-device communications platform for companies to address their employees.

**CHALLENGES:** In her first few months with the company, Wadsworth struggled to meet her quota. She worked hard and by her third month had booked twenty-six meetings—twice her team's average—but her conversions were still low. Adding to the pressure, 50 percent of her prospects either canceled or

**VIDYARD VIDEO-IN-EMAIL PLATFORM**

*If email is the preferred method for delivering video content, services like Vidyard are the solution. The platform enables users to embed personalized videos that include call-to-action screens and generate real-time metrics for viewership and engagement.*

missed their initial call. She was frustrated and felt burned out, and wondered if she'd have to work twelve-hour days all week long.

**CAMPAIGN SPECIFICS:** Regrouping, Lauren noticed her boss's reaction to an email containing a video. She decided to give that a test, using Go, Vidyard's free embedded-video-in-email service. To start, she sent fifty-five personalized videos to prospects, each featuring the recipient's name written on a whiteboard as the start screen.

**RESULTS:** Wadsworth's results immediately changed. The campaign generated a 37.5 percent response rate and 12.75 percent meeting rate, versus the company's average 1 percent and 2 percent call-to-meeting and email-to-meeting conversion rates. She noticed that while her response rates had suddenly increased, something else was happening: Her prospects were keeping their appointments; the cancel rate dropped from 58 percent to 7 percent. News of Wadsworth's success spread quickly, and soon her entire team was using the

**EMBEDDED VIDEO STATS IN REAL TIME**

*The Vidyard platform includes dashboard reports that show real-time stats for viewership and engagement with videos embedded in email messages. These enable users to connect with target contacts while they're watching the messages.*

Courtesy of Vidyard

Vidyard service. In their first month after making the switch, the team booked more meetings with vice presidents and C-level executives than it had in the previous year combined.

**KEY TAKEAWAY:** Wadsworth's story helps us see how valuable video-in-email can be. Her story combines elements of personalization with the magical effect of video to take the viewer anywhere in the world, to connect with the sender as though they've actually just met. When Wadsworth conducts her meetings, Vidyard also gives her key intelligence to know who has already viewed videos, how many times they were viewed, and what was watched. It's like a window into the buying committees' minds.

---

## VARIATION

I also use Vidyard in my content marketing tech stack. I find it fascinating and highly useful to monitor what's happening with the videos once they're sent. I use the higher level of membership to run clips in a seamless sequence in my emails. It starts with a personalized clip of me on the beach (but not in a bathing suit), holding a whiteboard personalized with the recipient's name. It then jumps to a professionally shot and edited segment about the weekend strategy sessions I offer on the island where I live. The final scene is a call-to-action slide of my book with a link to arrange a call on my calendar.

The effect of all this is dramatic. The mental image of spending the weekend brainstorming in the little seaside village of Langley, Washington, is priceless. And only video allows me to quickly introduce the concept in a way that makes viewers feel like they're already there.

---

## Adjusting to a Selfie World

As a nonmillennial, I have a bit of a hang-up about video. Growing up with television, I'm locked into a more formal view of presenting on camera. You should be impeccably dressed, not a hair out of place. You should have camera makeup on to look your best under the bright lights. Everything should be scripted and perfect.

Millennials, however, view the camera in an entirely different way. They're relaxed, more authentic, more free to express themselves. They simply turn on the camera and start talking. If there are scenes to be shot and edited, no problem. They've done it all their lives. They know how to be cool under the pressure of the camera because they don't even feel any pressure.

When Bizible enterprise business-development rep Alex Perkins points the camera his way, a guitar or ukulele is always close at hand. It might seem strange to quote Marilyn Manson in a book about business, but I will, because he truly has it right: "Music is the strongest form of magic."

It's a good way to describe what happens when Perkins sends one of his videos in an email. Recorded on the spot, in front of his computer in the office, he sings a custom-written song into the camera and sends it in an email from his Vidyard account.

"I write songs that are pretty much, 'Hey so-and-so at such-and-such company, let's meet up and talk about measuring ROI of your marketing activities,'" he explains. "And the effect has been like magic."

Perkins started using his singing videos when he first joined Bizible. He knew the challenges—B2B marketing is oversaturated with marketing tech sales reps trying to get through. He knew that cold-calling probably wouldn't help him break through, and that he needed to do something different to stand out. So he thought, "Why not use something I enjoy doing outside of work—singing and making videos?" And it worked.

## CASE STUDY
## Alex Perkins's Singing Videos

**BACKGROUND:** When Alex Perkins arrived as a new sales development rep at his new employer, Bizible, he knew he faced a massive struggle. In the B2B

Courtesy of Alex Perkins

**ALEX PERKINS SERENADES PROSPECTS IN VIDEOS**

*When Alex Perkins records personalized videos for his prospects, he puts his personality on full display. Alex likes to sing, so naturally his outreach efforts involve original songs about each recipient.*

space, buyers are inundated with requests for contact by sales reps. To succeed, he would have to find a way to stand out.

**CHALLENGES:** As a new sales rep, Perkins had nothing to differentiate himself, but he recently became aware of new techniques and strategies that might help. The challenge was to take stock of his own unique talents and attributes and channel those into a contact campaign no one else could duplicate.

**CAMPAIGN SPECIFICS:** Perkins's focus quickly went to his love of singing and music videos. Combining the two with the Vidyard platform, and with ukulele in hand, he started singing into the camera. Each song was personalized to each recipient with lyrics addressing their particular situation set to well-known melodies.

**RESULTS:** He immediately started breaking through. And companies started offering jobs, if Perkins ever cared to move on from Bizible. Prospects reached out to say how much they enjoyed his unique approach. One VP, who was coming to Seattle, told Perkins, "Remember you sent me this video? Let's hang out when I'm in town. I want to learn from you."

The videos produced a lot of meetings for the company's sales team, but Perkins says there are a few limitations. Singing videos seem to work best with companies that have fewer than five hundred employees, where it produces a 35 percent to 40 percent meeting rate.

**KEY TAKEAWAY:** I find song videos are a lot like cartoons. They express a point in such a way that the recipient is thrilled to take in the message. They giggle. They smile. They let you in. Music and humor are both powerful tools to create connections with the people we most want to connect with. They humanize us.

Perkins's use of his own qualities and talents is also brilliant. He isn't the world's best singer, but he doesn't need to be. He just needs to be himself and get it on video. And the marvelous thing about that? It's the same thing we can all do in our own videos. We don't need musical instruments. We just need to take our own self-inventory and put ourselves into our video messages.

In honing his process, Perkins has found it helps to focus the songs on the account rather than the recipient. The result is even more pass-along within target companies. He also finds it useful to produce song videos to address special circumstances—for instance, when someone hasn't returned his calls, or when he wants to send a very special thank-you message.

# VIDEO-IN-A-BOX

Putting your heart and soul into your videos makes sense, but can we put our videos into something other than email? Thanks to thin-screen micro-displays and innovations from companies like UVIAUS, Structural Graphics, and others, the answer is yes.

You could produce a theme box around a movie and send the DVD with a slim bag of microwave popcorn, but that's not what is meant by the term "video-in-a-box." Here, we're talking about a beautiful enclosure that features a built-in screen, usually on the lower surface of the top lid, set to play the moment the box is opened. This creates all sorts of possibilities for Contact Marketers.

The box can be almost any size or shape (as long as it accommodates the screen's quarter-inch thickness). They can be made of wood, metal, Styrofoam, even carbon fiber, but they're usually made of paper-wrapped cardboard, the kind of box that fine gifts are presented in.

When video becomes part of the packaging, the dynamic changes. The video becomes the narrator of the piece, the equivalent of a letter, but one that can take the viewer anywhere in the world, or beyond, to show—rather than describe—virtually anything. Perhaps it's a parade of customers giving their testimonials. That's a powerful way to open a box, and we haven't even filled it yet with the goods, the visual metaphors, gifts, and proposed agendas that will open doors.

UVIAUS founder and president Jaycen Thorgeirson figures, "If a picture is worth a thousand words, one minute of video is the equivalent of 1.8 million words—it gives you the ability to connect and inspire." While UVIAUS works with sales teams to connect with their most valuable accounts, it also helps brands connect with top social media influencers. Thorgeirson points out that "unboxing" videos are one of the most popular genres on YouTube. "Opening the box creates a shareable moment," he says, which is useful for any Contact Marketing mission.

Video-in-a-box is both a gift box that delivers a viral message and a digital medium that delivers a tangible experience. It is a rare combination of digital and physical that is sure to stand out and open doors.

## CASE STUDY
# Speaking Up

**BACKGROUND:** When C-Suite Network chairman and best-selling author Jeffrey Hayzlett wants to drum up new speaking engagements, he has challenges like the rest of us. The people most likely to hire Hayzlett to speak are meeting planners, heads of sales, and company presidents—and they're all hard to meet.

**CHALLENGES:** Speaking is a tough market and there is a limited demand for big-buck speaking engagements. As a potential speaker, Hayzlett competes with some of the best-known people on the planet—best-selling authors, television and film actors, world-record setters, even ex-presidents, to get onstage. Standing out among these people is an extreme challenge.

Adding to the difficulty, bookers are already familiar with many of the competitors Hayzlett faces. They already have a sense of who these speakers are, what they deliver, and how the audience will react. To break through, at minimum, Hayzlett must demonstrate his speaking ability and expertise within seconds. A simple letter with a brochure won't even the field.

**CAMPAIGN SPECIFICS:** Hayzlett uses a video-in-a-box campaign designed and produced by UVIAUS. The jet-black box features a video screen inside the top lid, which automatically plays when the box is opened. The video is both a

## VIDEO-IN-A-BOX DELIVERS STORY AND ELEMENTS

*It's hard to beat the combination of jewel boxing, video, and visual metaphor elements in this powerful contact piece. The video is triggered to play when the box is opened, while the printed elements within help tell the marketer's story.*

greeting and a sample of Hayzlett's speaking, onstage, before an audience, and on his proposed topic.

Inside the box is a signed copy of Hayzlett's latest book, *Think Big, Act Bigger*. The campaign is rather stark, with just two components: the video box and the book within. I think this is smart. It shows respect for the recipient's time and for their position of power. Get in, get on with the message, and get out.

**RESULTS:** The campaign produces a "more than 50 percent contact rate," Hayzlett reports, along with a constant shower of compliments. "Recipients keep these on their desks," he says, "and they stay there for years. They don't let go of them."

**KEY TAKEAWAY:** Hayzlett says he gets a lot of speaking gigs from the campaign, adding, "If you're a speaker, why not send a video?" The combination of a quick sampling of his speaking prowess and best-selling book to explain his thesis tell meeting officials all they need to know. This type of approach makes sense for anyone in a performance-based line of work.

# HOW TO MAKE A DESKTOP VIDEO
Create personalized videos from your PC

If you're using a platform like Vidyard to produce and send personalized videos as part of your outreach program, just connecting via Zoom or Skype for a video conference, or even appearing as a featured speaker on a webinar, producing professional-looking videos can greatly enhance your personal presentation.

> **WHAT YOU'LL NEED:** Desktop or laptop PC/Mac with in-monitor camera, external mic, three LED tripod-mounted videography lights with color temperature adjustment, and tracing paper.

Hollywood producer Greg Strom says most amateur video suffers from improper lighting and camera positioning. If you are a Hollywood professional yourself, you already know how to create fine-looking footage. For the rest of us, we could use a little help.

Strom says the best, most flattering angle for a desktop camera shoot is two to three feet away, positioned slightly lower than eye level. "This is the angle that produces the most natural image of your face," he explains, "about like what you see when you look in the mirror."

Another source of unsatisfactory video images stems from improper lighting. If you are shooting in an office or home study, the background might include a few windows or other light sources. These will make you appear as a darkened silhouette, which is hardly how you want to be seen on-screen.

To correct this, Strom advises placing one light facing toward you from a slight distance behind your camera, a bit above eye level. But you also don't want your background to disappear into darkness. The solution is to place two other lights out of frame, shining on the background behind you from both sides.

Even if you have a bright window directly behind you, you can light the rest of the structure and elements around it to create a natural scene, perhaps with trees showing through the window, blue sky, and so on. The extra illumination from the two background lights will allow you to balance it all for a beautiful, professional-looking scene.

You'll want to experiment before going live. Try using tracing paper overlays (with LED lights only) and adjusting lighting levels and temperatures to soften lighting patterns for the most natural look for you and your background. You'll be shooting like a pro in no time.

**1.** Place a small light behind the camera, slightly higher than eye level, to light your face. Position camera just below eye level for the most flattering angle.

**2.** Place larger lights out of frame to light the background. Adjust lighting levels and temperature for desired skin tone and setting. Lighting the background creates a more natural look.

**3.** Experiment with placement of folded tracing paper to diffuse light for a more natural look all around.

# VIDEO IN PRINT

In chapter five we examined jewel boxing, wrapping a gift or visual metaphor in a package that magnifies the effect of the item within. A box with an embedded video screen would certainly get my attention. If it's personalized to me, all the better.

When we send physical campaign devices, we're always compelled to include some sort of explanation of who we are and why we're reaching out. Handwritten notes are wonderful, but I have to wonder, could a video create an even stronger connection?

If video is to be an element of a physical package, the screen doesn't have to be part of the box, either. A similar micro–video screen can be a separate element in the box and have the same effect. That brings us to video-in-print.

In the old days, sending a video was accomplished by dropping a large, bulky cassette into a padded envelope, depositing it in the mail, and hoping it was in a format the recipient could play.

**COLOR AND LIGHT**

*Video in print is still in its infancy. Today's embedded video screens are bulky, but imagine the unbeatable effect of a seamless e-paper contact device that combines the beauty of print and the motion of video, like those seen in the movie* Minority Report.

One meeting can change everything.

RedPaperPlane.com (template); iStockPhoto (interior image)

Video-in-print is several generations beyond all this. These are dimensional pieces that open like brochures and incorporate thin-display technology to pack a self-contained video screen within the presentation.

The effect is quite different from anything else in print. The action of opening the piece triggers the video to play on its own, like a photograph in the brochure that incorporates sound, music, and action. Structural Graphics president Ethan Goller says, "Video causes more reaction than any other medium," which is a bit of a surprise, since his company is famous for producing astonishing 3-D paper sculptures, opening breathtaking worlds that burst forth from magazines and cards.

But that background has made Goller's team particularly adept at combining print and video into extraordinary new forms. One such campaign was produced with agency Hudson Rouge for Lincoln Motors, featuring an impressive triple-black corrugated box with a video-in-print brochure on a soon-to-be-released new model.

## CASE STUDY
# Lincoln Motors's Video-in-Print Campaign

**BACKGROUND:** Lincoln Motors knew that, on average, their owners shopped for new cars every 3.8 years. Agency Hudson Rouge was tapped to produce a contact campaign to reach their most loyal customers whose current vehicles were approaching that critical trigger point, to introduce the new model.

**CHALLENGES:** Since the buyers' identities and last purchase dates were already in the company's database, the real challenge was producing a device that would impress this most important audience. The contact piece had to convey a sense the recipient was an insider, part of a very select group who got to see the new model before anyone else. Ideally, the campaign would cause Lincoln's most loyal customers to line up to buy when it launched.

**CAMPAIGN SPECIFICS:** The campaign took shape as a dimensional mailer encased in a rich triple-black corrugated cardboard enclosure and mailed to approximately twenty-three thousand loyal customers. A zipper pull opened the box to reveal the video brochure within. Opening the lid activated the video player, which showed dramatic footage of the new flagship model running through its paces on a beautifully scenic road. Also inside was a letter explaining how special each recipient was to be able to place an order before the public even knew the car existed.

**RESULTS:** Loyal Lincoln buyers were certainly impressed by the presentation and their special opportunity to "get in first." As a result, nearly two-thirds of all preorders for the car came from the mailing. The US Postal Service was also impressed and featured the campaign in its "Irresistible Mail" hall of fame for the best marketing efforts sent through the mail every year, edging out efforts from Porsche and BMW.

Lincoln Motors's use of video-in-print is interesting from a Contact Marketing standpoint as well. By leveraging the relatively small list of recipients, the company multiplied the scale of the model launch by a factor of two. Even big marketers can use the power of microfocused campaigns to create a major impact on their results.

**KEY TAKEAWAY:** Truly effective Contact Marketing calls for multiple modes of communication. We instinctively know that email alone, social media alone, or phone calls alone aren't as effective as combinations of all three for creating meaningful contact. Contact Marketing gives us a broad range of tools and we should use them all.

Video-in-print is a perfect example. Combining the magic of print—the written word, the beauty of paper and form—with the magic of video, video-in-print can transport us anywhere. It allows us to humanize ourselves through expression and vulnerability not evident in words and pictures alone.

# WE ARE THE PROTAGONISTS

Regardless of how it's delivered, video must become an extension of ourselves. Hollywood knows the secret to audiences falling for a film is in the characters developed on-screen. Romantic comedies don't work unless the audience falls in love with the protagonists, too. Action films don't work unless we admire the hero and hate the villain. Horror movies depend upon our dread of a scary villain and our sympathy for the victim or hero.

In outreach videos, we must develop ourselves as characters. Not stuffy or staid, we need to come across as someone the target executive would enjoy working with, someone who is competent, accomplished, and full of ideas.

That brings to mind Ryan O'Hara. If he wasn't a sales development expert, he'd probably be making videos for Comedy Central. He's funny, strategic, and utterly comfortable in front of and behind the camera. He is a natural talent for video-based Contact Marketing.

Then again, O'Hara is typical of the people of his generation, having grown up on video and YouTube. He quickly found that his ease with video paid off when faced with the traditional December slowdown in business. With his boss's backing, O'Hara decided to take a bit more time to research each target contact and then develop a quirky set of outreach videos with music and film themes.

O'Hara addressed management's concerns about scalability of the videos by creating a three-segment arrangement, in which the first and third portions were generic and the middle segment personalized. The finished piece could be produced and adapted quickly to any recipient, while keeping the feeling of spontaneity.

Although they were asking for business meetings, the videos were anything but pitches, which is why the recipients found them refreshing and engaging. At the end of each video, O'Hara didn't ask for a meeting. Instead, he asked about their favorite movie.

## CASE STUDY
# Ryan O'Hara's Crazy Videos Produce Crazy Results

**BACKGROUND:** LeadIQ sales development rep Ryan O'Hara (now vice president of growth and marketing for the company) saw an opportunity to revamp the company's contact strategy during the end-of-year holiday slowdown. His theory was that a series of quirky videos could be used to encourage top accounts to open up more readily to conversations with LeadIQ sales reps.

**CHALLENGES:** LeadIQ's target was large, rapid-growth companies. Serious companies, like Hulu, Expedia, and Clearbuilt. Would they accept the playful nature of the outreach or reject it as unprofessional? O'Hara and team would be taking a serious risk of damaging their brand. Meanwhile, the company's management wondered, "If the test does work, can it be scaled?"

**CAMPAIGN SPECIFICS:** The plan was to test one video outreach per sales rep, targeting one of their major accounts. Some of the videos would be themed after '80s music videos, with reps lip-synching classic rock songs. Shot in three segments, only the middle fifteen seconds were personalized, making it easier to produce outreach videos at scale if they worked.

### RYAN O'HARA'S CASUAL WEBCAM VIDEOS

*In his prospecting videos, Ryan O'Hara favors minimal overhead with maximum fun. Here, he sets up a "fireside" chat with prospects, placing two monitors in the background, each playing a fireplace loop. Note the haphazard placement of connector cables. He's not going for polish—actually, just the opposite.*

Ryan O'Hara

Other videos were produced with a classical quartet playing favorites from Led Zeppelin, The Who, and Jethro Tull. Shot on a simple web camera, O'Hara opened the segment by announcing, "Hey, we'd like to work with you, but first, I thought I'd serenade you with some music." To give the campaign a further push, the videos were shared on social media as they were sent to prospects.

**RESULTS:** O'Hara explains, "Typically, our prospecting would produce a 15 percent connect rate, netting fifteen sales opportunities, then three to five would close per month." The video campaign changed those results drastically. In the first round of testing, 83 percent connected, booked meetings, and bought LeadIQ's service. Hulu's CEO liked the campaign so much, he congratulated O'Hara on the campaign and forwarded the video to CNN and *Fortune* magazine.

O'Hara figures the campaign cost $900 initially and about $200 per month to maintain. The test produced $40,000 in recurring monthly revenue, generating a roughly 53,000 percent ROI against nearly half a million dollars in new revenue.

Ryan O'Hara

### THE RYAN O'HARA MUSICAL SHOW

*For one series of prospecting videos, Ryan O'Hara hired a string quartet to play classic rock tunes by Jethro Tull, The Who, and Led Zeppelin. The videos were recorded on a webcam, with Ryan stepping in as the host, telling each prospect, "Hey, we want to work with you, but first I thought I'd serenade you with some music." The campaign generated a 40 percent meeting rate.*

**KEY TAKEAWAY:** The campaign—and the approach of using off-the-wall, very personal videos—has since become a fixture in the company's prospecting efforts. You never know what you'll see next from O'Hara and crew. In one piece, he's sitting in his office with a video of a fireplace and a cutout of actor Danny DeVito in the background. In another, a member of the crew shaves his head in an effort to get a meeting, although in fairness, he needed a haircut anyway.

O'Hara says while there is some risk of coming off as too silly, it's important to research the target contacts and deliver relevant messages. "The people you're going after are people, not the companies they work for," he explains, reminding us that people hate to say no to people they like. And that's the whole idea: Get them to like you first, do business after.

O'Hara strongly feels that personalization is not just about doing something about the prospect. He says, "You have to have your fingerprints all over that, too. Be yourself, put elements of yourself into what you're doing—and stay away from politics and religion." On that last one especially, great advice.

# PUTTING IT ALL TOGETHER

The power of video shouldn't be foreign to anyone alive today. Whether you grew up with television or YouTube, we're all familiar with the breadth of video styles and messaging. We understand the importance of storytelling and character development. We can see how video can create rapport and impress.

> *Get comfortable, but always keep in mind that you're there simply to share value, not to audition for a movie role. You don't have to be perfect. You just have to be genuine.*

To put it to use in our campaigns, we must become comfortable with getting in front of the camera as well as using the technology behind it. Anyone who has taken acting lessons or naturally has a beaming, effervescent personality is a step ahead, but really, we all have a story to tell, and we all deserve to tell those stories. Get comfortable, but always keep in mind that you're there simply to share value, not to audition for a movie role. You don't have to be perfect. You just have to be genuine.

Similarly, anyone who has taken videography classes or simply has a knack for shooting, editing, and distributing video content is well ahead of the pack. If you're of a certain age, this all comes as naturally to you as picking up a phone. But for those of another certain age, if you're not yet familiar with those skills, take classes, get help, and welcome yourself to the new, third level of literacy.

For our contact campaigns, we need to let go of the expectation that our videos should be perfectly acted, shot, and edited. Oddly enough, perfect video doesn't seem to excite recipients nearly as much as homespun shoots that replace perfection with a genuine personality. It's important to remember that, for this mission, we're not looking to impress; we're looking to make human-to-human connections.

To do that, take stock of who you are, of what makes you unique. Are you funny? Do you have an unusual talent? Do you live in a special place? What do you like to do for fun? Incorporate those into your videos—use them to define your own character to your target accounts.

# Critical Next Steps

*OBJECTIVE:* Master the third level of literacy—video—to break through to more prospects.

## *Step 1. Get comfortable with video.*

Some people naturally take to video, including many millennials. Others have no familiarity or comfort with it. If you fall into the latter category, you need to catch up. Imagine being unable to read or use a computer—imagine the overwhelming disadvantage that would create in your life. If you don't understand at least basic shooting and editing of video, you are at a similar disadvantage today.

## *Step 2. Do it yourself or hire a pro?*

If you are unfamiliar with shooting and editing video, you face a steep learning curve, but classes will have you filming within days. If you don't plan to do your own production, consider hiring a professional videographer. That way you'll be up and running immediately. Pros will ensure best-quality productions, but they are expensive. Either way, you should push to become proficient enough to make your own contact videos.

## *Step 3. Decide how you'll deliver your videos.*

Once you have your video produced, edited, and ready to go, you must decide how it will be delivered. Vidyard offers a simple method for embedding videos in emails, along with a dashboard to monitor viewership. The platform offers the added benefit of discovering who the influencers are, just by seeing who's watching. If you want to deliver the video as a physical piece, try video boxes and brochures—or perhaps delivering content on iPads.

# POINTS TO REMEMBER

✔ Video is the third level of literacy; proficiency is required for everyone in business today.

✔ Video is a proven tool for making important connections.

✔ It's not necessary to be a professional broadcaster or to have a professional studio to appear on camera. Authenticity trumps slick production values.

✔ Delivery of outreach videos has been made much easier with platforms that allow them to be embedded in emails.

✔ Embedded video emails can provide real-time contact intel, including who's opening, how long they're viewing, and where they're being forwarded.

✔ Video can be incorporated into boxes using thin-screen micro-technology.

✔ Video-in-a-box technology adds a new dimension to jewel boxing, covered in chapter five.

✔ It's important to let your personality shine through in your videos. Do you have a unique skill? Incorporate all of it into your videos.

✔ Video production is a highly technical skill. Take classes, practice, and don't be afraid to call in help from a professional videographer.

✔ There are three strategic questions to ask regarding contact campaign videos. What will they be about, what should they look like, and what is the desired effect?

✔ You must decide how your video will be delivered. Will you send it in email, as part of a box, or as a separate video-in-print element?

✔ You can put your video program together quite simply, using a smartphone, perhaps a few accessories, and a video editing program.

# CHAPTER 12

# AI / AR / VR

Elon Musk, Bill Gates, Stephen Hawking, and others have issued dire warnings about the potential evils of artificial intelligence (AI). They say AI will rob us of our jobs and make human work-for-pay obsolete.

Elon Musk famously tweeted, "Competition for AI superiority at a national level will most likely be the cause of World War 3." Gates has said, "Humans should be worried about the threat posed by artificial intelligence." Hawking told us, "The development of full artificial intelligence could spell the end of the human race."

But so far, the reality has been pretty good, with far greater promise ahead. There are already machine-learning platforms that analyze client relationships and recommend new contacts fitting the same profile. Some apps peer deeply into complex data streams and return insights about imminent purchases, with guidance on how and when to follow up. Others help us leverage not just our own networks, but all the relationships within an entire organization.

There are CRM platforms that use AI in the background to gather details from emails to properly populate client profiles, while expertly guiding the sales team to hidden opportunities. Another arranges appointments like an actual assistant.

This chapter looks toward the future of Contact Marketing. AI is already here, already helping a lot. But there are two other technologies that are still so new that they haven't yet shown up in Contact Marketing campaigns.

We've been seeing previews of augmented reality (AR) represented through sci-fi glasses and smartphone screens, thanks to Google, Apple, and others. Usually the views presented are of the user walking down the street with overlaid data points showing what's there to be eaten, bought, or consumed.

As the technology develops and matures, I've been wondering how it might serve our mission as Contact Marketers. I looked long and hard and found fascinating answers on the side of a wine bottle, of all places (more on that later).

The notion of virtual reality (VR) has been our reality for years. Today, it promises an alternate world where simulated, interactive experiences are delivered via immersive goggles. Some of these headsets cost several hundred dollars, but as you will see, there are some that cost just a few bucks and can be folded and sent through the mail.

VR is advancing rapidly. It may soon be the standard mode of delivery for Hollywood movies, news coverage, and, oh yes, meetings. There are already rudimentary VR meeting spaces being used to assemble programmers and engineers to collaborate as though they were right there in the same room. But they're not. They're scattered all over the globe.

It would be irresistible, in my opinion, to be invited to visit one of those raised huts over the opaline waters of Bora Bora to chat about anything. Or perhaps to join someone for a ride into space on Virgin Galactic's SpaceShipTwo. Or maybe just to visit a showroom somewhere to show a range of solutions someone might need.

Let's indulge a bit in an exploration of the future of Contact Marketing, shall we?

# MAKING THE CASE FOR ARTIFICIAL INTELLIGENCE

## Is AI the New Oracle?

If you had access to the fabled Delphic oracle of ancient Greek mythology today, you might ask her, "Which of my customers is likely to buy from me today?" Armed with such insights, you'd only need to make a few calls a day to have a very full deal book.

This is especially useful in a crowded market like technology solutions, which is what founder Justin Chugg had in mind when he developed the Ensable AI platform. Along the way, he discovered something far more powerful and relevant to our Contact Marketing mission.

Chugg and his team had a hunch. Actually, two. They started with the premise that buyers emit signals through social media, web searches, and in traditional media when they're about to make a purchase. And they figured AI could identify those signals across all relationships held by every member of a sales team, multiplying the sales opportunities already close at hand. The net effect was an AI coach with access to all contacts in the personal networks of every team member, which then analyzed each node for signs of imminent purchases.

That's the sort of intelligence and insight Contact Marketers can put to great use because one of our biggest challenges is deciding who to connect with and when. Ensable not only suggests who to connect with but who in our team can make an introduction, prioritized according to who's about to buy what we sell.

## CASE STUDY
# The Ensable AI Platform
# Pushes Sales Team Performance Higher

**BACKGROUND:** Artificial intelligence has the unique ability to peer into large streams of data and form critically important insights. This is having a profound effect on many endeavors, including sales. In this example, AI has been harnessed to probe and monitor activities—across a broad expanse—that indicate a planned purchase.

**CHALLENGES:** When we're interested in something, we often follow a pattern. We search on Google and Bing. We check reviews and read articles. We have conversations on social media. These are all buying signals. The theory is, if we can gain access to even a small portion of those signals, our sales calls can be immensely more productive. We would eliminate ill-timed calls and simply close massive amounts of business. The challenge is to collect enough buying signals and convert those into reliable insights to optimize sales activity.

**CAMPAIGN SPECIFICS:** The Ensable AI platform is a system that peers into network connections on social media and other sources. Its effectiveness rises substantially as more personal networks are accessed. Armed with those data sources, Ensable makes recommendations on who to contact, when to contact them, and who in the company's network can make introductions.

Ensable

### THIS IS WHAT BUYING SIGNALS LOOK LIKE

*The Ensable platform uses AI to scour social and traditional media and other sources to identify buying signals—searches for certain key terms, stories of new positions and promotions, expiring contracts, and more. They're spotted, tabulated, and displayed on the Ensable dashboard, where they can be used to make timely connections with potential buyers.*

**RESULTS:** Chugg says the Ensable platform has already had a dramatic effect on sales outcomes for a diverse customer base, ranging from smaller shops all the way up to enterprise-level companies, including IBM and CenturyLink. Since the system relies in part on the depth of networks aggregated across sales teams, the more people on your team, the more Ensable is able to lead that team to increased sales.

Chugg cites a managed services provider (MSP) client that offers outsourced IT services. Its staff includes eighty sales reps nationally who constantly consult Ensable for their most promising prospects. Chugg reports that the company has already seen a *doubling of revenue* within its current customer base.

**KEY TAKEAWAY:** AI is ready to bring deep insights and greatly enhanced timing to our selling regime. Ensable's platform shows AI can be an astonishing tool for recognizing buying signals, providing deep insight into who will soon be making purchases.

## The Benefits of Pairing AI with Your CRM Platform

While Ensable has its approach to gathering data from a team's personal networks, other AI platforms offer different ways to see and use customer data points. If your company has a CRM program, for example, you might assume customer relationships are being properly logged, tracked, and managed. But they're not. CRM platforms are only as good as the user-entered data within, and that data is always incomplete. Wouldn't it be better if a CRM program could collect data points all on its own and then draw insights and offer expert coaching to the sales team based on *all* the data on hand?

Perhaps Spiro.ai can help. Spiro is a CRM program with an AI overlay. Whenever you have an email conversation or post to social media, Spiro is taking notes and cleaning things up. Ditto for your calendar. If missing details show up in a contact's signature file, like phone numbers, addresses, titles, or email addresses, Spiro automatically scoops them up and enters the missing data into the CRM database. Records are updated and conversations are noted, stored, and flagged for later consideration. If deadlines are mentioned, Spiro will even create follow-up events.

Spiro is like a superhuman sales assistant. Except it's really quite a lot more.

By combining AI with CRM, the creators of Spiro have produced something that has never existed before. It keeps records up to date, while tracking the sales opportunities often locked within. Spiro becomes an all-seeing, all-knowing coach—a *mensch*—someone who has your back and always has your interests at heart.

If that sounds like a Jewish mother, that's by design. Spiro communicates its coaching directives via email, but the company wants to make sure they always connect. So they have given the Spiro platform a comedic voice. Each email can come in the language of a motivational coach, ditzy personality, a drunk Santa—even a Jewish mother. They figure if it's engaging to read, it'll get read.

## CASE STUDY
## CabinetM Uses Spiro.ai to Launch Marketing Tech Stack Service

**BACKGROUND:** CabinetM is a startup that provides an innovative platform to help marketers integrate, manage, and evaluate the various martech (marketing tech) apps in its technology stack by theme, with headings like content, social, video and webinars, analytics, and more.

**CHALLENGES:** In line with CabinetM's mission to streamline its clients' marketing processes, the seven-member team needed to streamline its sales process. Founder Sheryl Schultz found the leading CRM programs too burdensome; she and her team were constantly filling in forms rather than selling. "For a sales tool to work for our team," she explains, "it has to be easy. We don't want to work for the program, we want it to work for us."

**CAMPAIGN SPECIFICS:** Schultz heard about Spiro.ai and decided to give it a try. Upon setup, Spiro immediately started sucking out data from her emails, quickly discovering scores of opportunities and filling out data forms on its own. Entering new opportunities was also a greatly simplified task with Spiro's helpful AI hand there to fill in the blanks. According to Schultz, setup was as simple as popping open a screen, inputting new opportunities, and setting a few parameters.

**RESULTS:** The team has been selling its service for ten months so far but is not yet sure of the monetary value of Spiro's assistance. Schultz says the platform has made CabinetM's selling process far more defined and efficient—and it has

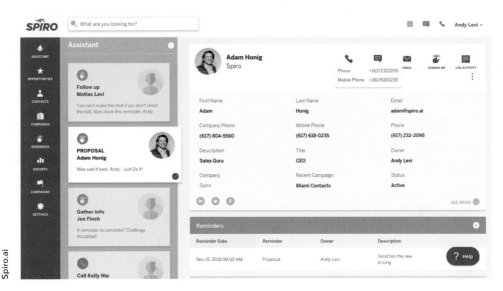

Spiro.ai

## THE NEW FACE OF COACHING

*The Spiro platform mixes CRM and AI to produce a new form of sales coaching. Data points are harvested from email and other activity and entered into account files. Opportunities are then tracked, producing timely prompts to help users maximize their sales efforts.*

also provided an unexpected benefit. She says Spiro has been able to give her a precise picture of what's happening within their funnel at all times and has created a map of what their process looks like. "It has defined a cadence for us and shown us what our typical sales cycle looks like." She adds, "If someone says they need to take a pause, we always know where to pick up and what to expect."

From its use of Spiro, CabinetM has learned that its sales cycle takes four months to complete. Spiro continues to learn as well, constantly pointing out opportunities and suggested daily steps. Schultz concludes, "This has simplified the tracking of opportunities so we have more time to focus on our best ones. And we're selling a lot as a result."

**KEY TAKEAWAY:** The simple act of syncing our email accounts and calendars to a CRM system makes perfect sense. Adding a layer of AI to coordinate the data points—then translating those into insights, prompts, and recommendations that lead to business—is an obvious choice for greater success.

The more we examine AI in sales and productivity, the more we see powerful new tools that can make us all perform at superhuman levels. AI has the ability to see into every dark corner of our messy business lives and not only make sense of it, but use every scrap of it to help us succeed. As we reach out to the people who can change the scale of our lives, we need tools like Spiro to keep things straight and ensure we never miss the deals that are already well within hand.

## Using AI to Track Relationships

While Spiro tracks CRM data to identify opportunities, Nudge.ai has a different approach. It uses AI to track the relationships themselves and knits together the total of those nodes across an enterprise's cumulative collection of personal networks to produce amazing results.

Warm introductions are often said to be the gold standard for getting important meetings. LinkedIn especially has greatly expanded our professional networks and even shows us who's connected with whom. But the viability of any introduction comes from the strength of the underlying connection. Wouldn't it be nice to have a way to monitor the strength of those relationships throughout our network and, even better, coach us to take actions that quickly improve those ties?

If you have thousands of connections, though, there is a limit to what you can track in your head. Anthropologist and evolutionary psychologist Robin Dunbar insists our brains are only capable of tracking a certain number of relationships, which is the basis of a principle known as "Dunbar's Number." It states, "150 is the number of individuals with whom any one person can maintain stable relationships."[1]

But if our brains can't maintain more than 150 relationships, how are we to optimize the thousands of connections we already have? That is the premise for Nudge.ai, the AI-based platform that not only helps you cope but also turns your network into a buzz saw of important referrals and opportunities.

"The best salespeople are natural connectors and networkers," says Nudge.ai Chief Technology Officer Steven Woods, "so the Nudge platform is designed to help average salespeople perform like the best." The platform constantly measures the strength of each relationship in each user's network, then delivers "Nuggets" every morning to help them reach out to their most important contacts with deep relevance.

Nudge multiplies the efficacy of personal networks, but it can go much further. It has the ability to link every personal network within a given company,

---

[1] "Dunbar's Number," Wikipedia, https://en.wikipedia.org/wiki/Dunbar%27s_number

so, suddenly, all users have an enormous new source for high-level introductions. If someone in accounting already knows the person you're trying to reach, Nudge knows and will help you make the connection. Without the amplification of AI, that would be a referral source you'd never have known existed. Nudge does this constantly, which can greatly improve chances for more business.

Suddenly, your sales team has a far greater network to draw upon in its mission to acquire new accounts and business.

## CASE STUDY
# Nudge.ai Extends Personal Networks and Sales

**BACKGROUND:** The company founders of what would become Nudge.ai set out to create an AI-based platform that would use an entire enterprise's set of personal networks to give each member access to the conjoined network. Beyond that, the goal was to have the AI component assess the strength of each relationship and suggest actions to make them stronger. The result was the Nudge.ai platform.

**CHALLENGES:** The goal of the platform is to give individual reps greater access to top accounts by discovering who in their organization already has ties within each company. The challenge was making those connections discoverable, which would be an entirely new capability in business.

**CAMPAIGN SPECIFICS:** The process starts by mapping relationships throughout each employee's network using social media interactions, email conversations, CRM data, and other factors. Each relationship is then modeled to determine its strength. Then the whole of the relationships and networks is rolled together into an aggregate of business relationships held throughout the enterprise. Finally, the collective network is analyzed for matches with targeted accounts.

**RESULTS:** Nudge's head of marketing, Jaxson Khan, reports that one client just generated $1 million in new business a week after installing Nudge. Another reported hammering away at an account for six weeks with no luck. Nudge identified a warm connection within the seller's organization and suddenly a six-figure deal ensued.

"The Nudge platform helps every salesperson become superhuman," explains Kahn. "Just within your own personal network, we figure it causes an immediate 40 percent growth in connections." Once applied to an entire organization's network of connections, that growth can be exponential.

**THE NETWORKED HIVE**

*What would it be like if every member of an organization's networks were converted into one huge network? Opportunities would multiply as connections emerge to reach virtually anyone. Remember the six degrees of separation from Kevin Bacon? That's what Nudge. ai does for any company or group.*

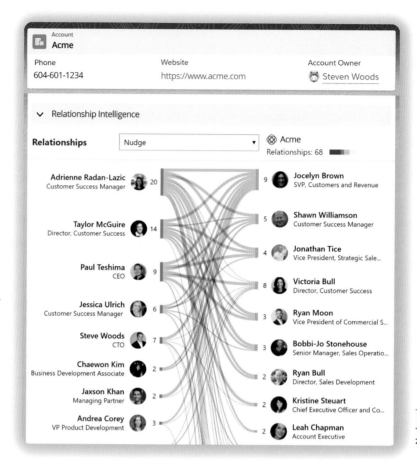

**KEY TAKEAWAY:** Without the superhero power of AI, we mere mortals can only maintain 150 relationships. But the Nudge.ai platform allows us to expand that sphere so that many multiples of that number of relationships can be maintained and acted upon—which can mean a lot more new business for us all.

# AI Does the Deep Dive

The irony of artificial intelligence is that through the use of technology, AI seems to make salespeople more human. As Ensable, Spiro.ai, and Nudge.ai show us, AI makes us far more perceptive of buying signals, it prompts us to follow up precisely when and where needed, and it expands the reach and impact of our networks exponentially. It even helps us boost the strength of our human relationships.

The power of AI derives from peering into and making sense of large sources of data. We see what's possible when AI looks at internal sources of data: personal networks, customer profiles, email communications, and more. So what happens when we direct its bright beam toward external sources of data?

That's what Brandon Bornancin and three ex-Google colleagues set out to discover when they formed Seamless.ai. The platform came from the founding four's desire to have a quick, reliable source of information on their targeted accounts they would otherwise spend weeks gathering by hand.

As sales reps for Google, they would often spend up to six months assembling a pitch deck for a client, including deep research into each contact's personal markers, and wondered if there was a way to shorten the process. So they built an AI-powered search engine that peers deeply into social media, the internet, offline news media, company reports, and more and delivers insights and verified contact details—in seconds.

Profile scrapes are not new. They are widely used, at times with a lot of imagination. Charlie Liang's bobblehead doll campaign, which used profile pictures from LinkedIn accounts to great effect, is one of many standout examples of using personal data to create contact. Profile scrapes are the basis of several stories of Deep personalization usage in chapter four.

## CASE STUDY
# Human vs. Seamless.ai Profile Scrape Comparison

**BACKGROUND:** There are a few options for producing profile scrapes for Contact Marketing campaigns. You can do the research yourself, hire a service, or use an AI-based platform. I set out to compare the three in a head-to-head test.

**CHALLENGES:** Google search and social media have made profile scrapes much easier than they would have been before the internet. Still, the process is tedious and made harder by a number of factors. Large companies are set up to keep people out. Live "switchboard" operators are rare, so there's no longer anyone to ask for help. Some phone systems ask for an extension and

## PROFILE SCRAPES IN A FLASH

*What used to take hours, even days, to research an important contact's vital personal information now takes seconds on the Seamless.ai. platform. Search by company, person, or title, and Seamless returns an entire dossier, including verified email, phone, and address details.*

hang up if none is given. If your contact happens to share the same name as a celebrity, good luck finding anything on the person you want. Even when all search factors align, finding and assembling information for a list of contacts is a tiresome process.

**CAMPAIGN SPECIFICS:** For the test, I assigned TaskDrive, a platform offering the services of human researchers in Eastern Europe, with the task of generating profile information on the chief marketing officers of one hundred Fortune 500 companies. After completing the task, I ran the same contacts through the Seamless.ai system to compare results and evaluate them for suitability in a campaign using Deep personalization.

**RESULTS:** The TaskDrive researcher took a week to complete a spreadsheet with the names of the target executives at the selected companies. Details included name, title, address, email, and phone numbers, but no further specifics were given. The same contacts were then run through the Seamless platform to compare resulting contact and other details.

The two tasks were wholly different. I didn't ask Seamless to find the CMOs of the Fortune 500. That was the assignment for the TaskDrive researcher, who used human expertise to gather the list. The head-to-head comparison was of the accuracy of the information returned. And on that score, the two resources were pretty even. Both returned similar contact information for the targeted executives.

But Seamless jumped well ahead in two important ways. Time-to-results was seconds for each contact, compared to the full week required by the human researcher. And the Seamless dashboard included scores of additional resources in its search results, including links to social media accounts and various traditional media and company resources.

**KEY TAKEAWAY:** Seamless was undoubtedly the quickest resource for scrapes and it accommodates searches by selectors other than just name. I could have asked for the list of Fortune 500 companies, individually, by name as well. What's intriguing, though, is that it's also comforting to have a human researcher to speak to, perhaps to clarify results or next steps.

Disambiguation is also a challenge for both AI platform and human researcher. Finding details for a target executive obscured by the results of a pop singer or sports figure with the same name remains a challenge for researcher and AI alike.

# SOME TACTICS FOR USING AI

AI hasn't been on the job for long, but everything it touches seems to become orders of magnitude easier, faster, and more effective. That's true for profile scrapes and managing relationships, networks, and emerging sales opportunities. But what about that source of so many new contacts in our lives, social media? Can AI help us operate like superhumans there, too?

Social media is now at the heart of selling. It has become our primary method for connecting and interacting with potential clients, vendors, and collaborators. It can be a source of massive opportunity, new business, and important connections. Many of us are posting daily content, fielding dozens of contact requests per day, and juggling dozens of daily conversations and follow-up tasks. Don't we need a CRM platform for that, too?

Yes, we do. Social media represents an unprecedented bloc of inbound opportunity, but it is also a source of time-wasting chaff that can leave us overwhelmed. It can drain us of time, focus, and productivity. We need a way to track what's important, and we need a way to tame it, to make sense of it. We need a way to make our efforts pay off. We could also use an AI overlay to optimize our use of the data bits to ensure it all converts to something useful. Let's look at some ways AI can help us with this as well as other tactics for using AI to better manage our time.

## TACTICAL EXAMPLE
# Using Nimble for Contact Marketing

**TACTIC:** Use Nimble to produce dossiers on your social media–sourced prospects so you have the contact info you need to start a campaign.

**WHAT IT IS:** Nimble is a social CRM-with-AI platform that gathers the details of followings and followers, tweets and posts, and connections and opportunities, and puts it all in an easy-to-use dashboard. From there, you can organize important contacts into categories based on the kinds of opportunities they represent. Some might be interview guests for your podcast. Others could be potential clients or speaking engagement possibilities. Or sponsors. Still others may be content collaborators or future strategic partners. Whatever they are, Nimble keeps them organized.

Like any good CRM program, Nimble tracks opportunities and reminds users of important tasks. And then the AI kicks in. With the Nimble widget installed, you can hover your cursor over any name in whatever social media platform you're in, and Nimble can identify the contact, add them to the database, and append their personal details, including verified contact information, other social media accounts, even their latest posts.

**WHY IT'S NEEDED:** The most persistent challenge we face as Contact Marketers is finding valid contact information for target contacts. Even with all our easy access to information, finding contact details has actually become harder. We used to be able to call the main number for a company, reach an operator, and ask to be directed or for contact details. Now we call the main number and reach an automated system. Remember when they used to say, "Please listen carefully, as our options have recently changed"? They finally have. Now there are just two options: If you have an extension, dial it now. Otherwise, get lost. We need a way to collect contact information for prospects and, ideally, not just their work number and email but their social media accounts and more.

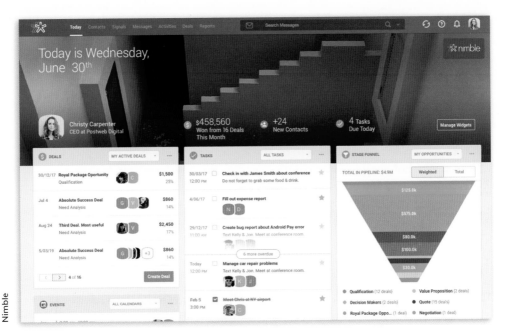

Nimble

## SOCIAL SELLING'S ULTIMATE DASHBOARD

*What Salesforce, HubSpot, and others have done for sales-oriented CRM, Nimble does for social selling. Social media relationships and opportunities are monitored and organized, while Nimble uses AI to gather intel and provide coaching. Beyond all that, it aggregates verified contact details for virtually any high-value target contact.*

Nimble is a social media CRM platform designed to help users track and manage their interactions. That is useful, but we can also use Nimble to connect with those hard-to-reach prospects.

**HOW IT WORKS:** Nimble installs as an extension on Gmail or Outlook. Upon loading, the Nimble widget appears on the program interface, allowing users to perform several neat tricks. Hover the cursor over any email address and the widget immediately displays a dossier on the person. The instantaneous results include related companies, links to all social media accounts, professional experience, areas of influence, and relevant websites. The panel allows you to add the person to your Nimble CRM to enhance engagement. Click another button and it displays email, title, website, location, and URLs for social media accounts.

**HOW I TESTED IT:** I was interested to see how Nimble's AI component could support the Contact Marketing mission. In particular, I wanted to see how it could help me reach VIP prospects like movie producer Brian Grazer. I needed his contact information so I could reach out to him for this book (see chapter three). As you can imagine, his details were hard to find.

Nimble proved to be invaluable. Grazer is a meeting junkie. He loves reaching out to fascinating people to have "curiosity conversations." Still, he is a celebrity himself and highly resistant to contact from others. Contact details are treated like a national secret in this crowd, but Nimble was able to give me his address, phone, and web details—even his personal email address.

**KEY TAKEAWAY:** We still have to do the legwork and engage in a persistence campaign, but Nimble can provide us with a slew of information that helps us connect. Like the other AI platforms discussed in this chapter, Nimble is something you will want to include in your tech tool kit.

## TACTICAL EXAMPLE
# Employing a Virtual Assistant: Amy Ingram in Action

**TACTIC:** Elevate your status and outsource your calendar to an AI assistant from x.ai.

**WHAT IT IS:** Amy (you can also assign the name Andrew) is the screen name for an extraordinary service from x.ai. Amy is an AI virtual assistant that sets up meetings for you. Forgive me, but from this point on, I will refer to it as "her." Or if you choose to set the persona to a male voice, Andrew will do the work just as efficiently; in that case, you can refer to it as "him."

**WHY IT'S NEEDED:** In a lot of ways, agreeing to meet or talk with someone is the easy part. The hard part is arranging the details without pulling your hair out. But from a programming standpoint, the challenge is to produce an AI platform that is never stumped by the thousands of possible impediments, objections, and complications that arise when trying to simply agree on a date, time, and call procedure or location.

Further complicating the task, the AI must be able to decipher intent from written language, including misspellings, oddball clichéd expressions, and poor writing skills. The ultimate goal is to present an AI platform that seamlessly works with people to coordinate their schedules, reach agreement for meetings, and register all of it in every participant's calendar. It's not an easy job, and it's never acceptable for Amy to return an error message. It must appear as though an intelligent human being is on the other end of the keyboard, efficiently making necessary arrangements.

**HOW IT WORKS:** As soon as you ask her to, Amy jumps into an email conversation and deals with the minutiae. What day and time work for you?

Oh, that won't work, how about this date and time? Do you want to call me or should I call you? What's your phone number? Do you want to see if Sarah wants to join us, too? Oh, neither of those dates is good for her? When can she meet? Should we move this to a phone bridge? What's the number and access code? Do you want to send calendar invites, or shall I?

You get the picture. It's hell to deal with, but Amy does it beautifully, always with the utmost professionalism, never with any trace of frustration.

The service is set up by establishing an account and syncing with your email and calendar applications. You set preferences for the times you're willing to accept appointments—not in the middle of the night or weekends, of course. And you're ready to go.

To invoke Amy's help, you simply "CC" her when you're conversing with someone via email and decide it's time to arrange a call or meeting. As soon as you include "Amy.Ingram@x.ai" in the CC field and send the email, x.ai springs into action.

Amy immediately checks your calendar for availabilities and writes back to your contact with three suggested appointment times. They'll usually respond, indicating which works best and Amy completes the calendar invitation. The next thing you know, Amy sends a notification that the meeting has been confirmed.

As a stand-in for a human assistant, Amy is so lifelike that she has fielded more than just appointments. Some contacts have responded with requests for dates; one even offered a proposal for marriage. Certainly, the aim is not to deceive but to present a viable alternative to the back-and-forth Ping-Pong game involved in setting up meetings.

**HOW I TESTED IT:** I first learned about "Amy" and x.ai just after the release of my book, *How to Get a Meeting with Anyone*. Word of a new AI assistant that would set your appointments had spread all over social media. Questions like "Have you tried Amy?" appeared throughout posts and discussions on Facebook and LinkedIn. I was one of the lucky ones who was able to try the beta version and was surprised by how humanlike she was.

I employed Amy's services extensively during the trial to set up meetings. It worked flawlessly, even when complications arose. Like a human assistant, if someone decides to be nonresponsive, Amy will persist for a time, then refer the problem back to the user. That happened a few times, and when I made the call to straighten it out, the system easily set the meetings.

It was also impressive to see how Amy worked the details of calls involving more than two people. The complexity of setting up such a call rises exponentially with each added person, and Amy easily handled it all.

But what happened when she received an entirely nonstandard set of responses? Would she be able to handle those, too, with humanlike perfection?

I once had a confirmed appointment set up, but on the morning of the call, the contact reached out to Amy to reschedule. He wrote, "I can't make the call this morning. When else can Stu talk?" It could have easily triggered an error message, but that never happened.

Instead, she accessed my calendar and responded with three alternative times. The contact gave another nonstandard directive. "I don't care," he responded. "Any of those will work." Again, Amy should have returned an error code, but didn't. She simply chose one of the time slots, sent a calendar invite, and the meeting was back on. Mere computer programs would not have been able to perform these tasks. Only AI—or a human—could decipher the meaning of the language and make choices on its own about when the meeting should take place and proactively send the revised invite.

**KEY TAKEAWAY:** X.ai's platform was an impressive glimpse into a future with AI-based platforms performing menial human tasks with flawless precision. Still, when the AI is presumed to be a live person and then later discovered not to be, there can be a backlash.

When I first started using Amy, I would write, "I'll have my assistant reach out and set something up." Amy would then run her routine and the meeting would be set. But when I revealed during the calls that Amy was not a real person, people were mostly put off. Sales trainer and consultant John Barrows says a better way to phrase it would be, "I'll have my virtual assistant get in touch." That way, there will be no misguided marriage proposals or offers

### HAVE YOUR "PEOPLE" CALL MY "PEOPLE"

*Arranging a time to meet or talk is surprisingly, frustratingly overcomplicated. Where should we meet? When? Should you call me or I call you? What number should I use? What's your email so I can send you an invite? X.ai makes that whole process simple, with an AI-powered virtual assistant who arranges everything. With x.ai, arranging a meeting or call is as simple as "CC-ing Amy."*

X.ai

of dates, and no flustered contacts on the calls. If I'd asked Amy to marry me, I'd be pretty disappointed to learn she wasn't real. And maybe a little embarrassed, too.

Dates, marriage proposals, and flummoxed prospects aside, we can see that virtual assistants can help us tame our schedules by letting AI deal with the details while we use our time for more strategic endeavors. And if you're a one-person show or work on a small team, having an assistant, even a virtual one, can make you seem more on par with your prospects who have real executive assistants.

AI has so much to offer sellers and marketers, and really, humanity as a whole. It can tame the entropy of massive data and details, and produce deep competitive advantages and opportunities. When it melds an entire organization's worth of personal networks, it creates magnitudes of new types of favorable outcomes where none existed before.

From my perspective, AI is a very good thing. At least so far. But it's not the only big, new technology disruption heading our way. Keep in mind, disruption is a very good thing if you're able to harness it to create new possibilities in your business or career.

# WELCOME TO AUGMENTED REALITY

## Augmented Reality in Action: Pick Up a Bottle of Wine

A wine shop is an odd place to find the future of Contact Marketing, but if you happen to find a bottle of 19 Crimes wine on the store shelf, bring it home. And prepare to be amazed. The bottle is actually an augmented reality (AR) experience waiting to be unleashed.

Each label features an antique sepia-tone photograph of a criminal condemned to exile in Australia in the early 1800s. View the label through the Living Wine Label app on your phone and the image goes from still to live action. Suddenly the old photograph comes to life, with each featured criminal telling his or her story. The characters are fully animated, so they blink, gesture, and move about as though actually there, speaking from the label through your phone.

## CASE STUDY
# Augmented Reality Explodes Brand Reach

**BACKGROUND:** Augmented reality is a new set of technologies that will enhance our view of the real world with a visual overlay of data points and entertainment experiences. Here, those are applied to the challenge of making a brand of wine stand out in a very crowded field of competitors.

**CHALLENGES:** Wine brands have a tough obstacle to overcome. Walk into any wine shop and you'll be blinded by the assortment. Since they all go into essentially the same sort of bottle, the only way to make a last-second appeal to the consumer is with a thoroughly captivating label. The branding process starts well before the consumer visits the store, but the challenge remains: How does the marketer stand out among so many competitors who seem so alike? This is often the challenge we face as Contact Marketers, too.

**CAMPAIGN SPECIFICS:** Treasury Wine Estates (TWE), the parent of 19 Crimes wine, developed the first implementation of a wine label with an AR experience. The idea was to have consumers view the labels through an AR app on their smartphones in order to unlock an utterly unique experience. To accomplish this, TWE tapped agency JWT to create animated versions of the criminals on each label, along with a custom app to unlock the experiences. At the heart of the effect is new image-recognition technology that sees a trigger image and launches the experience.

All of this was applied to a delightfully compelling theme. In eighteenth-century England, there was a list of nineteen specific crimes that would cause violators to be banished to Australia, when it was a dusty, remote penal colony. On each bottle, the label presents an antique "wanted" poster motif, with a single convicted criminal shown as a sepia-tone daguerreotype. With the company's Living Wine Label app activated, users point their phones toward the bottle and watch the characters come to life to tell their stories.

**RESULTS:** The company hoped tech-enabled consumers would find the backstory of the brand compelling, along with the delivery of a one-of-a-kind AR brand experience. They did. Company CMO Michelle Terry says the labels have already generated *more than four hundred million views*, indicating an enormously successful viral awareness campaign. More than that, 19 Crimes has dominated every award for the world's hottest wine brands for the past two years. And it's still catching on.

The program has been so successful, TWE is rolling out AR wine labels for its other brands, including The Walking Dead, Gentlemen's Collection, Beringer Brothers, and Chateau St. Jean, with more on the way. It's also rolling out Mandarin Chinese and Spanish language versions.

**KEY TAKEAWAY:** We've read articles and seen videos teasing the promise of AR, but it never seems to materialize. Treasury Wine Estates just caused it to land on our dinner tables, and has done a superb job of it. TWE has shown us that AR is now ready to be used and explored in our own Contact Marketing missions. AR can expand our reach in unprecedented ways.

Terry advises, "The AR experience must be very, very good." That makes sense, as with everything we do as Contact Marketers. We're always looking

### THE FUTURE OF CONTACT MARKETING?

*Treasury Wine Estates (TWE), parent company of 19 Crimes wines, has just shown the world the future of augmented reality in marketing. Using the company's Living Wine Labels app, aficionados can view captivating AR experiences from the bottle labels, watching as characters come to life to tell of their criminal pasts. It is an enthralling introduction to the brand that has led to exponential sales growth.*

for a big win and that doesn't happen with weak concepts or shoddy implementation. As with everything else we do, our desired effect is to have target contacts nodding their heads in approval as they decide for themselves, "I love the way this person thinks. This is someone I need on my team."

## VARIATION

During our interview, I asked Terry if the same AR experience had been integrated into the company's business cards. After all, when their reps hand their cards to wine retailers all over the world, wouldn't it make sense to use that same AR device to spread their brand to the people who move their wines? Wholesale buyers could activate the experience, set the tracking pixel, and suddenly they're seeing 19 Crimes ads wherever they go on the web. (This is the basis for the Pocket Campaigns in chapter seven.)

"Good idea," she responded. I imagine soon TWE reps will not only have the coolest wine brands to sell, but the coolest business cards . . . er, Pocket Campaign devices to hand out while they sell it. And we all have that same opportunity with our own Contact Marketing campaigns.

# VIRTUAL REALITY IN CONTACT MARKETING

On the old *Star Trek: The Next Generation* television series, featuring Captain Jean-Luc Picard and my old college party friend LeVar Burton as Lieutenant Commander Geordi La Forge with the crazy mod glasses, we were given a fascinating preview of what is now called virtual reality (VR). That glimpse came in the form of La Forge's synthetic-vision goggles and the holodeck, a blank room where users could load any experience they desired and step into another world.

Today we don't have holodecks, but we do have two remarkable devices that seem like they've come straight from the *Star Trek* set. Those would be smartphones and VR goggles, from makers like HTC, Oculus, and Samsung. The question is, can VR help us get meetings or even conduct those meetings in virtual reality?

I believe it holds great promise to do just that.

But to get there, we must first understand the current state of the art. Virtual reality comes in two forms, known as 360-degree video and walk-around. As Emblematic Group VR producer Cedric Gamelin explains, "360-degree video is like wearing a fishbowl over your head. You can look around, but you can't move through the experience." The higher-spec version is walk-around VR, which allows you to move through the experience as though you are moving through the real world. In both forms, the greater the detail, the more lifelike the experience, which increases complexity and expense.

To produce a photorealistic, three-dimensional hologram of yourself in a similarly detailed environment for a five-minute experience would cost roughly $75,000 and involve a lengthy session in a volumetric capture studio, with green screens and a ring of fifty cameras recording you from all angles. But VR is coming to Main Street. Emblematic is about to launch a new platform, REACH, which will allow you to produce your own VR experience using just your smartphone and a pop-up green screen.

Distributing your VR experience is also a challenge, but there are many interesting options, some costing as little as ten dollars. The ultimate VR Contact Marketing campaign might involve sending a set of high-end VR goggles with the invitation, "Put on the goggles and meet me on the beach in Tahiti." Once there, the contact would be greeted by a photorealistic, volumetric representation of you, sharing something of great value and intrigue.

High-end VR goggles are expensive, but there is a novel, low-cost option using cardboard VR goggles that ship flat and unfold to accommodate the recipient's smartphone. Smartphone-based VR will surely be of the fishbowl variety, but still a novel way of connecting. RedPaperPlane.com has fold-out cardboard goggles for under five dollars apiece that can be custom printed with your own brand identity.

That's all fine as a novel outreach to secure a meeting at a later time, but what if you could simply pick up your own headset and have a meeting in the VR world as casually as picking up the phone for a call? It's already happening.

## TACTICAL EXAMPLE
# Having Real Meetings in Virtual Reality

**TACTIC:** Put a new spin on face-to-face meetings by connecting with anyone anywhere in a virtual world.

**CHALLENGES:** To simply jump into a VR meeting, businesspeople owning goggles must be commonplace, like having a mobile phone. Once that is achieved, or if the googles are furnished as part of an outreach campaign, the possibilities are endless. That is, as long as there is a budget to support it.

**WHAT'S IN THE WORKS:** David Karlak is currently developing new VR experiences for legendary film director Ridley Scott to coincide with several new movie releases. He is also creative director for Nurulize, which has just developed a collaborative tool called Nu Design. The VR platform uses rudimentary avatars of collaborators who are all present in a black room with grids, much like *Star Trek*'s holodeck. This is the beginning of meeting spaces in virtual reality.

**WHY IT'S NEEDED:** Face-to-face meetings require a lot of overhead. To get there you may have to fly, take an Uber, then find the right space in an unfamiliar building. You check in and wait till the other parties are ready, then you finally meet. And then you repeat the process to return home. Even in the meeting room, there are time sucks and distractions. There are pleasantries and interpersonal friction points that delay the work. But think of the possibilities if you could put on a pair of goggles and check in from wherever you are, like making a phone call and literally stepping into the same room from anywhere on the planet.

"Using VR as a collaborative space removes all of the distractions and impediments of real world meetings," explains Karlak. He says the VR meeting experience introduces a much greater level of focus and productivity.

Ultimately and somewhat paradoxically, Karlak believes VR will bring far greater *actual* reality to our lives. When we

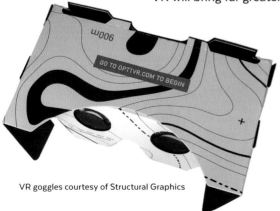

VR goggles courtesy of Structural Graphics

**VIRTUAL REALITY THROUGH THE MAIL**

*These VR goggles cost five dollars apiece and fold flat to be sent through the mail. Recipients download an app, insert their smartphone into the goggles, and immerse themselves in a VR experience. It is a powerful way to invite someone to meet and understand the value you propose to bring.*

**MEET ME ON THE BEACH IN TAHITI**

*Imagine receiving a beautiful wooden box, opening it, and finding this pair of Oculus Go VR goggles with an invitation to meet, right now, "in person," on the beach in Tahiti. How could anyone resist?*

Custom box by Wayfaren; VR goggles by Oculus

immerse ourselves in each location, where news events happen, for example, we won't simply view it, we will experience it firsthand. He sees great promise for VR to heighten experiences in all fields, particularly news and entertainment. I see the same promise for getting meetings.

**KEY TAKEAWAY:** For our Contact Marketing purposes, VR is a tool we should be using to generate high-level meetings—if budgets allow it. In our virtual worlds, we can create anything, show anything, demonstrate anything. Delivering the experiences is also an opportunity to stand out. A high-end set of goggles in a beautiful, custom box is a powerful way to start any contact. Inviting recipients to jump into a virtual world to learn or try something they've never experienced before will be hard to resist.

Virtual reality will take on an increasingly important role in our lives. It will heighten our own sense of reality. And it will open entirely new ways of connecting with people anywhere on the globe. As Contact Marketers, we need to be constantly watching for new ways to stand out and make meaningful connections. It won't be easy, nor will it be cheap, but VR needs to become part of how we introduce ourselves, our ideas, and our value.

Just as VR will lend a greater sense of reality—of "being there"—to news coverage, entertainment, and more, it will allow Contact Marketers to create powerful new experiences, opening entirely new opportunities to make meaningful connections.

Using VR also demonstrates something powerful about us as Contact Marketers. It says we're people who embrace new tech to create commanding results, and that we're not afraid to step into the unknown. It makes us highly desirable partners in our target contacts' own success stories.

# PUTTING IT ALL TOGETHER

I suspect you may have started reading this book from the same place I did when writing it. I didn't know much about artificial intelligence, augmented reality, or virtual reality, and it certainly hadn't entered my life other than certain references to it in ads, science fiction movies, and television series.

The experience of examining these near-future technologies has been profound. I now understand them more and have already started integrating some in my own Contact Marketing campaigns. I even invested in one of the companies after hearing their story (full disclosure: Seamless.ai).

What a sharp turnabout from where I started. Hawking, Gates, and Musk were proclaiming AI to be the biggest threat to humankind. But I see AI as a chaos-taming friendly hand, a coach that can connect bits of information to help us all spot and capitalize on opportunities more efficiently than ever before.

It just makes sense to add a layer of deep machine learning to the torrent of information and tasks we cope with every day. It makes us better and more efficient at our jobs.

# Critical Next Steps

**OBJECTIVE:** Use AI, AR, and VR to step into the future of Contact Marketing.

### Step 1. Make AI an essential part of your strategy now.

The AI-powered platforms discussed in this chapter should become part of your technology suite *immediately*. Collectively, these platforms will enable your team to spot hidden buying signals, run deep profile scrapes in seconds, accelerate access to top accounts, and convert more opportunities into sales faster. Each represents a spectacularly unfair advantage to be enjoyed either by you or your competitors.

### Step 2. Become an expert on augmented reality before everyone else does.

Augmented reality is not in widespread use, which is what makes it so compelling for Contact Marketing missions. One exciting aspect is how AR works. It requires both an experience and an app to view the live animation. The digital interface, while serving up the experience, gives us an opportunity to set a tracking pixel and trigger our persistence campaign. The AR experience can be used as the main contact campaign, reps' Pocket Campaigns, or both. Start exploring this technology now and watch for ways to bend it to your contact mission.

### Step 3. Get a pair of goggles and step fully into virtual reality.

Chances are, the only thing you know about virtual reality is what you've seen lately on the news or in commercials—people wearing goofy goggles and making awkward gestures as they express awe and wonder. It's time to take your turn behind the goggles. Get a pair of Oculus Go goggles and start experiencing this new reality. You'll be amazed, but you'll also be equipped to have virtual meetings right away with Facebook connections (if they, too, have Oculus goggles). If you have the budget, consider having a custom experience developed so you can invite prospects to take their next meeting with you on a beach in Tahiti. Or wherever else you can imagine. If you remember *Star Trek*, it'll be like taking meetings on the holodeck from anywhere in the world.

# POINTS TO REMEMBER

- ✔ Great minds of our day have been telling us AI will be the destruction of mankind, but so far it's proved to be quite helpful to sellers and marketers—and it's only getting better.

- ✔ In the very near future, the adoption of AI in selling processes will define who wins and who loses in markets all over the world.

- ✔ Augmented reality (AR) and virtual reality (VR) are not yet being used in Contact Marketing but will soon offer unprecedented new experiences and tools to help us gain important meetings.

- ✔ The function of AI in sales and marketing is to conjure useful, timely insights and actions from vast amounts of data.

- ✔ Ensable uses AI to identify buying signals that would otherwise be invisible to guide sales team actions to close more business. Unfortunately, the platform pertains only to technology purchases for the moment.

- ✔ Spiro.ai combines AI with a customer-relationship management (CRM) platform that gathers missing information, identifies opportunities, and coaches sales team members.

- ✔ Nudge.ai combines the personal social networks of all members of an organization into a single collective network, then coaches reps to create new pathways to accounts and prospects.

- ✔ Seamless.ai condenses the immense task of scraping profiles for Deep personalization or gathering verified contact details for Wide personalization applications into mere seconds.

- ✔ Nimble uses AI and CRM to help us tame and create order in the deluge of connections, posts, and opportunities encountered on social media.

- ✔ X.ai, or "Amy," uses AI to set up meetings through an utterly convincing, professional, and effective virtual assistant. "She" can be an invaluable asset in your quest for high-level meetings.

- ✔ Many of these AI platforms offer free memberships or trials. It is in your interest to bring them all into your Contact Marketing process.

# PART 4

## PUTTING IT ALL TOGETHER

# CHAPTER 13

# THE PERFECT CONTACT CAMPAIGN

The perfect contact campaign. What should that look like?

My thinking has shifted since writing the original *How to Get a Meeting with Anyone*. When I wrote it, I thought contact campaigns should break through to as many recipients as possible on the first effort and that was that. There was plenty of evidence that it was an effective strategy as campaigns have been producing response rates as high as 100 percent, which is orders of magnitude beyond any other form of marketing.

Still, it bothered me that, if we were identifying high-value prospects and connecting with 50 percent, that still left 50 percent unconnected. If those people truly are high-value contacts, why lose any of them? Especially when there are tools and strategies to ensure no one goes to waste.

But that would mean recalibrating our response baseline to 100 percent. That's crazy. It's marketing heresy. Still, there was the case of Poul Nielsen's rubber business cards. Those stretchy little devices were generating three to four new clients every time he handed one out. That's a 300 to 400 percent response rate. The same sort of results occurred with Dr. Lechmann's sliding dentist cards. Every time they were handed out, they netted new clients.

Those business cards weren't acting like cards at all. They were functioning as campaigns. Like contact campaigns, they were leaving recipients with the same "I love the way you think" response while achieving something more: evangelism. Recipients didn't just love the way Nielsen and Lechmann thought, they were moved to the point of sharing the campaign with friends and pushing them to respond as well, thus multiplying opportunities beyond the original recipients.

In this book, I have identified strategies and tools to easily leverage persistence into our campaigns. These will serve throughout the contact and sales cycles, consistently pushing toward 100 percent response rates every time. There are also tactics to stimulate evangelism in our campaigns, perhaps routinely enabling response rates well beyond 100 percent. That's extraordinary. Nothing else like that exists in any other form of marketing.

So persistence, evangelism, and hyper-response are now part of our tool kit, added to the twenty Contact Marketing campaign categories of the original book. And our business cards will never be the same. We now have more tactics, tools, and strategies. As the depth of the Contact Marketing discipline grows, we're able to make connections and affect the outcome of sales opportunities. Gather up your notes from all the previous chapters and let's take a look at what it all means.

*Note:* As I describe the strategies and steps to be taken in this chapter, I refer to "you" and "your team" interchangeably. You could be a team of one or leading a crew of hundreds of reps. You could be leading a startup with a constantly changing lineup of players. I have structured the information in this way because I know that you are part of a diverse group of readers, ranging from single reps to business owners to sales and marketing executives. Your title might be CEO and founder all the way through the C-suite and the entire ranks of vice presidents, directors, and managers to the SDRs themselves, who are all focused on the mission of growing the enterprise.

# CONTACT MARKETING: THE NEW MANIFESTO

To achieve perfection in our contact campaigns, we must recalibrate our thinking. We *will* break through. Every time and to every account. Our campaigns will be ever-evolving and always astonishing. Our follow-up will be thorough, timely, and hyper focused on maximized production. Our persistence will be resolute, filled with value and deeply appreciated by recipients of our campaigns. Our outcomes—of hyper-response, greatly accelerated sales, explosive ROI, and rapid growth—will be inevitable. To get there, these are the twelve new principles we must incorporate into our thinking.

1. **100 PERCENT RESPONSE RATES ARE THE NEW BASELINE:** From now on, we should assume 100 percent contact rates in the planning and execution of our Contact Marketing campaigns. To achieve that goal, we will incorporate varied, multiple waves of contact efforts with new persistence campaign elements.

   > *There is no "old-school," no "new-school." There is only what works.*

2. **EXCEEDING 100 PERCENT RESPONSE IS THE NEW GOAL:** NASA's probes reach great velocities by slingshotting around planets, using their gravitational pull to achieve new heights. Similarly, we will design our contact campaigns to inspire not just response, but evangelism among our most important contacts, leading to shares, hand-offs, and referrals, resulting in response rates beyond 100 percent.

3. **AI BECOMES A CONTACT MULTIPLIER:** Use AI tools and platforms to produce deep profile scrapes, track and enhance opportunities, and lend beyond-human guidance with enterprise-wide awareness of opportunities and shared connections.

4. **CONSTANT PERSISTENCE CAMPAIGN IN THE BACKGROUND:** Follow up based on trigger events, scheduled contact, and AI prompts, while digital persistence campaigns run in the background using retargeting, geofencing, and other tools.

5. **MULTIWAVE, MULTIMODAL, MULTISENSORY:** The campaign doesn't stop at one effort and is not confined to a single mode of communication. Recognize that people respond to information differently—visual, aural, tactile—and incorporate them all to make your campaign compelling, unexpected, and stimulating. Use everything; waste nothing.

6. **MIX OF WIDE AND DEEP PERSONALIZATION:** The utility of personalization has expanded. Use Wide personalization to reach contacts rapidly, with tightly controlled branding and messaging. Combine it with Deep personalization to include personal insights or to deliver one-off experiences.

7. **CONSTANT INNOVATION, EXPERIMENTATION, AND TESTING:** There is no "old-school," no "new-school." There is only what works. Always seek new tools, technologies, and approaches to produce new levels of audacity, astonishment, response, and evangelism.

8. **LISTS AND LINKEDIN ARE YOUR PRIMARY SOURCES:** Compiled lists of accounts and high-value LinkedIn connections are our best sources of VIP prospects. Use mega-engagement and regular posts on LinkedIn to connect with unexpected sources of potential new business, then quickly take the communication off-platform for significant levels of connection.

9. **COMMIT TO THE CONTACT MARKETING TRAINING/PROCESS:** Process and training are the mechanisms that instill best practices and deep expertise across teams. When Contact Marketing becomes an integral part of your sales team's mode of operation, sales and market share growth are inevitable.

10. **CENTRALIZED AND IN-THE-FIELD CAMPAIGN TOOLS:** Campaigns should be created and managed centrally to ensure proper economies of scale, brand integrity, and maximized performance. But video, print, and document management tools should also be made directly available to reps in the field to gather intel and respond quickly to emerging events.

**11. POCKET CAMPAIGNS, NOT BUSINESS CARDS:** No more tapping phones together; no more dead-end business cards, no matter how fancy. Capture business, generate evangelism, unlock potential from every in-person meeting or drop-off with a campaign launched from your pocket. This is a campaign that looks like a business card, but generates measurable sales, ROI, and viral pass-along.

## THE NEW CONTACT MARKETING MODEL

| Phase | ❶ RESEARCH | ❷ PRE-CONTACT | ❸ CONTACT | ❹ SALES CYCLE | ❺ POST-SALE/ RETENTION |
|---|---|---|---|---|---|
| **Old Model** | Gather list/Manual profile scrape | | | | |
| | | Produce/Launch campaign | | | |
| | | | Follow-up/Tally response | | |
| | | | | Move on to next on list, no further support of sale or client retention | |
| **New Model** | List/Research/Reach enhanced with AI | | | | |
| | | Produce/launch contact campaign, initiate ongoing persistence campaign element (digital, AI, and manual) | | | |
| | | | Follow-thru to 100% response | | |
| | | | | Response/Test cycle/Maximize ROI/Aim for evangelism effect | |
| | | Pocket Campaign | Launch campaign, set tracking pixel | | |
| | | | | Initiate ongoing persistence campaign element (digital, AI, and manual) | |
| | | | | Response/Test cycle/Maximize ROI/Aim for evangelism effect | |

**THE NEW CONTACT MARKETING MODEL**

*The new base response rate for Contact Marketing campaigns is 100 percent, accomplished with the addition of new AI-enhanced research and follow-up tools, digital persistence elements, and Pocket Campaigns in place of business cards to convert qualified face-to-face encounters into new business.*

**12. SHIFT BEYOND "I LOVE THE WAY YOU THINK":** The goal of contact campaigns has always been to inspire recipients to say, "I love the way you think." It's time to step it up. The desired response now is "Wow! Hey, everyone, check this out! This is amazing!"

This is an extremely aggressive, even radical vision. For traditional marketers, it will be shocking that anyone would suggest 100 percent response rates, especially as a baseline, and then to suggest those should actually go higher. We know it just isn't how marketing works. I'm a little shocked by it myself.

Still, the conclusions come from what's in this book. It's a revelation to think that pressing for anything less than 100 percent response rates may now represent setting our sights too low as Contact Marketers. Everywhere I look, I now see evidence of having aimed too low, even though Contact Marketing already outperforms any other form of marketing.

> *LinkedIn has magnified our ability to find, track, research, and load qualified prospects into our campaigns.*

Our outreach efforts can now be bolstered with passive, automated background persistence campaigns, making it far more likely to break through than ever before. Artificial intelligence can make it even more likely to break through with its ability to create a collective network among team members and spot emerging opportunities we would otherwise miss. Personalization, technology, even business cards will have helped create a richer palette for innovation.

LinkedIn has upended what it means to compile a list of VIP contacts. Like personalization, which has split and multiplied, LinkedIn has magnified our ability to find, track, research, and load qualified prospects into our campaigns. All this should be like rocket fuel for our Contact Marketing efforts. But in order to blast off, we'll need to put some structure to our elevated mode of outreach.

# YOUR SIX-STAGE PROCESS

## Stage 1: Planning

To mount a perfect Contact Marketing campaign, you must start with a solid plan. Lead with the questions "Who do we want to reach, and how are we going to generate at least a 100 percent response rate and turn our most important contacts not just into new clients, but evangelists?" The answers should be applied to five areas of planning: strategy, audience, process, training, and execution.

**STRATEGY:** Defining a winning strategy starts with more questions. What is the purpose or desired gain from the campaign? Is it straight revenue growth, rapid expansion into a new market, greater market share, or in the case of a startup, a rapid spool-up addressing potential investors, strategic partners, and key initial clients? Who are these critically important people and how do we find them? And finally, what is the desired financial impact of the campaign? *What is its value?*

Addressing the last question first, I suggest starting with a budget of 1 percent of the desired financial result. If you spend 1 percent of the projected financial result and hit the goals of the campaign precisely, that's a 10,000 percent ROI. Thus, for every million dollars of revenue you hope to gain, plan on spending $10,000.

Before committing to your campaign, give consideration to what you expect to generate (based on test results, not assumptions) and the minimum response/ROI you're willing to tolerate. If you aren't willing to allow anything below a 10 percent response rate, note it and move forward in your campaign planning.

But wait, haven't I just been talking about 100 percent baselines and hyper-response at multiples of that level? Yes, but for budget purposes, you should be conservative until you see actual performance figures. Hyper-response will come from adding the persistence element, designing evangelism into your campaign, and setting performance expectations with your team.

Still, how do you credibly set the expectation of a 100 percent or greater response rate? If you're leading a team, they will need to be briefed on the strategies of digital persistence and evangelism as well as the expected effect. But there is also the psychological effect of setting a lower goal and the team performing just to that level. Bring them in on the plan; let them know what you're trying to achieve.

Your answers to the other questions, about purpose and audience, will combine to create a direction and framework for the campaign. If you're after a general increase in revenue and market share, which are the companies that can get you there the fastest? Who within those companies will you need to connect with to produce the desired outcome? How many of those companies will you need to convert to clients, partners, or referral sources to achieve your goals?

And finally, you'll need to address the prospect's needs, interests, and areas of pain in your campaign. What are they and how does your solution apply? How does it compare to your competitors' solutions? How competitive is your market? Can you see how these will combine to produce a direction for your Contact Marketing efforts?

**AUDIENCE:** This is where the process starts to become fun. Which companies would absolutely blow your mind if they became your clients? Which organizations could transform your scale immediately with their business or access to their sales channels? Who would you really like to connect and partner with?

Those are the people you should target for your campaign. Define who they are, compile or purchase data, and confirm their contact details. Research what they're saying (are they posting on social media, for example?) and get a sense of their passions and personalities. Use AI platforms like Seamless and Nimble to produce complete dossiers on these critically important people.

With that, you will have a data set to use in your campaign. But you're not done. Your campaign strategy should include ready tools to respond to opportunities that arise from your use of LinkedIn and other social media platforms. Many potential sources of business are lurking, watching and waiting to see who you are and what you can bring to their operations. When ready, they'll reach out, and you (or your entire team) should be ready with a dazzling campaign response that takes the conversation off-platform and to the next level.

**PROCESS:** Let's consider nature for a moment, weeds in particular. They easily spread to new territory, quickly colonize it while displacing competitors, and protect their turf when challenged. They use strategies that have been honed over eons of evolution, but they don't formulate strategy themselves. Instead, they are programmed to exhibit certain attributes while relentlessly executing the strategies already programmed into their fiber. In nature, *process* is the mechanism that enables the entire population of weeds to act in unison, deftly executing the strategies set for them. In this way, each instance of the plant performs like a seasoned expert.

In our world, the tools of process are diagrams, scripts, and platform. The ideal contact campaign will have several tracks, serving multiple strategies. One might address creating viable relationships with each new LinkedIn connection. Another would be an automated background persistence campaign. And certainly the primary outreach campaign should be directed to the contacts on your top accounts list.

Each of these must be defined to the users of the campaigns in great detail, so they know the steps involved. Flow charts demonstrate how you want each campaign to be used and define if-then steps as it progresses. Scripts will define what is to be said during interactions with receptionists, assistants, influencers, and principals to help reps navigate the process and standardize a framework for conversations with contacts.

The team will need a way to efficiently enroll new prospects in each of the campaigns. Pocket Campaigns should be put in the hands of all reps who interact with high-value prospects.

**TRAINING:** Process is useless unless followed precisely as designed. It shouldn't be assumed that reps will simply encounter the process, materials, and tools, and know how to integrate themselves into the campaign. At minimum, they require training to understand the nature, goals, and operation of all campaign elements.

But wouldn't it be nice to know they're already trained Contact Marketing operatives who thoroughly understand the mission and their expected contributions? That level of understanding and expertise can be invaluable, as it allows team members to autonomously run the process. Training becomes even more critical when reps are given freedom to use desktop video platforms, document management platforms, and Deep personalization.

Basic elements must also be reinforced. Call precisely when you say you will. Develop a VIP statement. Know precisely what an ideal sale looks like across the spectrum of your products or services. Reps should be thoroughly versed in the company's go-to-market and Contact Marketing strategies, how they fit in, and what's expected of them.

Without training, process becomes worthless. Weeds don't need training to participate perfectly within their process. They're already hardwired and fully optimized to run their process, operate with certain attributes, and use their tools to aggressively advance. If we want our reps to perform similarly within the Contact Marketing mission, training is a must.

**EXECUTION:** The strategies you define for your campaign, based on the questions above, will dictate how the campaign should function. But what form should it take? I've shared a lot of examples in this book, showing how Contact Marketers have approached the planning of their campaigns. The purpose of all the preceding chapters is to inspire your own ideas that uniquely fit your strategy, audience, and market conditions. The new Contact Marketing "manifesto" in this chapter is meant to inspire you to take a multitiered, multimodal, and multisensory creative approach to your campaign, to ensure the greatest levels of performance and response.

Producing a complex campaign with a high degree of innovation and exceptional creativity is not easy. You can take it on yourself or hire specialized help to make it happen.

As a Contact Marketing agency owner, I have my opinions, but they might not be what you'd expect. Plenty of marketers come up with brilliant campaign strategies on their own. Doing it yourself may imbue a handmade quality that can be very effective. If you do hire an agency or consultant, you should expect a quicker path to getting the campaign right and into your marketplace.

But that brings up an important point. Who should be managing your Contact Marketing program? If you're doing it on your own, the answer is obvious. If you have a small team or staff, you probably won't have a marketing or sales specialist available, but you will need to give someone bottom-line responsibility for the program. Someone has to be the internal go-to person for the campaign.

For much larger companies, it's likely there is someone in a sales enablement or sales operations role. They are the most likely candidates for running your Contact Marketing program. They will need budgetary authority and responsibility for improving the performance of the sales team.

Campaign runners will need to operate the programs as marketers with performance and budgetary responsibility. They will need to mastermind the creation, implementation, and management of the campaigns. It will involve testing various assumptions and creative approaches and monitoring results to continually hone the campaign. Ultimately, they should be strategic growth managers or executives.

Once your campaign has been created, the responsible manager must oversee the distribution of campaign assets. Will everyone participate or just a few members of the sales team? Which campaign assets will be administered and fulfilled centrally and which from the field?

## Stage 2: Precampaign

The campaign is about to start, or it's already operational, but new target accounts and contacts are to be added. In the new Contact Marketing model, a digital persistence element is presumed to be part of the campaign.

Two weeks prior to outreach, target executives should be activated in the digital persistence element of the campaign. This will predispose recipients to connect quickly, using ads that introduce your company, your solution, and eventually your reason for reaching out.

Your ads will start showing up on the right rail on the most popular sites on the web, wherever the prospects go, seemingly all over the web. Your campaign might also run Google Ads targeting your prospect's full name. Start following and responding to their social media posts, particularly on LinkedIn. The idea is to create a positive impression and awareness, and a ramp-up for the campaign ahead.

# Stage 3: Contact Campaign

Your campaign, as you know by now, can take any number of forms. There are twenty-two categories discussed in this book and twenty in the original *How to Get a Meeting with Anyone*. All are valid, useful, and powerful. Between the two books and now more than thirty campaign categories, there are plenty of options.

The flow of your campaign *must* incorporate different modes of communication. Many marketers seem to stick to one mode, usually email, and wonder why it's not working (remember Einstein's definition of insanity?). Switching between email, phone, and physical campaign elements is far more stimulating to the recipient but also takes into account that people are specialized in the way they absorb information. Some are tactile, others visual or aural. Use them all.

A sample campaign might incorporate video in email (Vidyard), a series of visual metaphors, and a Deep personalization gift effort while the digital persistence campaign runs in the background. Or it could mix Wide and Deep personalization with a video from the rep, holding a cartoon BigBoard or gift theme box, announcing that the contact piece is coming. As always, the persistence element would be running in the background. Both campaigns should include a schedule of email, voice, and written messaging to keep the contact effort rolling, each adding incremental value to the conversation along with a push for contact.

Your campaign should integrate centralized and decentralized elements, the latter being critical for the flexibility reps will need to respond to developments rapidly. If using Deep personalization, the campaign should include standardized, branded packaging so it always appears to be coming from your company in a coordinated, buttoned-up fashion. Try producing various sizes of Tyvek shipping envelopes printed with your brand for nonbreakable items, plus a few sizes of branded shipping boxes for fragile gifts.

Reps should have the ability to produce professional-looking cards that can be generated on a color laser printer in their office. In the "How to Make a Greeting Card" sidebar on page 80, I diagram how to produce professional-grade greeting cards with a few pieces of desktop graphic-studio equipment. For my agency clients, I provide editable PDF files so they can personalize the cartoon on the front panel to the recipient. You can find other ways to incorporate personalization into your in-the-field cards that will give you and the reps on your team a useful tool for building contact.

Reps should have the ability, training, and autonomy to use video for impromptu messaging. Vidyard makes this easy and provides valuable contact intel, as discussed in chapter eleven. It allows you to quickly address issues in a way that stands out.

Consider using a calendar app that allows you to monitor activity and capture data at the administrator level. TimeTrade and other calendar apps are an excellent add-on to video call-to-action screens, leading to directly booked appointments.

And finally, all customer-facing reps should be using a Pocket Campaign for the company, replacing business cards. As discussed in chapter seven, Pocket Campaigns launch like business cards, inviting an entirely new level of fascination, play, and interaction while integrating with your Contact Marketing program. The cards can be handed out or dropped off, bringing face-to-face meetings into the persistence element of your campaign.

By converting to a Pocket Campaign strategy, reps will turn virtually any in-person encounter they have with important prospects into a measurable contact effort. Pocket Campaigns, by nature, will be involvement devices meant to trigger evangelism, persistence, and hyper-response.

## Stage 4: Persistence Campaign

We've already started the persistence element in the precampaign stage, to lessen prospects' natural resistance to connecting with strangers prior to outreach. The persistence element will continue to support outreach all the way through the sale, perhaps even through a client retention phase.

That starts with the digital measures discussed in chapter nine—geofencing, social media ads, and the use of tracking pixels to place an ongoing set of retargeting ads through the Google Display Network. The result will be ads showing up essentially anywhere the target executive visits on the web, including all the major news sites.

At first, we're not concerned with clicks. We just want the target executive to start noticing us. The practice will make smaller marketers look like national advertisers, and larger firms will appear surprisingly relevant to their needs, because we're addressing them directly. Either way, they'll be impressed, ready to connect, and eager to do business.

The ads will need to change over time to reflect the phases of contact. Ideally, in pre-contact mode, prospects see one version, then during contact mode, they'll see another. Once contact is established and a sale is pending, they'll see perhaps a series of ads reinforcing the sale. The process should even extend to existing clients, in an after-sale or ongoing retention and brand-enhancement effort.

The persistence campaign should not be entirely digital ads. A separate program of value-driven communication should continue once the main contact effort has been initiated, to build and reinforce your stature as a trusted source. This might take the form of regular content updates on LinkedIn or podcasts, or perhaps come in the style of Tom Searcy's mailed letters delivering glimpses of the future or David Brock's insightful use of public information from chapter eight. Social media interactions can also raise awareness and profile.

The persistence element should be every bit as multimodal and multisensory as your primary contact campaign. The persistence portion of the campaign is a key element leading to hyper-response results, ensuring none of the contacts go to waste. If they're all important, they should all be addressed through your campaign. The persistence element will help make that happen.

## Stage 5: Postcampaign

Once the campaign is up and running, it's time to institute an ongoing cycle of measurement, evaluation, and testing. This should occur on all levels of the campaign. Test different ads in the persistence campaign. Test various approaches and efforts within the primary contact campaign. Test varied approaches to the Pocket Campaign.

The evaluation process is ongoing. New strategies emerge as results and sales figures emerge. Did we hit our goal for contact/response? Did we hit the sale figures we originally set? What didn't work? What went right? How can we tighten it all up? The entire program, stages one through five, should repeat with every test cycle.

# Stage 6: Evolution and Innovation

When the original *How to Get a Meeting with Anyone* book reached critical mass and people started talking about it on LinkedIn, I noticed one disturbing trend in the comments. Some marketers, who I assume have been in their careers less than three years, began to dismiss some of the contact techniques as "old-school." If digital marketing is all you've known in your career and you see it as the only mode of marketing, you have a seriously limited view.

Digital marketing has been around long enough that it has itself become traditional. You could say, if you really needed to pass such judgments, that SEO, digital display, social media, and certainly email are now rather old-school themselves. Contact Marketing can involve virtually *anything* as long as it delivers the desired result. It could be a block of wood sent through the mail or a handwritten letter, or it could be an augmented reality/virtual reality experience or a hologram projecting from a campaign device not yet invented. It could be a model airplane, fake dog poop, a giant cartoon on a foam core board—or it could be an experience like sending a prospect to racing school. It could be a brilliant unsolicited proposal, or some wildly intricate unboxing experience, or a video using any number of delivery schemes.

What we want is to dazzle the people who are the focus of our outreach. These are not mere targets. They are the people who will work with us, help us reach new levels, and elevate our lives.

# LAST WORD

What a long journey this has been. When I wrote my groundbreaking book on Contact Marketing, *How to Get a Meeting with Anyone*, I was still thinking about novel campaign approaches that were opening doors. It was entertaining stuff, but also a marketing anomaly. Coming from the direct marketing world, where 1 percent is considered a "good" response rate, the metrics of Contact Marketing must be hard to believe for many fellow marketers.

When I started this book, my intention was to produce a compilation of case studies with photographs. I wasn't expecting the great leap of progress, the enhanced Contact Marketing model, or the new baseline goals that have materialized.

I've since realized this is not just a way to make connections. This is not some obscure offshoot of marketing. I now fully appreciate that the ability to make important connections, for everyone in business, whether they sell or not, is a critical mission that runs across the entire enterprise. Contact Marketing is now a decisive change-management program with deep implications for the success and growth of any business or career.

The belief that everyone should be involved is reflected in some of the new AI tools. When Nudge.ai integrates all personal networks in an organization into one enterprise-wide network, more meetings and sales occur. When Spiro.ai automatically fills gaps in CRM data from emails, then monitors opportunities and directs sales team members in their follow-up, more meetings and sales occur. When Ensable scans the digital universe to detect buying signals and forwards those to the team, more meetings and more sales occur. After writing this book, I can't imagine doing business without AI-enhanced tools.

The benefits and virtues of persistence have been known for a very long time. Lately, we hear it takes seven to fourteen outreach efforts before someone responds. While the aim of Contact Marketing is to greatly accelerate that

---

## LET'S CONNECT

If you'd like to connect, or if you'd like to explore your own campaign, please do reach out. We're living in a wonderful new age when readers can instantly connect with authors and strike up conversations about what they've read or are inspired to do next.

You can easily reach me on LinkedIn—www.linkedin.com/in/stuheinecke. If you do, mention you bought and read my book, and let me know how you put these tools and strategies to work. Nothing thrills me more than to know that someone has read one of my books and it had a positive effect on their life. You can also listen to the *How to Get a Meeting with Anyone* podcast, found on the C-Suite Radio Network, iTunes, Stitcher, and other outlets. I regularly update and announce my podcast on LinkedIn, so follow me there to get those updates. Also watch for new videos on YouTube that share the Contact Marketing stories of your fellow readers or follow mastermind members during their weekend strategy sessions here on Whidbey Island, in the beautiful Pacific Northwest.

And finally, if you want me involved in your campaign, I'd be delighted to discuss it. I serve a wide range of clients as their consultant, agency, mastermind coach, or trainer.

Whatever form that might take, I want to offer my sincerest thanks for buying and reading this book. You're part of a very select group of people who invest in their careers and intellect. And I am truly humbled to be part of your journey.

process, perhaps getting those meetings on the first attempt, it's obvious that persistence and multiple touches are necessary to routinely reach 100 percent response rates.

Being persistent used to mean diligent, ongoing, in-person follow-up. It still does, but we now have powerful new tools to automate some of the workload. When our most important contacts start seeing our retargeting ads before our outreach, they are far more likely to respond positively. As the ads persist and evolve with the conversation, they will support our efforts to make a sale—and more.

We now have a new model to apply, a set of steps to follow, and an astonishing new set of tools to ply. It's going to be a lot of fun to use them while we generate metrics and results that defy belief. As a Contact Marketer, your contributions will become more essential than ever before. I can't wait to see how you put it to use.

# ACKNOWLEDGMENTS

A book like this doesn't happen without a lot of contact with a lot of people who have shared their stories, wisdom, and audacious thinking. It would also not exist without the generous support of many people to whom I am deeply grateful.

To the publishing team, especially Debbie Harmsen, for guiding this project so deftly; Glenn Yeffeth, Adrienne Lang, Alicia Kania, and Leah Wilson for your deep expertise, wisdom, and encouragement; and Sarah Avinger for your keen eye and mind that brought visual brilliance to the book, thank you also to Kit Sweeney, Miki Alexandra Caputo, and Jessika Rieck for applying your talents and expertise to add polish to the project. Thank you all for making yet another dream come true. And to Jim Carroll, master of film, light, and lens, thank you for shooting my favorite headshot of all time.

My deep thanks also go to Russ Klein, CEO of the American Marketing Association, for lending his voice and authority to the Contact Marketing story. I am very proud to have your words accompany mine as the foreword to this book.

To the many people who supported my efforts to complete this yearlong effort, I thank you. Al Williams, Amy Egtvet, Andy Paul, Anne Thornley-Brown,

Blake O'Neill, Bruce Johnson, Bridget Vanyo, Charles Preston, Cherie Ware, Courtney Pierce, Craig Lack, David Rosuck, Diedre Moore, Drew Joiner, Drew Schwartzhoff, Duane Dunk, Dylan Abbott, Gerry Call, Gregg Wallick, Jason Thomas, Jeffrey Krivis, Jeremy Wellman, Jerry Timmerman, Joel Lissick, Lauren Mead, Logan Lyles, Mariam Zadeh, Mareo McCracken, M. C. Mills, Mark Derks, Matt McNamara, Mike Goldner, Randy Bernard, Rick Dees, Ron Braley, Sam Watson, Scott Lieck, Siddharth Sawkar, and Tom Cramer—thank you all for your support, ideas, and inspiration.

And to Jeff Sheehan, Kare Anderson, Sangram Vajre, Rikke Heinecke, and others, thank you for reaching deep within your personal networks to introduce me to fascinating people who greatly enriched the story this book shares.

The Contact Marketing story is a broad one that reaches every part of the world. People are using truly audacious means to break through to those who can most assist them with their own goals. This book is their story. And so, for sharing their brilliance, tips, techniques, and stories, there are many to thank.

Thank you Adam Schoenfeld, Alec Brownstein, Alex Perkins, Amanda Harkness, Art Sobczak, Andrew Samuel, Anthony Iannarino, Austin Craig, Barry Mills, Ben Chiriboga, Benny Albert, Brett Chester, Brandon Bornancin, Brendan Alan Barrett, Brian Buffini, Brian Wallace, Cedric Gamelin, Charlie Liang, Charlie Moon, Chelsea Stoelting, Chris Hirsch, Chris Roehm, Connor Dube, Curtis Brooks, Dameon Green, Dan Waldschmidt, Daniel Skiffington, David Brock, Dave Koslow, Dave Mullins, David Henzel, David Karlak, Dawn Knox, Dennis Brown, Dennis Mortensen, Dom Steinmann, Donna Serdula, and Doug Liddle.

Thank you also Eileen Brady, Ethan Goller, Evelio Mattos, Fabio Milito, Howard Silvermintz, Ian Grais, J. Barrows, Jacquelyn Dheere, James Carbary, Jason Hagemeister, Jaycen Thorgeirson, Jaxson Khan, Jeff Davis, Jeff Harmon, Jeff Holmes, Jeff McGhee, Jeffrey Hayzlett, John Hitt, John Jentsch, Joe Snell, John Ruhlin, Jon Ferrara, Justin Chugg, Justin Dumois, Justin Croxton, Kate Blumberg, Katy Hart, Keaton Scadden, Keenan, Ken Thoreson, Kenny Madden, Kevin Mitnick, Kristin Gallucci, James Mahon, Jeni Mattson, Lauren Wadsworth, Lee Hancock, Les Cowie, Lori Richardson, Luz Enseñat, Mark Babbitt, Mark Birch, Mark Hunter, Mark S. A. Smith, Matt Heinz, Matt Reuter, Max Altschuler, and Michael Kim.

And more thanks to Michaela Underdahl, Michelle Terry, Mike Syring, Mike Weinberg, Mikey Pawell, Miles Austin, Nate Barr, Nicolé Royer, Noah Gold, Patrick Hodgdon, Phil Gerbyshak, Poul Nielsen, Remo Caminada, Rick Tobin, Robert Smith, Russ Klein, Ryan Lohman, Ryan O'Hara, Sam Buxton, Sean Airhart, Sharon Gutowski, Sheryl Schultz, Stephanie Wiriahardja, Steven Woods, Taice Perrotti, Tamara Saviano, Terry Miller, Tibor Shanto, Tito Bohrt, Tom Williams, Tom Searcy, Trent Palmer, Trish Bertuzzi, Tsufit, Tyler Lessard, Yasar Daglar, and Zach Barney.

Thanks also to the companies that supported this effort with their stories, platforms, and products that contribute to the Contact Marketing story. To Display Fake Foods, DocSend, Ensable, Jukebox, MikesFalconry.com, NBBJ, Nimble, Nudge.ai, PocketMonkey, Rob Hetler, Seamless.ai, Spiro.ai, Stetson, TaskDrive, Terminus, TimeTrade, Treasury Wine Estates, Vidyard, Wayfaren, WoodGiftBox.com, x.ai, and Z-Card North America, I say thank you.

And finally, to my family, friends, and especially my wife, thank you for putting up with my constant holing up in the studio, unable to participate in whatever you generously brought to my attention. Charlotte, after more than a year straight of interviewing, compiling, writing, and editing seven days a week, I'm finally available for yard work again. I can't wait to get back out there with the mower.

# INDEX

# ABOUT THE AUTHOR

**STU HEINECKE** is an author, *Wall Street Journal* cartoonist, and hall of fame–nominated marketer. When *How to Get a Meeting with Anyone* debuted in 2016, it ignited an international sales and marketing movement. In the book, he coined the term "Contact Marketing," a powerful form of outreach employing clever "contact campaigns" to create the sort of connections that can change the scale of careers, businesses, and lives.

Since then, tens of thousands of sales reps, business owners, job seekers, entrepreneurs—even CEOs themselves—have used Contact Marketing to generate stunning numbers of high-level connections, meetings, and surges in revenue and investment.

Heinecke is based on a beautiful island in the Pacific Northwest, where he provides agency services, consulting, mastermind coaching, training, and weekend strategy sessions to help sales teams break through to their top accounts faster and more effectively. He also hosts the *How to Get a Meeting with Anyone* podcast weekly on the C-Suite Radio Network, iTunes, Stitcher, and Libsyn and is the founder of Cartoonists.org, a group of prominent cartoonists from *The Wall Street Journal* and *The New Yorker* who are dedicated to using their art to help charities raise funds, while reframing single-panel cartoons as collectible art.

# The hard part just got **easy**.

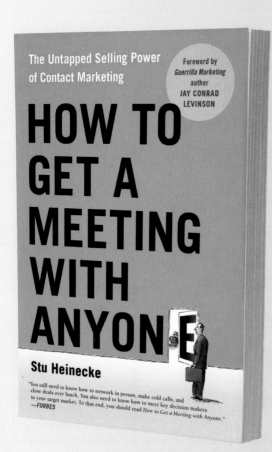

The Untapped Selling Power of Contact Marketing

Foreword by *Guerrilla Marketing* author **JAY CONRAD LEVINSON**

# HOW TO GET A MEETING WITH ANYONE

**Stu Heinecke**

"You still need to know how to network in person, make cold calls, and close deals over lunch. You also need to know how to meet key decision makers in your target market. To that end, you should read *How to Get a Meeting with Anyone*."
—*FORBES*

"Stu Heinecke may be a one-of-a-kind cartoonist and marketeer, but his ideas and examples for one-to-one marketing and selling should have any marketer creating their own audacious goals and asking themselves, 'Why not?'"

**—FORBES**

# STUHEINECKE.COM